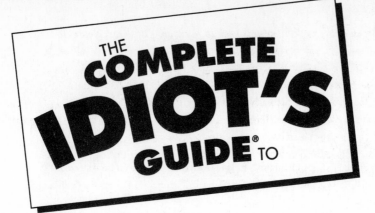

THE COMPLETE IDIOT'S GUIDE® TO

Adoption

Second Edition

by Christine Adamec

ALPHA

A member of Penguin Group (USA) Inc.

I would like to dedicate this book to my loving husband, John Adamec.

ALPHA BOOKS

Published by the Penguin Group

Penguin Group (USA) Inc., 375 Hudson Street, New York, New York 10014, U.S.A.

Penguin Group (Canada), 10 Alcorn Avenue, Toronto, Ontario, Canada M4V 3B2 (a division of Pearson Penguin Canada Inc.)

Penguin Books Ltd, 80 Strand, London WC2R 0RL, England

Penguin Ireland, 25 St Stephen's Green, Dublin 2, Ireland (a division of Penguin Books Ltd)

Penguin Group (Australia), 250 Camberwell Road, Camberwell, Victoria 3124, Australia (a division of Pearson Australia Group Pty Ltd)

Penguin Books India Pvt Ltd, 11 Community Centre, Panchsheel Park, New Delhi—110 017, India

Penguin Group (NZ), cnr Airborne and Rosedale Roads, Albany, Auckland 1310, New Zealand (a division of Pearson New Zealand Ltd)

Penguin Books (South Africa) (Pty) Ltd, 24 Sturdee Avenue, Rosebank, Johannesburg 2196, South Africa

Penguin Books Ltd, Registered Offices: 80 Strand, London WC2R 0RL, England

Copyright © 2004 by Christine Adamec

International Standard Book Number: 1-59257-274-X
Library of Congress Catalog Card Number: 2004113214

07 06 05   8 7 6 5 4 3 2

Interpretation of the printing code: The rightmost number of the first series of numbers is the year of the book's printing; the rightmost number of the second series of numbers is the number of the book's printing. For example, a printing code of 04-1 shows that the first printing occurred in 2004.

Printed in the United States of America

Note: This publication contains the opinions and ideas of its author. It is intended to provide helpful and informative material on the subject matter covered. It is sold with the understanding that the author and publisher are not engaged in rendering professional services in the book. If the reader requires personal assistance or advice, a competent professional should be consulted.

Most Alpha books are available at special quantity discounts for bulk purchases for sales promotions, premiums, fundraising, or educational use. Special books, or book excerpts, can also be created to fit specific needs.

For details, write: Special Markets, Alpha Books, 375 Hudson Street, New York, NY 10014.

Publisher: *Marie Butler-Knight*
Product Manager: *Phil Kitchel*
Senior Managing Editor: *Jennifer Chisholm*
Senior Acquisitions Editor: *Randy Ladenheim-Gil*
Development Editor: *Jennifer Moore*
Production Editor: *Janette Lynn*

Copy Editor: *Kelly D. Henthorne*
Cartoonist: *Richard King*
Cover/Book Designer: *Trina Wurst*
Indexer: *Angie Bess*
Layout: *Angela Calvert*
Proofreading: *John Etchison*

Contents at a Glance

Contents

Appendixes

Foreword

After nearly 30 years in the child welfare field, I've seen adoption become a more and more acceptable option for people who want to start or add to their families. These days, many people are adopting or talking about adopting; open a newspaper or magazine, or turn on a TV talk show, and chances are you'll come across some story related to adoption.

While adoption has become more widespread, the adoption process has grown more difficult. Chris Adamec's book does a very good job of providing a beacon through the often tangled and varied paths to parenting through adoption. (I should mention here that Chris and I co-authored a reference book and have been colleagues on a number of projects.)

As you read *The Complete Idiot's Guide to Adoption, Second Edition*, it will become clear that there are at least two (sometimes more) differing opinions about nearly every subject related to adoption. Because adoption is so intensely personal and so directly linked to many of the controversial topics of our day, this diversity of opinion is inevitable. In this book, Chris does a good job of reflecting that diversity in a fair and even-handed manner.

There are two suggestions I'd like to make as you think about, or prepare for, an adoption. First, you need to take responsibility for your own actions. Second, you need to listen to sound advice.

On the first point, always use your common sense. Be cautious if an expert says something that strikes you as dubious. Use your instincts. Ask questions. Be skeptical, especially of those who come across as slick or facile or who may have no solid basis for their claims (in my opinion, that includes much of what is on the Internet). Only do what you're comfortable with.

On the other hand, as you read this book (and after), check out the resources that Chris has listed for you. Many thoughtful, careful, and astute observers of the adoption scene have summarized decades of experience for your critical consideration. You can especially benefit by taking heed of their cautionary notes.

The adoption process will require a great deal of time, thought, and careful research. Remember, adoption will not just require a substantial investment of money. It will change your life.

—William Pierce

President, National Council for Adoption

Introduction

I'm assuming that you've picked up this book because you would like to become an adoptive parent. What a great idea! I'm an adoptive parent myself, and I wrote this book to help steer you through the rough spots and move you onward to smooth sailing—with some extra guidance for a few unexpected rocky moments that may occur as your child grows into adulthood. I wrote the first edition in 1997 and by 2004, plenty of changes had occurred in adoption, both internationally and in the United States, so I've updated this second edition very thoroughly.

Why do you need this book? Because to succeed at adoption and adoptive parenting, you need to understand how it is like and unlike biological parenting. Many people who are trying to adopt don't realize that adoption is a system with its own special rules and terminology. You don't have to master it all (few people do!). But if you want to "win" at adoption, you first have to learn the basics.

If your goal and dream is to parent an adopted child, I hope you find that the information here steers you toward a very happy and successful adoptive parenthood. And that you'll enjoy some of the silly stories as well as the heart-tuggers within these pages.

One thought I must share with you, as a kind of mantra for you to adopt: Never give up! Whether you're in the process of adopting or you're trying to cope with issues as an adoptive parent—the answers are out there. Good luck!

How the Book Is Organized

This book is organized to make it easy for you to find what you need when you need it.

Part 1: "Adoption: A Wonderful Option!" Why do people adopt? How do you know whether you're ready to adopt? Why do birthparents place children for adoption? And who are the children who need families? This part provides you with an overview, as well as information on finding adoptive parent groups on the Internet.

Part 2: "What Are Your Options?" This valuable part will help you discover which kind of adoption arranger is right for you. I've also included valuable information on how to avoid adoption scams. It's crucially important to realize that adoption laws vary radically from state to state, which is explained and also illustrated with a state-by-state adoption law chart. Finally, I devote an entire chapter to international adoption, an increasingly popular option.

Part 3: "Finding Your Child." You've decided to adopt, found your adoption arranger, and launched yourself on the path to adoption. This part walks you through the process. You'll learn how to survive a *home study* background investigation. You'll also learn how to apply if you are a nontraditional parent—that is, if you are single, gay or lesbian, disabled, or older than you might think you can be to adopt. This part also shows you what you need to know about birthparents and about a child you may adopt.

Part 4: "Raising Your Adopted Child." Congratulations! There's a child for you! From the day you first hear the news, to the day you bring your new child home, and beyond, this part covers key issues involved with parenting an adopted child. I'll show you how to introduce your child to the family, explain adoption to the child at different ages, and deal with problems that may come up.

Part 5: "If Your Adult Child Searches." Plenty of material has been written for adopted adults searching for birthparents. But how do adoptive parents feel about this and what should they do? If your adopted child searches, does that mean you've failed as a parent? Will your child abandon you? This part explains why and how adult children search.

Extras

In addition to the main narrative of *The Complete Idiot's Guide to Adoption*, you'll find other types of useful information in sidebars throughout the book.

Adopterms

Definitions of adoption words and phrases that are used frequently by experts in the field. Get a heads-up and learn the jargon! It'll help.

Real Life Snapshots

Anecdotes about real adoptive parents or adopted children. Sometimes heartwarming and other times startling, these stories should make you stop and think.

Familybuilding Tips

Tips on how to deal with common problems and issues.

Adoption Alert

Situations to watch out for. The information in these boxes may save you from minor (and sometimes major) problems.

Adoptinfo

Adoption research or newsworthy topics that can help or interest you.

Acknowledgments

To research and write a book covering many aspects of adoption, you can't do it alone! You need the emotional support of someone close to you, and I have always had that in my husband, John Adamec.

You also need assistance with information gathering and advice. In particular, I would like to single out Deborah Borchers, M.D., a pediatrician from Cincinnati, Ohio, who has generously reviewed medical passages in several chapters and offered very helpful suggestions.

Thank you to Nancy Ashe, editor for Adoption.com (a service of Adoption Media, LLC) for advising me on Internet issues.

Special heartfelt thanks to Mary Beth Style, a social worker by training and the former vice president of the National Council For Adoption. Mary Beth is a strong believer in adoption, and she has generously given me a great deal of valuable advice and assistance in updating this edition.

I am extremely grateful to the following attorneys who provided me with information on state adoption laws throughout the country and who also enabled me to prepare my adoption law chart. Of course I am responsible for the interpretation of the data that was provided to me.

Thanks to Vika Andrel, Austin, Texas; Carolyn Arnett, Louisville, Kentucky; Harold O. Atencio, Albuquerque, New Mexico; David Allen Barnette, Charleston, West Virginia; Martin W. Bauer, Wichita, Kansas; W. Thomas Beltz, Colorado Springs, Colorado; Judith M. Berry, Gorham, Maine; Lynn Bodi, Madison, Wisconsin; Maxine M. Buckmeier, Sioux City, Iowa; Deborah Crouse Cobb, Collinsville, Illinois; Frederick Corley, Beaufort, South Carolina; Dan J. Davis, Tupelo, Mississippi; Catherine M. Dexter, Portland, Oregon; Mark M. Demaray, Edmonds, Washington; Rhonda Fishbein, Atlanta, Georgia; Robert Flint, Anchorage, Alaska; Alison A. Foster, Modesto, California; Susan Garner Eisenman, Columbus, Ohio; Gregory A. Franklin, Rochester, New York; Elisabeth Goldman, Lexington, Kentucky; Karen K. Greenberg, Wellesley Hills, Massachusetts; William Harrie, Fargo, North Dakota; John Hawley, Boise, Idaho; Elizabeth Hopkins, Tinton Falls, New Jersey; Kurt M. Hughes, Burlington, Vermont; Larry Jenkins, Salt Lake City, Utah; Steven M. Kirsh, Indianapolis, Indiana; Lori Klockau, Iowa City, Iowa; Monica Farris Linkner, Ann Arbor, Michigan; Laurie Loomis, Honolulu, Hawaii; Kaye H. McLeod, Little Rock, Arkansas; Mark T. McDermott, Washington, D.C.; Ann McLane Kuster, Concord, New Hampshire; Ellen S. Meyer, Wilmington, Delaware; Diane Michelsen, Lafayette, California; Scott E. Myers, Tucson, Arizona; Jack Petty, Bethany, Oklahoma; Douglas Reiniger, Bondurant, Wyoming; Allan Stewart, Clayton, Missouri; Susan L. Stockham, Sarasota, Florida;

Eric Stovall, Reno, Nevada; Janet S. Stulting, West Hartford, Connecticut; Jeanne T. Tate, Tampa, Florida; W. David Thurman, Charlotte, North Carolina, Robert D. Tuke, Nashville, Tennessee; Samuel Totaro, Bensalem, Pennsylvania; Noel Vargas, New Orleans, Louisiana; Judith Vincent, Minneapolis, Minnesota; Michael Washburn, Omaha, Nebraska; and Bryant Whitmire, Birmingham, Alabama. I hope that I have not inadvertently left out anyone's name.

Trademarks

All terms mentioned in this book that are known to be or are suspected of being trademarks or service marks have been appropriately capitalized. Alpha Books and Penguin Group (USA) Inc. cannot attest to the accuracy of this information. Use of a term in this book should not be regarded as affecting the validity of any trademark or service mark.

Part 1

Adoption:
A Wonderful Option!

This part gives you the who, what, when, where, and why of adoption: who needs to be adopted and why, where they are, and more. The chapters in this part give you essential information on adoption, whether you're a "wannabe" adopter or someone that has already succeeded at adoption before and wants to adopt again.

This part will also help bust some common myths about adoption. So forget everything you've read or heard before, and read on to gain important core knowledge from which to build.

Chapter 1

All About Adoption

In This Chapter

- ◆ Adoption by the numbers
- ◆ How adoption affects adopted children
- ◆ Who adopts and why
- ◆ What the adoption process is like

Steve and Lori wanted a baby, but they couldn't have a child biologically. They considered their options and chose to adopt. Friends of theirs had recently adopted a baby through an attorney, Ms. Nize, so they made an appointment with her. After an hour-long interview, Ms. Nize said she'd put them on her list and let them know if a situation came up. A few months later, Ms. Nize called to tell them about a pregnant woman who wanted a family for her baby. Were they interested? Yes! They asked about a million questions; later, a social worker asked *them* what seemed like a million questions. Three months after Ms. Nize's call, Lori and Steve took home their newborn girl.

Tim and Amy were thrilled about adopting a baby from Russia. They'd agreed to pay an adoption agency more than $25,000 right away and eagerly awaited their healthy infant. Six months later, the agency called about a child selected for them. The agency sent a videotape, and Tim and Amy saw that the child, who was nearly a year old, moved very little and couldn't walk or crawl. A pediatrician who watched the tape said that the child had severe problems. The agency director refused to give Amy and Tim any more information—unless they were willing to pay more money. She also said they could either take the child or not take him: The agency would keep the money no matter what. Tim and Amy didn't know what to do.

Dan and Lucy were in their late forties and had talked about adopting older kids. They had seen a TV show about three brothers who needed a family, with a number for interested viewers to call. Dan and Lucy phoned, asked for information, and they soon began adoption classes. Several months later, their new sons came home.

What do all these people have in common? They all attempted to build their families through adoption. Adoption is a successful familybuilding institution that has created millions of very happy families nationwide. It's also a widespread family choice. Most of the time, adoptions work out well. Sometimes, however, they don't. This book will show you how to create your own successful adoption and how to sidestep problems that might occur if you attempt to adopt. (Watch out for the Internet, which has put a whole new wrinkle into adoption! Be sure to read my advice on smart ways to use the Internet to help you adopt, in Chapter 5, and read about Internet adoption scams in Chapter 9.)

In this chapter, I'll help you understand why adoption is such a popular family-building option today and provide some basic information that anyone considering it should know. In addition, I'll try to explain the most common fears people have about adoption.

How Many People Choose Adoption?

No one knows for sure how many people adopt children in any given year, in part because children are adopted in a variety of different ways and no single group or agency tracks all of them. However, thanks to information released by the U.S. Census Bureau in late 2003, we do know that about 1.6 million adopted children younger than age 18 were living in the United States in 2000. We also know that nearly 98,000 adopted children (from the United States and other countries) age 1 and under were living in the United States in the year 2000.

Adopted children represented about 2.5 percent of all children under age 18 in the United States in 2000, and this percentage probably hasn't changed much since then.

According to the Census Bureau, about 473,000 adopted adults were living in the United States. This means that about 2 million men, women, and children were adopted as babies or older children. They all have biological parents and adoptive parents (many of them living), and many of them have biological and adoptive siblings as well as grandparents, aunts, uncles, cousins—and, well, you get the idea. A *lot* of people are affected by adoption.

Adopterms

Adoption refers to the complete transfer of parental rights and obligations from one family to another family. The adoptive family assumes all the legal obligations and responsibilities of raising the adopted child, and the adoption ends the rights and responsibilities of the biological family to the child.

In many cases, the transfer of rights and responsibilities is not direct from the biological parents to adoptive parents; for example, the responsibility for the child may be initially transferred from the birthparents to an agency. Ultimately, however, the adoptive parents become the parents by law, and the biological parents have no further legal rights.

You might not think you know many adopted people or adoptive parents, because many people affected by adoption don't talk about it that much. If you bring up the subject, however, you just might be surprised to hear Aunt Mary tell you that your cousin Billy was adopted. Or she might confide in you about the child she placed for adoption 40 years ago. When I mention that I'm an adoptive parent, people very often share these kinds of stories with me.

Table 1-1, which includes data provided by the U.S. Census Bureau, shows the numbers of adopted children under age 18 in the United States, as well as the numbers born in the U.S. and other countries. Table 1-2 shows the numbers of adopted children in each state, compared to the numbers of nonadopted children. As you can see, minor variations of the percentages of adopted children exist from state to state.

Real Life Snapshots

At a school outing a few years ago, another mother and I sat on a park bench watching our children. After I made a positive comment about adoption in passing, she told me about the baby that she had placed for adoption years ago. She also told me that she herself was adopted and was very happy with her own adoptive parents. I said to her, "So you knew that adoption would be a good choice for your child, too." She responded with one of the most radiant smiles I've ever received. It said to me, "You understand me."

If you are considering adoption, try an experiment: Mention the subject to a few close friends or relatives. Then sit back and see what kind of response you get.

Table 1-1: Selected Characteristics of Adopted Children Under Age 18 in the United States, 2000

	Total	Male	Female
Total number of children	1,586,004	750,528	835,476
Age			
Under 1 year	41,795	19,447	22,348
1 year	55,857	25,310	30,547
2 years	63,250	28,549	34,701
3 years	71,211	32,071	39,140
4 years	74,717	33,832	40,885
5 years	82,466	38,334	44,132
6 years	85,298	40,123	45,175
7 years	92,634	44,325	48,309
8 years	100,144	47,771	52,373
9 years	106,403	59,491	55,912
10 years	106,626	51,320	55,306
11 years	107,221	51,908	55,313
12 years	106,116	51,161	54,955
13 years	105,336	50,856	54,480
14 years	105,184	49,662	55,522
15 years	98,249	46,715	51,534
16 years	93,859	45,319	48,540
17 years	89,638	43,334	46,304
Native or Foreign-born			
Native	1,386,868	666,452	720,416
Foreign-born	199,136	84,076	115,060

Table 1-2: Number and Percent of All Children and Adopted Children, State by State: 2000

	Total number of all children under age 18	Number of adopted children	Percent of adopted children of total children
United States	64,651,959	1,586,004	2.5
Alabama	995,282	24,944	2.5
Alaska	175,315	6,910	3.9
Arizona	1,197,953	28,966	2.4
Arkansas	604,462	15,973	2.6
California	8,027,573	167,190	2.1
Colorado	1,006,573	29,438	2.9
Connecticut	775,214	19,239	2.5
Delaware	172,427	3,452	2.0
District of Columbia	87,890	2,649	3.0
Florida	3,204,362	82,179	2.6
Georgia	1,903,475	49,194	2.6
Hawaii	238,287	6,941	2.9
Idaho	344,494	9,562	2.8
Illinois	2,886,152	73,638	2.6
Indiana	1,441,338	37,004	2.6
Iowa	688,589	18,569	2.7
Kansas	662,249	19,733	3.0
Kentucky	906,933	20,661	2.3
Louisiana	1,051,564	22,827	2.2
Maine	280,763	7,137	2.5
Maryland	1,197,553	32,269	2.7
Massachusetts	1,383,945	35,647	2.6
Michigan	2,356,202	61,232	2.6
Minnesota	1,215,739	31,378	2.6
Mississippi	660,190	16,300	2.5
Missouri	1,300,281	33,156	2.5
Montana	212,401	6,803	3.2
Nebraska	421,429	11,812	2.8
Nevada	452,493	10,588	2.3

continues

Table 1-2: Number and Percent of All Children and Adopted Children, State by State: 2000 (continued)

	Total number of all children under age 18	Number of adopted children	Percent of adopted children of total children
New Hampshire	290,564	6,864	2.4
New Jersey	1,881,428	42,614	2.3
New Mexico	447,024	11,764	2.6
New York	4,153,245	100,736	2.4
North Carolina	1,753,973	42,911	2.4
North Dakota	152,943	3,647	2.4
Ohio	2,643,807	62,653	2.4
Oklahoma	798,929	23,518	2.9
Oregon	770,173	23,901	3.1
Pennsylvania	2,659,562	62,328	2.3
Rhode Island	229,017	5,496	2.4
South Carolina	881,583	22,027	2.5
South Dakota	186,772	5,691	3.0
Tennessee	1,244,838	30,980	2.5
Texas	5,178,912	110,275	2.1
Utah	664,965	19,430	2.9
Vermont	139,324	4,181	3.0
Virginia	1,567,983	38,289	2.4
Washington	1,392,445	38,879	2.8
West Virginia	365,657	9,849	2.7
Wisconsin	1,278,901	30,583	2.4
Wyoming	118,786	3,997	3.4
Puerto Rico	937,408	10,696	1.1

Source: Rose M. Kreider, "Adopted Children and Stepchildren: 2000, Census 2000 Special Report," CNSR-6RV, U.S. Census Bureau, issued October 2003.

Adoption Is Forever

Adoption is a *permanent* option. Even though this sounds self-evident, some people confuse adoption with foster parenting or other temporary situations. An adopted child has the same legal rights and privileges as a biological child. Adoption is not the same as *foster care* or *guardianship*, both of which are usually temporary (or are supposed to be). Instead, adoption is forever. In fact, many adoptive families refer to themselves as "forever families."

Adopterms

A **foster child** is a child who is placed with another family for days, months, or even years. The government or private adoption agency that arranges foster care retains primary legal custody of the child while in care. A foster child cannot be adopted except by consent of a parent or by order of the court.

A **legal guardian** of a child is a person who can make legal (and often parental) decisions for the minor child. The legal guardians cannot adopt the child and become full parents unless the biological parents (or whomever has custody) agrees.

When you adopt, the child becomes your "real" child, and you're regarded (or should be) as "real" parents. I place *real* in quotation marks because this word is a sore point to many adoptive parents and adopted children. (If you adopt a child, you may be surprised at how heated the issue becomes in your own mind.)

What's the big deal? Well, if you're not the "real" parent, the implication to some is that you're a "fake" parent. The term "natural parent" is also quite unpopular with adoptive parents and many adopted people. If you're not natural, then you must be … unnatural. That has a very negative connotation.

How Happy Are Adopted Children?

Many media stories and made-for-TV movies present adopted children as alienated, unhappy, or even criminal. The truth is, however, most adopted children grow up to be normal adults who blend in with everyone else.

In 1994, the Search Institute in Minneapolis released the results of "Growing Up Adopted," a four-year study of 881 adopted adolescents, 1,262 adoptive parents, and 78 nonadopted siblings. The study found that the majority of the adopted teens were strongly attached to their families and psychologically healthy. (If they're doing well in adolescence—a tough time for most of us—imagine what they might achieve as adults!)

In fact, the adopted teens in the study scored *better* than their nonadopted siblings or a sample of their peers in …

◆ Connectedness—having three or more friends and having access to two or more nonparent adults for advice.

◆ Caring—placing a high value on helping other people.

◆ Social competency—friendship-making and assertiveness skills.

Adopted teens also scored higher than nonadopted adolescents in …

◆ School achievement—having a B average or better and aspiring to higher education.

◆ Optimism—expecting to be happy in 10 years and expecting to be successful as an adult.

◆ Support—having a high level of support from parents and from school.

Real Life Snapshots

Here are some famous adopted adults:

Halle Berry (actress)

Robert Byrd (U.S. senator)

Peter and Kitty Caruthers (figure skaters)

Eric Dickerson (football player)

Former president Gerald Ford

Melissa Gilbert (actress)

Scott Hamilton (Olympic gold medalist skater)

Debbie Harry (singer, a.k.a. Blondie)

Faith Hill (singer)

Steve Jobs (co-founder of Apple Computers)

Jim Lightfoot (congressman)

Jim Palmer (professional baseball player)

Nancy Reagan (former First Lady)

More recent are the preliminary results from an ongoing study of nearly 1,000 children, including adopted adolescents and their siblings. This study, funded by the National Institute of Mental Health, is called the Siblings Interaction and Behavior Study (SIBS), and it is led by Matt McGue, Ph.D, at the University of Minnesota.

All the adopted children were under the age of two years old when adopted. In 2003, researchers reported some preliminary results from their study: The adopted kids and their siblings had as close a relationship as nonadopted children. In addition, the researchers said they found no greater risk for emotional problems among the adopted kids than among the nonadopted children. You can read more about siblings and adoption in *Parenting Your Adopted Child: A Positive Approach to Building a Strong Family* by Andrew Adesman, M.D. (McGraw-Hill, 2004).

Most people don't realize that many adopted adults are quite successful and famous. This doesn't mean that an adopted child should be expected to be some kind of super-achiever. But you never know what might happen!

Successful Adoptions: A Well-Kept Secret?

These positive findings seem to contradict those of some older studies on adoption, which indicated that adopted people had a higher rate of problems than nonadopted people. Why the discrepancy? Here's the primary reason.

Older studies on adoption (and even a few newer ones) almost invariably lumped together kids who were adopted as infants with kids who lived in troubled situations (sometimes for years) before they were adopted. These included kids who were abused, for example, or kids who were shuffled from foster home to foster home until they were finally adopted when they were 10 or 11 years old or older.

Children who were adopted as foster children are usually children with heavy emotional baggage. They are very different from kids who are adopted as infants! But too many researchers group all adopted children or adults together.

Another problem is that many other older studies contain subtle biases against adoptive parents or adopted children and adults. For example, in 1960, psychiatrist Marshall Schecter conducted a study that has been misunderstand and is still, unfortunately, cited frequently. In a population of 120 child mental patients, Dr. Schecter noted that 16 had been adopted, or 13 percent. This 13 percent statistic was mistakenly interpreted by some researchers to mean that 13 percent of *all* adopted people are mentally ill, an error Dr. Schecter himself tried to correct. (Other studies have found few differences between adopted and nonadopted children—even those studies that examine only psychiatric patients. For more information on troubled adopted children, read Chapter 21.)

Another complicating factor in the Schecter study and others is that researchers didn't differentiate between problems that children had that may have been related to adoption versus problems related to nonadoption issues.

Some of the adoptive parents in the Schecter study were given bad advice that contributed to (if not caused) problems the children were experiencing; for example, a pediatrician told one family adopting a 14-month-old child to force toilet training immediately. (Most experts today don't push potty training at such a young age.) It's not surprising the child had trouble with potty training and with adjustment into her family. Had she been born to the family and had they pursued potty training with the same zealotry, it's likely she would have also experienced problems.

What I'm trying to say here is that many of the myths surrounding adoption—that adopted children do not thrive or that all adopted families are unhappy—can be traced back to flawed research or unfounded generalizations. Adoption isn't perfect. But millions of Americans have used adoption to create happy, successful, and loving families.

Media Bias

Some suggest that another reason adopted children may get a bad rap is because the media has a bias against adoption. In 1988, Dr. George Gerbner, a researcher at the Annenberg School of Communications at the University of Pennsylvania, found evidence of negative bias against adopted children in many movies and TV shows. He found that these programs often portrayed adopted kids as "problem children"—drug addicts, victims, and so on. Unfortunately, many people get their ideas about adoption from such shows. Do you *really* think that life is like a soap opera? If you do, then maybe you have been married eight times, have suffered amnesia or a multiple personality disorder, have had dozens of affairs, and have forgotten the co-creators of your biological children. If you're like most of the rest of us, this does not describe you.

Adoption Alert

You've just watched *A New Day Dawning*, your favorite soap, and Felicity Ferule has suddenly changed her mind—she wants her adopted son back! (He was placed with the Halfmain family six years ago.)

Can that happen in real life? No way! Most states have a time period during which a birthparent can challenge an adoption; depending on the state, that time period can be hours, days, or even months. But after an adoption is finalized, it can only very rarely be overturned.

The news media has also been guilty of showing a bias against adopted people in its news reports of actual events. For example, if an adopted person commits a crime, the adoptive status is often accentuated. (In one case, a reporter wrote that an adopted man had committed a crime because he had been torn from his "roots" as a baby. This was news to the criminal. He stated frankly that he thought it was because he'd been high on crack cocaine and alcohol. Silly him.)

The fact is that most adopted people are not more criminally inclined, nor more violent, than nonadopted people. When we're talking about several million people who were adopted, from those who are infants to those who are elderly, it's impossible to generalize. Some are very talented or brilliant, some are less capable. Most are within the normal range, just like most nonadopted people of the world.

The media also tends to pounce on adoption horror stories. Sensation sells. For example, you may have heard or read stories about adoptions that went wrong because of some horrific dispute. These stories are newsworthy because they *are* unusual. Most adoptions go through without a hitch and would be considered very unnewsworthy by media.

That's not to say that the scary media stories about unusual situations can't be helpful if they teach everyone involved one key lesson: It's important to be careful in adopting, and if something that you are involved in (or are thinking about becoming involved in) doesn't seem quite right, you should ask questions. Lead with your heart, but don't throw your brain out of the equation.

Very few challenges are made to most of the thousands of infant adoptions that take place in the United States each year, particularly after the babies are placed with adoptive families.

Adopters: Is It a Club You Would Want to Join?

Adoptive parents come from all walks of life. Most are middle-class people; they're not especially rich or famous. (Tom Cruise, Calista Flockhart, and Nicole Kidman are adoptive parents, but you don't have to be gorgeous to adopt!)

Age-wise, new adoptive parents generally range from their mid- to late 30s to mid-40s; however, some are younger, and some are older. Many are married—most adoption agencies and attorneys like to place children with couples who have been married at least three years—but it's also true that single people adopt kids. (For more information on adopting as a single parent, read Chapter 13.) Adopters are both religious and indifferent to religion. They are extroverted and introverted, short and tall, chubby and thin. Their common denominator is that they want to be parents.

Familybuilding Tips

It's a well-kept secret, but some agencies and attorneys *need* adoptive parents. For one thing, untold numbers of infants and children in foreign orphanages need families. In other cases, sometimes birthmothers seek a particular kind of adoptive parent. Bottom line, no matter what your profile, *do not* assume adoption is impossible for you. It usually isn't.

Real Life Snapshots

Here are some famous adoptive parents:

Mona Charen (columnist and TV commentator)

Jamie Lee Curtis (actress)

Calista Flockhart (actress)

Patti LaBelle (singer)

Mary Landrieux (U.S. congressperson)

Rosie O'Donnell (actress)

Marie Osmond (singer)

Sally Jessy Raphael (talk show host)

Gail Sheehy (author)

Barbara Walters (reporter)

There are some categories, however, that adoptive parents generally *do not* fall into. They are not criminals or drug addicts or child abusers—social workers check out the backgrounds of adopting parents to make sure that irresponsible or unsuitable people are not allowed to adopt. However, the adoption system and the people who work in it are not infallible. On rare occasions, unsuitable parents are allowed to adopt.

Adoptions Inside and Outside the Family

When most people think of adoption, they envision a set of parents adopting a child who is a complete stranger to them. Yet this is often not the case. *Relative adoptions—* in which the adopted child is related to the adoptive parents—are almost as prevalent as *nonrelative adoptions.* I'll explain both kinds in more detail.

Adopterms

A **relative adoption** refers to an adoption in which the adopter is biologically related to the adopted child or is married to the child's parent. A stepparent adoption is also usually considered a relative adoption.

In a **nonrelative adoption,** the adoptive parent is a biological stranger to the child, with no common genetic bonds, and is not a stepparent.

All in the Family

Of the many American children who are adopted by Americans each year, some are adopted by relatives such as grandparents, aunts, and uncles. For example, actor Jack Nicholson was adopted by his grandparents. (But he didn't learn this until adulthood—not a good idea. I'll talk more about discussing adoption with children in Chapter 20.)

In a relative adoption, grandparents can become the legal parents of their grandchildren; aunts or uncles can adopt their nieces and nephews; and so on. Some children will refer to their adoptive parent as "Grandma" or "Uncle Bob"; others consider the adoptive relative to be "Mommy" or "Daddy."

Why do people adopt children from within their biological family? Here are a few reasons:

♦ The birthmother is too young to be a parent, and her own parents decide to adopt the child (grandparent adoption).

♦ The birthparent is ill.

♦ The birthparent has abandoned the child.

♦ The birthparent is considering adoption, and the adopting relative disapproves of nonrelative adoption.

♦ The adopter thinks relative adoption is easier than nonrelative adoption.

♦ The birthparent wishes to remain in touch with the child.

Grafting Onto Your Family Tree

People adopt children who are not in their biological family for a host of reasons, but by far the number-one reason people adopt is because they want to have a family but are infertile.

Here are a few more reasons people adopt children not related to them:

♦ They want to help a child.

♦ They feel "called" to adopt.

♦ They already have a child of one gender and want a child of another gender.

♦ They want a sibling for another child.

Familybuilding Tips

Probably 95 percent or more of people who adopt children are infertile.

Most adoption professionals agree that the best reasons to adopt, whether inside or outside the family, are because the adopter wants a child to love and wants to provide a good family for that child.

The Adoption Process: What's It Like?

A lot of people—perhaps you're one of them?—are interested in adoption, but they are afraid of going through the adoption process. If you think you'd like to become a parent by adoption but you're afraid to take the first step, join the crowd. It's not at all unusual for people considering adoption to have the following concerns and fears:

- The adoption process will take too long—at least five years.

- They will be rejected as potential parents by either birthparents or the adoption arranger.

- They won't be able to find an adoption agency.

- After they find a potential adoptive child, the birthparents will suddenly change their minds.

- They won't be able to afford adoption fees.

- The child could have medical or genetic issues/problems.

- They might not be able to love a child unrelated to them.

Most of these fears simply aren't justified, as I'll explain in the following sections as well as other chapters.

How Long Does It Take?

Some people succeed in adopting a child within a few months or a year; for others, it can take several years or more. Numerous factors are involved in the adoption time frame:

- The age of the child you want to adopt. You may have to wait an extended period to adopt a toddler born in the United States. Why? Because most birthmothers choose adoption when their children are babies. After that, they become too attached to them. However, toddlers are available for adoption in foreign orphanages.

- The amount of information you demand about the child. With international adoptions, for example, often very little is known about the child's history before he or she arrived in the orphanage.

- Your own willingness to contact a variety of agencies and attorneys.

- Your own circumstances: age, health history, marital status, financial stability, and so on.

- How flexible you are willing to be in terms of the type of child you will adopt.

In addition to the preceding factors, the adoption arrangers—the agencies, attorneys, and others who help people find and adopt children—play a part in how quickly you are able to adopt.

Will You Look Good on Paper?

Your individual circumstances affect the adoption process. Healthy married people between the ages of 30 and 45 or so are generally considered the most desirable by agencies, attorneys, and birthparents who place children for adoption. But you are *not* automatically shut out of the adoption process if you are single, disabled, gay or lesbian, or over 45! Contrary to popular belief, it's very possible for most people to adopt a child. I'll talk more about how nontraditional applicants can successfully adopt in Chapter 13.

Life (and Adoption) Are Not Perfect

As for how flexible you're willing to be about the child you want to adopt, it's okay to want a healthy child. Most people do, whether they have children biologically or through adoption. But if you want an absolutely risk-free adoption, with the perfect child and the perfect birthparents, you may have a long wait—maybe forever.

The Least You Need to Know

- Adoption is a permanent way to build your family.

- Most adopted children grow up healthy and well adjusted.

- Adoptive parents come from many walks of life. There is no single profile of a "successful" adoptive parent.

- Adoptions don't necessarily take a long time; nor will you automatically be rejected if you aren't a perfect potential parent.

- Despite the negative myths and stories emphasized in the media, most real-life adoptions are positive.

Chapter 2

Is Adoption Right for You?

In This Chapter

- Determining your reasons for choosing adoption
- Affecting your life through adoption
- Figuring out whether your partner wants to adopt
- Undergoing the screening process
- Looking at the financial costs of adoption
- Discussing adoption with family and friends

Many of us are raised to think of a family as a biological unit: Mom, Dad, and the 2.3 kids born to them. Nobody talks much about infertility or adoption. Therefore, it's one thing to think that, in general, adoption is a good thing. It's a whole other ball game to think about actually adopting a child yourself.

For example, how you feel about infertility—if you are infertile—is a major issue. Then there's how your extended family might react to a new person joining the family through adoption. You also have to think about the day-to-day constraints that would be placed upon you as a parent.

These are just a few issues that need to be mentally and emotionally processed before you adopt. This chapter will help you do that.

In this chapter, I help you figure out whether adoption is a realistic choice for you. In addition, I suggest ways you can balance the various influences that push you toward and pull you away from adoption.

Fiction Is Stranger Than Truth: Realities of Adoption

In the first chapter, I talked about outlandish adoption stories on soap operas and also about rare but highly publicized adoption scandals that make the news. Here's the process that an actual adoption takes for most adopters:

1. They decide to adopt.

2. They apply to an agency or attorney.

3. They are investigated by a social worker.

4. They are approved.

5. A child is placed with them.

6. They become a forever family.

Of course, the path between the starting point and the finish line can be nerve-wracking and fraught with fears. For many people, the fears and anxiety stem from their own attitudes and emotions rather than anything that actually happens during the process. Throughout the rest of this chapter, I'll help you examine some of the common fears and issues you need to face before you begin.

Why Adopt?

Most people adopt children because they are infertile. However, many people who could have biological children choose to adopt anyway. (Some call such people *preferential adopters*.) Here are some reasons fertile people opt for adoption:

◆ They think it makes more sense to adopt a child "already here" than to bring another child into the world.

◆ They don't want the hassles of caring for a baby and would rather adopt an older child.

◆ They have a genetic problem that they don't want to pass on to biological children.

♦ The woman has a medical problem that would make pregnancy difficult.

♦ The person is single and doesn't wish to create a pregnancy outside of marriage.

Many adoption agencies in the United States will turn down couples who are fertile. How do they know? They may require a statement from a physician describing an infertility problem. Preferential adopters generally adopt a child from another country, or they find agencies or attorneys willing to work with them.

Is Adoption Good Enough for You?

Here's another tough issue that most people don't like to think about: Will you be satisfied with an adopted child?

Maybe you want a biological child but can't have one, so you decide to adopt. Will you be able to love an adopted child as much as you would love a biological child?

To help you answer this question, first consider the fact that you are able to love lots of people who aren't related to you—your spouse and your close friends, for example. Also, consider the true importance of biological relationships to you. If you feel that what is most important is to have a child who resembles you or carries forth your genes, then adoption wouldn't be right for you. If the primary reason you want to adopt is to become a parent, then adoption might be right for you.

In addition, know that nearly all adoptive parents believe their children are the right ones for them, the ones they were meant to parent.

Are You Ready for Adoption?

A person's readiness to adopt is based on rational as well as completely emotional issues, fears, concerns, and constraints. You need to achieve a state of adoption-readiness, which enables you to then become very proactive and directed—what I call having an *adoption mind-set*. However, not everyone who experiences adoption-readiness moves into the adoption mind-set. This can happen for a number of reasons—perhaps a spouse doesn't want to adopt, or they decide that they can't afford the fees. Conversely, some people jump into the adoption mind-set

Adopterms

Adoption-readiness refers to your state of mind when you feel ready to explore adoption. The **adoption mind-set** is an attitude in which you not only *want* to adopt a child, but you *need* to adopt a child, and you plan to act on this need.

without ever going through the adoption-readiness phase. These people may not be ready to adopt.

Here are just a few of the issues you must confront before moving into the adoption mind-set—many of which are the same or similar to issues people face (or should face) if they are thinking about biological parenthood:

♦ Marital issues. If you are married, is your marriage stable?

♦ Lifestyle issues. Can you change your life to accommodate a child?

♦ Your health. You don't have to be an Olympic athlete, but can you manage the hard work involved in parenting? Also, is your health good enough that you can reasonably expect to be able to parent a child for the next 18 years or until the child's adulthood?

♦ Financial issues. Can you afford the costs associated with clothes, toys, furniture, child care, and other expenses?

♦ Your job. How does a child fit with your career?

Let's explore some of these issues in more detail.

Marital Bliss

Adopting a child primarily because you are unhappy with a spouse is a bad idea. Here are just a few of the problems that can occur if you adopt to "save your marriage":

♦ The child might sense that he or she's supposed to hold your relationship together, a burden that no child should feel.

♦ If your marriage does fail, the child will feel that he or she failed you. (Children think a lot of bad things are their fault.)

♦ Parenting is hard work. If your marriage is under strain already, adopting a child could be the final straw.

♦ Children need a stable environment in which they feel emotionally safe.

Does this mean that if sometimes you get annoyed with your spouse for snoring or for forgetting to pick up bread and milk on the way home from work, your marriage isn't good enough? Of course not. All marriages have ups and downs. What matters is that you and your spouse feel a strong, positive, lifelong bond to each other.

Lifestyle Changes

Whether you adopt an infant or an older child, you can be sure that your life and your lifestyle will change. Is that okay with you?

Are you ready to devote yourself to your child? When you become a parent—whether through birth or through adoption—there's this other person who needs constant attention and care. Are you prepared to fulfill a child's physical and emotional needs on a daily basis? Will you resent forgoing the night out on the town with friends when your child gets ill or the babysitter cancels at the last minute? Scientists say that children are born with temperaments—outgoing, shy, and so forth. What if you're very outgoing and carefree, but the child you adopt turns out to be shy and clingy? A good parent must adjust to the child's personality. (If you think this is only a problem for adoptive parents, think again! Many biological parents are baffled by their children's personalities, which are radically different from their own.)

Is Your Partner Adoption-Ready?

By now you should have a good sense of whether you're adoption-ready. If you have a partner, now it's time to think about whether he or she is also ready to consider adoption as an option. One way to do this is simply to ask. But sometimes people, especially those we love, don't want to hurt our feelings or make us angry with them and so tell us what they think we want to hear, rather than what they are really thinking. That's why you and your partner should take the following Adoption Readiness Quiz. The questions are designed to elicit true feelings as well as to encourage you and your partner to actually think about adopting.

It's good for couples to try to imagine their lives as adoptive parents and then to talk about those visions. You might be surprised to learn that your partner will be happy only with an infant. Or an older child. You might find out that your partner is receptive to adopting a child with special needs or a child from another country. You might also find that your partner doesn't want to think about this imaginary child at all— maybe your partner isn't ready to make a decision about adoption yet, or maybe he or she is dead set against the idea. No matter what you learn from this process, it's much better to find out before you begin the adoption process than after.

Adoption Readiness Quiz

You and your partner should both take some time to answer the following questions to determine your state of adoption-readiness. After you've completed the quiz, ask your partner to do the same. Then read the next section to help interpret your and your partner's answers.

1. Imagine that we *do* adopt a child. What is our life like?

_____

_____

_____

2. What do you think are the main pros and cons of adopting?

Pros: _____

_____

Cons: _____

_____

3. What do you think are the main pros and cons of parenting?

Pros: _____

_____

Cons: _____

_____

4. What would we do as a family in our spare time and on vacations?

_____

_____

_____

5. What would our biological child be like if we had one? (Even if there is no chance that you could have one.)

_____

_____

_____

6. What would our adopted child be like?

_____

_____

_____

Interpreting the Quiz

Questions 1 and 4: These questions can give you a good idea of how you and your partner envision parenting. If either of you think nothing will be different, you're being unrealistic. If you're both already thinking about family trips, picnics, and other outings, then adoption might be right for you.

Questions 2 and 3: The quiz asks about the pros and cons of adopting as well as the pros and cons of parenting. If your answers to both questions are the same or similar, then it might mean that you view adoption as equal to biological parenting. If the answers are radically different, you might not be receptive to adoption.

Questions 5 and 6: Your and your partner's answers to these questions can give you important information about how you both view adoption. If your answers describe the biological child and adopted child in favorable terms, then you're probably at least open to considering the adoption option. If the biological child is described in glowing terms, and the adopted child is described more negatively, this may indicate a problem. Of course, if the adopted child is described in idealistic terms, that isn't good either. What you're looking for is realism and balance.

Getting Screened

Figuring out whether you are adoption-ready takes some serious thinking and a clear-eyed look at yourself, at your spouse (if you are married), and also at your life situation. This kind of thinking is rarely, if ever, required of people who have biological children. (Although it certainly would be nice if more people did think harder about it before becoming parents!)

When you adopt a child, social workers expect you to undergo some serious introspection, as well as to share information about yourself. You may feel like you're under a microscope, an interesting specimen for the social worker to analyze, catalog, and ultimately approve or not (no matter how nice the social worker is). Maybe you're successful in the business world, academia, or elsewhere. It doesn't matter. When you enter the adoption system, you go in at "Start," along with everyone else.

I talk about the screening process in detail in Chapter 12, so I'm not going to delve deeply into it here. Rather, I want to talk about the anger and irritation that many people have about the "unfairness" of being asked what seem to be a multigazillion questions when they want to adopt.

Some people believe it should be much easier to adopt than it is, and they think that going through background investigations, physical examinations, reams of paperwork, and talks with social workers is just too much trouble and it shouldn't be so hard.

> ![CAUTION] **Adoption Alert** _____
>
> Occasionally, even with screening, potential adoptive parents fail to seriously evaluate themselves. They make it through the adoption process on automatic pilot, without ever considering various issues. They think that chanting the party line on adoption is the right thing to do.
>
> The problem with spouting the party line is that people who somehow manage to jump into adoption without much thinking never attain that "state of grace" that I call adoption-readiness. This is not good. Adoption should be preceded by both adoption-readiness and the adoption mind-set.

I understand their frustration and can empathize with how they feel, but I simply do not agree with people who think it should be easy to adopt. I think that adoptive parents should be evaluated for three basic reasons:

- ◆ A screening can help avoid abuses of the system, such as baby selling to the highest bidder or putting undue pressure on a birthmother.

- ◆ A screening can help adoptive parents think about whether adoption is truly right for their family and to prepare for the adoption if they decide that it is.

- ◆ Screening usually can protect the child from very inappropriate adopters.

Sure, it's no fun to be evaluated, and some people—maybe most people—feel very insecure when they are being judged as potential parents. They fear they won't make the grade.

And yet, I still think it's important for adoptive parents to be screened. Children deserve the best chance they can get. With adoption, this can and should be the goal. The evaluation process is a big part of all that.

The Financial Costs of Adoption

Is it fair to charge fees to adopt a child? Many people don't think so. Although I'll talk more about adoption fees and how to afford adoption in Chapter 8, let's look at the financial issue, which is another blocking point for many potential adoptive parents.

Biological Babies Are Free

A lot of people mistakenly think that if they had a biological child, it would be free— because they have health insurance. However, it's not free to bear a child—somebody is paying for all of the doctor's visits during the nine months of pregnancy and the hospital fees when the child is actually born.

Birthmothers who place their children for adoption often don't have health insurance, and somebody has to pay for their medical expenses. When you adopt a child, you may be the one footing the medical bills.

In addition, adoption agencies and adoption attorneys have expenses. It might not be all that pleasant to think about this, but adoption providers have business expenses. It's not evil; it's life.

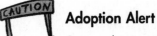

Adoption Alert

Some adoption arrangers charge much higher fees than everyone else. I wouldn't go to such people, and before you do, read Chapter 6 on adoption arrangers and also read Chapter 9 on adoption scammers.

Don't Want to Break the Bank

Okay, so you don't want to drain your savings account or borrow money to pay for a child. Who does? But let's face it: You must operate in the reality that the rest of us live in.

Adoption Is a Benefit to Society

What about adoption as a benefit to society? I agree that adoption *is* a social good. But do you think that social goods are free? Think again. Without getting too political here, think about public assistance and other programs to help those in need. Think about the arts. Think about your favorite charity. None of these worthy organizations can function without financial support.

As for the argument that the child won't have to go into foster care because you are benevolently adopting him or her, think again. If the child isn't already in the foster care system, then in most cases someone else will adopt him or her if you don't. Most birthmothers will seek other adoptive parents if you don't work out.

Paying Fees to Adopt Is Like Buying a Child

Is paying to adopt equal to buying a child? Not unless you're doing something illegal. What you're paying for are the services of the attorney or agency. Sometimes you may be paying for the birthmother's living expenses or her medical expenses, too. But you are *not* paying for your child. Besides, thanks to Congress, the Internal Revenue

Service now allows a $10,160 tax credit for adopting! Would the IRS allow a credit for something illegal? (Read more about the IRS tax credit in Chapter 8.)

Family Values

You can be sure that if you're thinking about adoption, just about everyone you know will have an opinion about whether you should (or shouldn't) adopt. But the problem with listening to everyone else is that you will receive conflicting advice. Also, the people telling you what to do probably don't know squat about adoption. They all want what they think is best for you—but how can they know what truly is the right choice for your situation? *Answer:* It must be your decision.

Only you (and your partner, if you have one) can make such an important and life-changing decision as to whether or not you are ready to adopt a child. After all, no matter how much you love your family and friends, who's going to stagger out of bed at 2 A.M. to feed the baby? It's *you* who will be responsible for your child, and no one else.

If you decide to adopt a child who is of a different race or from another country, you may get additional flak from your family. You may also receive family disapproval if you are single and wish to adopt. If you've explained what you want to do to your friends and family and their objections seem unreasonable to you, you must decide whether and how their feelings will affect your decision to adopt and your future relationship with them.

Breaking the News

Here are some tips for telling your family that you plan to adopt:

◆ Listen for the underlying emotions and try to restate them. "Mom, it sounds like you are saying that you're worried the birthmother will change her mind, and we'll be brokenhearted."

◆ Tell your family that you are learning about adoption and adopted kids and soon you'll be able to share information.

◆ If they seem worried, try to find out what the underlying concern is *really* about. My mother seemed to have doubts about adoption, but I couldn't figure out why. She finally told me she thought it would be hard to parent a disabled child. But I had no plan to adopt a child with special needs. Problem solved.

Opinions After Adoption

There are always going to be people who ask aggravating questions and make stupid comments. What's more, these questions and concerns will continue long after you've adopted a child. So, can you take it? Most adoptive parents answer with a resounding "Yes!" But I suggest that all potential adoptive parents imagine ahead of time how they might feel.

Adoption Alert _____

Adoptive families are the recipients of some uniquely strange comments. Think about how you'd feel if your family was discussed this way:

"Isn't it wonderful that they gave that little orphan a home?"

"She is so cute! Good thing her real mother can't see her, she'd snatch her right away from you."

"I bet he is hyperactive because all those adopted kids have that attention deficit thing."

"You are such a good mother. It's almost like he was really your own."

"You're so lucky you didn't have to go through labor to have her. You did it the easy way."

For example, would it bother you if people challenged your "realness," your entitlement to be a parent when you adopt? Or if they make wrongheaded comments based on silly ideas? If you aren't confident that you could tolerate such remarks, well, fasten your seat belt. You may be in for a rocky ride.

Am I trying to talk you *out* of adoption? No way! But to my mind, the most successful adoptions take place when families are prepared for situations that commonly occur.

Selflessness and Selfishness

Despite how many times you hear about adoptive parents who are "saints" because they "took in" the poor little darlings—and, incidentally, this imagery makes most adoptive parents nearly retch—adoption is in many ways a selfish action. If a parent believes that adoption is totally selfless, it can be very problematic for the child.

Many people who have adopted children did seek to have a biological child first, which is okay. But it's important that people who do adopt accept their children as the first-class beings that they are. If you think you "should" adopt so you can help a poor little orphan somewhere, even though you know in your heart you could never love her the same as "your own," my advice is: Don't adopt.

The best reason to adopt a child is because you want to become a good parent to a child who needs a family. You want to adopt because you want to give your love to a child and provide as happy a life as you can. But you are also selfish in that you want to receive love from the child as well and to enjoy watching your child grow up. The trick is finding the balance.

Here's another important point, one worth ending this chapter. Adopt the kind of child you want, not the child that is pressed upon you by social workers or others. If you want to adopt a healthy infant of the same race as you, fine. If you want to adopt a child from another country, also fine. And if your goal is to adopt an older child—from the United States or abroad—that's okay, too.

The Least You Need to Know

♦ As a potential adoptive parent, you need to assess your adoption-readiness.

♦ Talk to your partner to find out how he or she really feels about adoption.

♦ Understand the financial costs of adoption.

♦ Realize that your family and friends may offer unsolicited advice about your adoption.

♦ Make sure that you are adopting for the right reasons.

Chapter 3

Children Who Need Families

In This Chapter

- ◆ Adopting an infant
- ◆ Defining children with special needs
- ◆ Understanding the foster care system
- ◆ Adopting an older child
- ◆ Adopting a disabled child
- ◆ Adopting a child of a different race

Marie is single, pregnant, and thinking about adoption. She wants a good family for her baby, preferably a couple of the same religion with strong values. The Adorable Babies Adoption Agency has given Marie five resumés of approved couples to consider. She wants to select a family now so that everything will be settled when it's time to deliver.

Tommy, 8, and Timmy, 10, have been with several foster families over the past few years, sometimes living together, sometimes living apart. The rights of their parents have been terminated by the court, and the boys need a family who can love two active brothers.

Natasha is a nine-month-old Russian child who has lived in an orphanage since just after birth. She seems active and healthy, but she hasn't been adopted so far because she is a little small for her age.

These are just a few of the many different scenarios describing children (and children-to-be!) who need families all around the globe. Some of these children will be adopted quickly. For others, it will take much longer to find their families. This chapter will provide you an overview of the different kinds of children who need permanent, loving families.

Where the Babies Are

Many people want to adopt an infant, preferably a healthy baby and preferably tomorrow—if not today.

At least 30,000 American-born babies are adopted each year (called *domestic adoption*), and more than 20,000 children, mostly babies, are adopted from other countries (called *international adoption*). These numbers are not an upper limit—more babies and children could be adopted if more birthparents in the United States chose adoption over struggling to raise children they are unready to parent, or if more adoptive parents could be identified to adopt the many thousands of babies and toddlers living in overseas orphanages who need parents.

Infants who need adoptive families come in all colors. Most are healthy or have correctable health problems, but some are very ill. It may be a little easier and faster to adopt a child who is of mixed race or black, but whites who want to adopt white children certainly can succeed, as can families of other races or ethnicities who want to adopt children of the same race or ethnicity as they are.

If you want to adopt an infant, you have a variety of choices. Here are the major options available:

◆ You can adopt an American infant through an adoption agency in your state or another state.

◆ You can adopt an American baby independently, with the assistance of an attorney.

◆ You can adopt a child from another country through an adoption agency in your state or another state.

Familybuilding Tips

The adoption process is fraught with rules and regulations and an entire system to deal with. Learn the ins and outs of the adoption system, and you will succeed much faster and with less emotional and financial pain than the people who rush in to accept any offer.

In many cases of domestic infant adoption, the child hasn't even been born when the adoption arrangements are made. The reason for this is simple: The pregnant woman wants to know that her child will be placed with an adoptive family immediately—straight from the hospital. Some birthmothers are very adamant about this.

> **CAUTION**
>
> ### Adoption Alert _____
>
> Should people adopt only children with special needs because such children urgently need a family, and there are lots of them?
>
> My position is that a family should adopt the type of child they want to adopt. If they want to adopt a healthy same-race infant, I believe it is wrong to attempt to coerce them into adopting a child of another race, or with medical problems, or an older child. However, if the family does want to adopt a child with a special need and they understand the pros and cons of whatever the problem is, they shouldn't be dissuaded.

Why Adopt an Infant?

It's self-evident to many people why adopters want infants, but the question is a valid one. After all, people sometimes point out, many older kids and abused kids need families. So why don't most people want to adopt an older child?

Here are some reasons why people want to adopt infants rather than older children:

- ◆ They want to provide a continuously positive environment beginning when the child is young, believing that they will have a greater influence that way.

- ◆ They like babies.

- ◆ They don't want to deal with the after-effects of abuse and neglect that older children may have suffered.

- ◆ They want to watch the child grow from a tiny infant.

How to Adopt an Infant

Few infant adoptions occur through state government agencies, although some babies with serious medical problems are adopted this way. Instead, most infant adoptions are arranged either by adoption agencies, by the adopters and birthparents themselves, or by adoption attorneys. An estimated one half to two thirds of all infant adoptions in the United States are independent, nonagency adoptions.

An *agency adoption* is arranged by workers at a licensed adoption agency. This term usually refers to private adoption agencies, rather than state or county government (public) agencies. In an agency adoption, the agency is the primary facilitator of the adoption.

An *independent adoption* is a non-agency adoption. Often, however, adoption agencies are involved, in that they will do home study investigations of the prospective adopters, and they may also provide counseling services to the birthparents.

Kids with Special Needs

Many people adopt children with *special needs*, including older kids, children with medical problems, siblings, multiracial kids, and others. Some children with special needs are right here in the United States; others languish in foreign orphanages. All urgently need parents.

Adopterms

Agencies designate children who they believe are hard to place as children with **special needs**, although each agency differs on what constitutes a special need. What some agencies regard as special needs are not viewed that way by other agencies—and often not by hopeful adoptive parents. For example, healthy black or biracial infants and older children are often categorized as having special needs simply because the agency has trouble finding parents for them.

State agencies may have a legal definition of the term special needs. Some states may include the definition in their state law.

Children who fit the categories defined by law as special needs may qualify for state and/or federal benefits, such as Medicaid and monthly subsidy payments.

In addition, as of 2004, if you adopt one or more children with special needs from the U.S. foster care system—and nearly all kids in foster care are regarded as having special needs because of their age, race, being part of a sibling group or for some other reason—you are entitled to take a tax credit of $10,160 per child whom you adopt. This is true whether you have any adoption-related expenses or not. (People who adopt children from foster care rarely, if ever, pay any fees.) The reason for this astonishingly generous tax break is that the federal government is actively encouraging people to adopt foster children. (Read more about the tax credit in Chapter 8.)

Adoptinfo

In a fascinating study of 1,343 children adopted from the foster care system in Illinois, reported by researchers Jeanne A. Howard and Susan Livingston Smith in *After Adoption: The Needs of Adopted Youth* (CWLA Press, 2003), most of the children had been removed from their biological families because of severe neglect or because of substance abuse.

Despite the problems the children started out with in their lives, according to their adoptive parents, 92 percent of the adopted children were in good or excellent health. In addition, 93 percent of the adopters said they would definitely or probably adopt again, knowing what they know about the child. Most adoptive parents had been the child's foster parent prior to the adoption, and the majority of children had been placed with them as infants or small children, although they were not adopted until they were age six or older.

The biggest problem area the children had was in school functioning, and about 40 percent of the children were in special classes in school. The researchers found that the most significant risk factor in predicting a behavior problem in the children was prenatal substance abuse of the birthmother, and some adoptive parents wished they had been given more information about this topic. In contrast, the greatest predictive/protective factor *against* a child experiencing later serious behavior problems was the child's ability to receive and give affection.

Here is a general summary of children who are often defined as having special needs (keep in mind that children may have more than one special need and that the definition of special need varies from agency to agency):

- ◆ Children with a minor or serious medical problem—everything from a correctable birthmark to being HIV-positive

- ◆ Children who were abused, neglected, or abandoned in the past

- ◆ Children over the age of six or seven

- ◆ Children who have siblings (and whom the agency hopes to place together in one family)

- ◆ Children who are African-American or biracial

- ◆ Children with serious psychological or psychiatric problems

 Familybuilding Tips

Often (but not always), private agencies charge lower fees to families planning to adopt children with special needs. State government social service agencies (formerly called the welfare department) don't charge fees, but most of the children they place have special needs, by virtually anyone's definition. Attorneys who place children with special needs generally don't lower their fees.

doption agencies sometimes offer descriptions of their special-needs kids in advertisements of on their websites. The National Adoption Center website (www.adopt.org/waitingchildren) as well as the websites of many states, provide photos and pictures of children who need families, describing their hobbies, their problems, and the type of family that is being sought for them.

Infants with Special Needs

Families and agencies vary a lot in what they think constitutes a special need in an infant, so it's essential that you know how it's being defined when considering a special-needs infant.

> **Familybuilding Tips**
>
> In the past, many abused and neglected children entered foster care and were later returned to their abusive parents. Then they were reabused or neglected and, far too frequently, these same children entered the foster care system yet again. For many children, this revolving door cycle continued until they "aged out" at age 18. Because of federal parental "reunification" laws, which affected state foster care funding, states bent over backward to give parents chance after chance to resolve whatever problems they had that led to the abuse or neglect. (Primarily substance abuse and/or emotional disorders.)
>
> But what was forgotten by many people was that the most vulnerable individuals, the children, were growing up in emotional pain and hardship, often shuttled from foster home to foster home. By the time they were age 18, many were very troubled individuals. At long last, it was realized that, although it was very important to protect the rights of parents, they should not be given a child's entire life to resolve their issues. This recognition led to the Adoption and Safe Families Act of 1997, which put the interests of children first.
>
> Since the passage of the Adoption and Safe Families Act, which offered states financial incentives for the adoptions of foster children, the numbers of children adopted from foster care have increased from about 31,000 nationwide in 1997 to nearly 51,000 in 2002.

International Babies with Special Needs

An infant born in another country may have a problem like a cleft palate or some other medical condition that would be considered easily correctable in the United States but is a major problem that probably won't ever be corrected in the child's country. As a result, some families decide to adopt a child from overseas with a special need that might be treatable in this country.

Children born overseas may also suffer from malnutrition, hepatitis, tuberculosis, rickets, intestinal parasites, or other illnesses. Sometimes the effects of past deprivation can be overcome by good nutrition and lots of TLC. However, this is *not* always true—it should never be assumed that love conquers all. Consult with your pediatrician *before* you adopt a child with special needs—whether inside or outside of the United States. (Be sure to read Chapter 11 on children adopted from other countries and Chapter 15 on health issues in adoption.)

Waiting Children in Foster Care

Thousands of kids in foster care need adoptive families. State agencies generally refer to them as *waiting children*, and you may see their photos in local newspapers, on agency websites, or even on television programs. According to statistics from the Adoption and Foster Care Analysis Reporting System (AFCARS) from the federal government, in 2001 (the latest data as of this writing), the average child who was adopted from foster care in the United States was 7 years old. Most of the children (80 percent) were in foster care for more than 11 months before they were adopted.

The numbers of foster children needing families vary from state to state, but every state has foster kids who need parents. (You can also adopt a foster child from another state, although it's more complicated than adopting from your own state. I recommend looking homeward first.)

Adopterms

Waiting children refers to kids in foster care who need adoptive families. The parental rights have been legally terminated.

As you can see on the following table, the number of children adopted from foster care ("public child welfare involvement") have doubled or increased even more in many states since 1995, primarily because the federal government, at long last, made adoption a favorable choice for states. For example, 3,094 children were adopted from foster care in California in 1995, and that number increased to 8,713 children by 2002. In Missouri, 538 foster children were adopted in 1995, and 1,542 were adopted in 2002. North Dakota also saw triple increases in adoptions from 1995 to 2002, as did South Dakota and Wisconsin.

Some states had dramatic increases, such as in North Carolina, where 289 children were adopted from foster care in 1995, and by 2002, that number had increased to 1,324! That's almost a five-fold increase. Find your own state on the chart to see how your state is doing.

Keep in mind that even though adoptions of foster children have increased greatly, many children still in the system need families because so many children enter foster care. For example, according to national statistics released by the Children's Bureau of the Department of Health and Human Services, in fiscal year 2002, 302,000 children entered foster care, up from 295,000 children entering the system in 2001. An estimated 126,000 foster children nationwide were ready and waiting to be adopted, but less than half (51,000 kids) were adopted.

Adoptions of Children with Public Child Welfare Involvement by State, Fiscal Year (FY) 1995–2002

State	FY 1995	FY 1996	FY 1997	FY 1998	FY 1999	FY 2000	FY 2001	FY 2002
Alabama	128	153	136	115	153	202	238	249
Alaska	103	112	109	95	137	202	278	190
Arizona	215	383	474	n/a	761	853	938	793
Arkansas	84	185	146	258	318	325	362	297
California	3,094	3,153	3,614	4,418	6,344	8,776	9,180	8,713
Colorado	338	454	458	576	713	691	611	840
Connecticut	198	146	278	314	403	499	444	617
Delaware	38	46	33	62	33	103	117	133
District of Columbia	86	113	132	139	166	319	230	252
Florida	904	1,064	992	1,549	1,355	1,629	1,493	2,206
Georgia	383	537	558	724	1,129	1,080	899	934
Hawaii	42	64	150	301	281	280	260	349
Idaho	46	40	47	57	107	140	132	118
Illinois	1,759	2,146	2,695	4,656	7,028	5,664	4,107	3,585
Indiana	520	373	592	795	759	1,147	878	920
Iowa	227	383	440	525	764	729	661	871
Kansas	333	292	421	419	566	468	428	450
Kentucky	197	214	222	209	360	398	573	552
Louisiana	292	321	310	311	356	476	470	487
Maine	85	144	96	125	202	379	364	285
Maryland	324	413	290	478	592	548	815	631
Massachusetts	1,073	1,113	1,161	1,100	922	861	778	808

State	FY 1995	FY 1996	FY 1997	FY 1998	FY 1999	FY 2000	FY 2001	FY 2002
Michigan	1,717	1,950	2,047	2,257	2,446	2,804	2,979	2,826
Minnesota	232	239	302	429	633	614	567	626
Mississippi	109	101	131	170	237	288	266	216
Missouri	538	600	533	640	849	1,265	1,102	1,542
Montana	104	98	143	149	187	238	275	234
Nebraska	208	168	180	n/a	279	293	292	308
Nevada	155	145	148	n/a	123	231	243	251
New Hampshire	51	59	24	51	62	97	95	114
New Jersey	616	678	570	815	732	832	1,028	1,365
New Mexico	141	148	152	197	258	347	369	275
New York	4,579	4,590	4,979	4,819	4,864	4,234	3,934	3,160
North Carolina	289	417	694	882	949	1,337	1,327	1,324
North Dakota	42	41	57	111	139	105	145	137
Ohio	1,202	1,258	1,400	1,015	1,868	2,044	2,230	2,396
Oklahoma	226	371	418	505	825	1,067	956	987
Oregon	427	468	441	665	765	831	1,071	1,115
Pennsylvania	1,018	1,127	1,526	1,516	1,454	1,712	1,564	2,020
Rhode Island	216	341	226	222	292	260	267	256
South Carolina	231	220	318	465	456	378	384	340
South Dakota	42	72	55	55	84	94	97	145
Tennessee	458	330	195	337	382	431	646	922
Texas	804	746	1,091	1,602	2,054	2,040	2,319	2,295
Utah	283	124	268	334	369	303	349	335
Vermont	62	83	80	118	139	122	116	153
Virginia	320	298	276	235	326	448	495	424
Washington	645	521	656	878	1,047	1,141	1,204	1,077
West Virginia	139	188	220	211	312	352	362	361
Wisconsin	360	511	530	643	642	736	754	1,028
Wyoming	10	20	16	32	45	61	46	50
Puerto Rico	n/a	n/a	n/a	480	483	415	475	388
Total	**25,693**	**27,761**	**31,030**	**37,059**	**46,750**	**50,889**	**50,213**	**50,950**

Source: U.S. Department of Health and Human Services, Administration for Children and Families, Youth and Families, Children's Bureau, October 2003.

How Do Kids Enter Foster Care?

When a child is abused, neglected, or abandoned and the protective services division of the state or county learns of the problem, the parents or primary caregivers are investigated. The child may also be removed from the family while the investigation occurs, especially if severe physical abuse or sexual abuse is suspected. Sometimes the child is placed in an emergency shelter or group home while social workers determine whether the child needs longer term care or not. If the child appears to need longer-term care because it would be unsafe to return her to the biological family, she then may be placed with a foster family.

If the state or county finds that no abuse or other serious problems have occurred, the child is returned to the family (although sometimes red tape delays the return).

The abusive or neglectful family is given a *performance agreement* or a goal, which is a plan to change their behavior so they will be able to be reunited with the child. They may be given a time limit or target date to complete these goals. Often, however, a sympathetic judge will extend the time period.

Real Life Snapshots

I asked a group of state adoption specialists, "What is the biggest mistake or misunderstanding people have about children placed for adoption through the state?" Here are a few of the responses I received.

"Not all older children considered special needs are 'problem' children. Though they may have suffered abuse or have multiple needs, most respond *very* well to a loving, structured home." (New York)

"They think that 'Love cures everything' and expect some level of gratitude for having 'rescued' a child from foster care." (Washington)

I also asked what was the most important thing to know about the children their agencies had placed for adoption.

"Most have experienced serious abuse and/or neglect with lifelong consequences. Nevertheless, most show dramatic improvement with stability and committed adoptive parents." (Washington)

"These are children who have been *victims* of neglect, abuse, and other circumstances beyond their control, and who need and deserve a safe and loving family in which to grow and thrive. They bring great joy and sometimes great challenges to families waiting to share their lives with a child." (Florida)

Many abusive parents have problems with drug or alcohol abuse. In addition, they might have criminal records and jail time on their dossier. A performance agreement could include such stipulations as staying off drugs or alcohol, getting a job, and staying out of trouble. Parents are also often required to take parenting classes.

If all attempts to preserve the biological family fail, the biological parents might consent to an adoption or, as more commonly happens, the parents' rights are involuntarily terminated. Termination of parental rights (TPR) is *not* taken lightly by the courts, and in most cases, courts bend over backward to give biological parents chance after chance to overcome whatever problem caused their children to be placed in foster care. However, since the passage of the federal Adoption and Safe Families Act in 1997, states have revised their laws to restrict the time that parents are given to resolve their problems, and more foster children are available for adoption than in the past. Consequently, thousands of children in foster care nationwide are free to be adopted now. If and when a foster child *is* released for adoption, the child might be emotionally distressed by years of going in and out of foster care. Adoptive parents must prepare for the probability that the child will need therapy and extra support as he or she learns to trust in the permanency of the adoptive family.

Foster kids who need families are included in special photolisting books that state agencies maintain for prospective parents and might also be listed on Internet websites. The books or websites might include short descriptions of the child. Sometimes videotapes of children are also available, and these can be very helpful.

Legal Risk Adoptions

Some states offer *legal risk* (sometimes called *fost/adopt*) programs. This means that you might become a foster parent to a child who the state or county agency believes will soon become available for adoption.

Familybuilding Tips

Social workers say that many prospective adoptive families make mistakes at two extremes when it comes to adopting foster kids: They either assume that foster children have no problems that can't be cured by lots of love *or* that they are children who cannot recover from the abuse and neglect. In most cases, neither is true.

Adopterms

Legal risk refers to a program in which parents become foster parents to children who might become available for adoption. Some states also use the term "fost/adopt" to describe the same program. The intent is that the agency will seek to terminate the biological parents' rights to the child. Some attorneys use the term *legal risk* to denote the time frame during which a child could be legally reclaimed by a birthparent; for example, during the days allowed by a state (if any) to revoke consent.

This program is called a "risk" because the biological parent might fight the loss of parental rights. Another risk is that social workers change, and a new social worker might decide to try to reunite the child with the biological family—no matter how many workers in the past have tried and failed. So it's possible that the child will never become available for adoption.

Adopting Older Children

Usually the public agencies (state and county government services) consider an older child to be over six or seven, but sometimes they raise the bar higher to age eleven or twelve. So it's important to ask for a definition of what is an older child from every agency that you contact.

Older Children Overseas

Some international agencies also place older kids, usually kids who've been living in orphanages for years. They, too, may have been abused, but the physical, emotional, or sexual abuse could have occurred at the orphanage rather than at the hands of their birthparents or other relatives. Some families think that orphanages overseas are better than foster homes in the United States. The fact is that some overseas orphanages are well run and staffed by caring people, and others are not. One over-all truth, however, is that no orphanage is as good as a family.

Older Children in Nonagency Adoptions

Very occasionally, adoption attorneys place older children in families. In these un-usual cases, the biological parents find themselves unable to parent and often they don't trust the state social services division. They want to feel they have some control over the adoption process. It's also true that in many cases the state agency will refuse involvement unless the child is abused or neglected. As a result, a private agency or attorney is the only way to go for a nonabusive but overburdened biological parent.

In most cases, however, it's preferable for an agency to be involved in the placement of older children to ensure that counseling is provided. With an older child adoption, the birthparents and adoptive parents are not the only ones who need counseling—the children, if they are old enough, will need counseling as well. They need counseling to learn to understand that it's not their fault that their birthparents couldn't care for them. Counseling also can help children deal with the loss of their biological parents while at the same time enabling them to learn to trust in the permanency of their new family.

Real Life Snapshots

Several years ago, I learned about a mother who discovered she had terminal cancer. She had three young children, no living relatives, and the children's father had died. So the mother concluded the only answer for her children was adoption, and she began to look for a family.

She contacted a local adoption agency, but the agency didn't understand or accept that she wanted to choose the family herself. Her reasoning was this: Who knew her children better than she did? So she resolved to locate the right family. She found several possible families and personally interviewed them all.

One of the families had older children and seemed kind, friendly, and upbeat. They contacted an attorney who handled all the details for them, and they found an agency to do the home study. The mother prepared her children as best she could, and the family sought the help of a counselor to help the children and the mother. The mother and the family decided they'd finalize the adoptions before the mother died, so she would know the kids were safe, but the family swore that the mother could see her kids until the end of her life. They kept their promise.

Adopting Disabled Children

Some children who are adopted have medical problems, ranging from relatively minor and temporary conditions all the way up to terminal illnesses. In fact, parents sometimes adopt children from foreign countries whom they know must have surgery as soon as they arrive in the United States to correct life-threatening conditions. (Be sure to also read Chapter 15 on health issues and adopted children.)

Some people adopt children with medical problems because they (a) love children and (b) have medical expertise to care for such children.

Of course, not all medical problems are life-threatening, and some problems may even seem silly to some people. If you wanted to adopt an older child, would you turn down a child who had mild attention deficit disorder? Or a mild speech impediment? Or a cleft palate? These conditions would be minor to some people, but beyond toleration for others. Luckily, some wonderful adoption social workers can figure out which kids fit with which parents.

Real Life Snapshots

Years ago, I led a small adoptive parent support group and published a monthly newsletter. An agency contacted me about a baby girl who had a correctable hernia problem—they didn't have a family who wanted to adopt her. I published the information in my newsletter, and a family contacted the agency. They adopted her! They didn't consider the girl's problem to be a reason to not adopt her.

Why Adopt Special-Needs Kids?

People adopt children with medical, psychological, or other problems or kids who are older for many reasons. Here are a few of those reasons:

- Their biological children are grown, and they feel they have more love to give a child.

- They feel they can empathize with the child's problems.

- They believe they are "called" to adopt the child(ren), by a higher power or by their own conscience (or both).

- They have expertise in teaching, social work, or another field they feel can help the child.

As discussed earlier, some special-needs children have survived physical, emotional, or sexual abuse (and often all of these). These problems are not automatically wiped out the day they are adopted, no matter how loving and helpful the adopters are.

Some adopters want to ignore the past and pretend the child was born the day he entered their family. This is a bad idea, and adoptive parents should work to maintain realistic expectations of themselves and their children. I bring this up now because it's important to think of such issues even before you adopt a child. (For more information on parenting older adopted children, read Chapter 21.)

Real Life Snapshots

In an unpublished article written in 1996, psychiatrist Aaron Lazare described the arrival of his adopted daughter, Hien, age 4½, in 1973. She was a mixed-race child born to a Vietnamese mother and an African-American soldier.

When the prospective parents were told about this child, a volunteer wrote, "I hope you like strong-willed children."

When Hien arrived, she was "frightened and angry. She was homely and appeared malnourished with a protruding stomach. She made funny sounds that made me think she was mentally retarded. All of her teeth were decayed, and she occasionally held her jaw as if to soothe the pain. She then became mute for several weeks." Although she did have a learning disability, Hien later graduated from college with a 3.5 average.

Said her father, "Hien is no longer the homely child I described earlier. She is the attractive, strong-willed, determined survivor as forecast in the letter we had received earlier."

(Reprinted with permission of Aaron Lazare, M.D., Chancellor, University of Massachusetts Medical Center.)

However, with love, attention, and sometimes counseling, many special-needs children can and do turn their lives around.

Are We There Yet–Racially Speaking?

It's an unfortunate fact that it's harder to find adoptive families for nonwhite children. Yet, whether biracial or African-American children should be adopted by whites has been a subject of intense debate. In 1994 and again in 1996, the federal government passed laws that forbade racial consideration as the sole reason to deny a prospective adopter a chance to adopt a child of another race.

Despite changes in the law, white families who want to adopt children of another race or children who are biracial might find it easier to adopt them through a private adoption agency, rather than through the state social services department, because of bureaucratic resistance to transracial adoption. Sometimes families adopt a child of another race through an adoption attorney. Agencies (but not attorneys, usually) might charge lower fees for children who are nonwhite.

Here are a few issues to consider if you are thinking about adopting a child of another race from your own, regardless of your race or the child's race:

♦ Your child probably will face some racial slurs, as may you and other family members.

♦ People will ask you intrusive questions.

♦ Some people will be very positive toward you, and others very negative.

People who support *transracial adoption* say that what children need is a loving family and that too many African-American children remain in foster care while African-American adoptive families are sought for them. Some people (like me) believe that if people of a certain race are good enough to be long-term, stable foster parents, then they are also good enough to become adoptive parents. But unfortunately, many foster children who are placed with families of a different race have been eventually removed to a same-race placement, purely for racial reasons. Of course, this does *not* mean that children should always be placed outside their race. Whenever possible, foster children should be placed with appropriate foster/adoptive families of their

Adopterms ____

Transracial adoption refers to the situation in which a family adopts a child of another race. Generally, transracial adoption specifically alludes to whites adopting African-American children.

Familybuilding Tips

Families interested in transracial adoption should read *Inside Transracial Adoption* by Gail Steinberg and Beth Hall (Perspectives Press, 2000). This book is packed with anecdotes and positive, helpful advice for transracial adopters.

own race. However, race should not prevent a child from having a family.

Those who oppose transracial adoption believe that it's important for a child to be parented by people of the same race. They think the child would be racially and culturally deprived—some call it racial genocide—if the child were adopted by parents not of the same race. They also believe that the parents could not understand how to deal with racial insults and slurs and that such insults would be more prevalent in a child adopted transracially than in a child adopted by parents of the same race or ethnicity.

Opponents of transracial adoption believe that children of other races cannot develop an ethnic identity or sense of racial heritage when they are raised by white parents. They argue that these children will feel inferior or will not be comfortable with their own racial culture.

Adoption Alert

Special laws govern the adoption of any child who has parents, grandparents, or even great grandparents who are Native American. The Indian Child Welfare Act of 1978 treats all Native American lands as if they were separate countries within the United States. As a result, in most cases the consent of the birthparents alone is not enough to adopt a child—you must also obtain the consent of the tribe.

Adoptions have been stopped in their tracks and even overturned after years when a tribe has complained that the Indian Child Welfare Act was not complied with.

(If you are part Native American yourself, or eligible for tribal membership, the way to adopt an Indian child may be considerably eased.)

Some studies suggest that this may not be the case. Rita Simon and Howard Altstein have been studying a group of black children adopted by white families since 1971. Their most recent book, *Adoption Across Borders: Serving the Children in Transracial and Intercountry Adoptions* (Rowman & Littlefield, 2000), indicates that the majority of children adopted transracially have a strong sense of self-esteem and a positive sense of their identity.

Although Simon and Altstein found that most of the transracially adopted children have done well, they don't deny that transracial adoptions can cause problems. Unfortunately, racial slurs and inequalities still happen at all levels in our society.

Transracially adopted children may be subjected to teasing and may sometimes feel like they don't fit in. It is also likely that the parents in Simon and Altstein's study were especially sensitive to racial issues and took care to deal with them as effectively as possible.

Real Life Snapshots

African-American comedian Tommy Davidson (formerly of the TV program *In Living Color*) was adopted by a white family as a child. In a 1996 interview with *Jet* magazine, he talked frankly about the pros and cons of his own experience. His mom had two biological children, and Tommy said that he was often questioned about why he and his siblings had different skin colors and that he often had to face racism. But there were also some advantages.

Said Davidson, "When I hear blacks talking about white people, saying, 'White people are this and white people are that,' I say to myself, 'that is not true.' ... And when I hear white people saying, 'Black people are this or that,' I'll say, 'I know that is not true because I'm black.' That's what makes me me. It's a very cool thing."

Multiracial Children

A logical problem arises when a child is of mixed racial heritage—what then? Some people, like professional golfer Tiger Woods, who is part Asian, part African-American, and part Native American, don't like to be identified with any particular race. As a result, a new category, *multiracial*, has been created.

Tiger Woods wasn't adopted, but when multiracial people like him are adopted, the opponents of transracial adoption like to insist that they be placed in a nonwhite home. Their position is that when a child is multiracial, you should default to the minority race that seems physically most obvious. (Not always an easy call!)

Thus, by this reasoning, a child born to a white parent and an African-American parent should be adopted by only African-American parents. In fact, this has been the generally accepted practice in public agencies for years—although enforcement of new laws might eventually change these policies. As a result, in most cases where white parents want to adopt a child of mixed race, they may find it easier to adopt through a private adoption agency, no matter how many mixed-race children wait in foster care for families.

Adopterms _____

A **multiracial** child has a heritage of more than two races in her background.

Long-term studies of children adopted transracially indicate that most of the children adopted as infants do well in their adoptive families. As with other children, the children at most risk for future problems are those who are adopted over the age of two or three—although many older adopted children adjust well to their new families.

Two other at-risk groups are children abused at any age and those who lived with many families before their adoption occurred.

The Least You Need to Know

♦ Babies and older children in the United States and overseas need families.

♦ Agencies and attorneys are the primary adoption arrangers.

♦ Some children with special needs need families—but the definition of special needs can vary a great deal.

♦ Children in foster care can be adopted after the rights of their biological parents have been terminated.

♦ Adopting a child of another race is an option, but it is opposed by some people.

Chapter 4

Birthparents Who Choose Adoption

In This Chapter

- Why birthparents choose adoption
- Birthfathers and their rights
- How birthmothers feel about their babies
- How birthparents and adopters find each other
- When birthmothers change their minds

Mary Ann and Brian loved each other, but both agreed that in no way were they ready to get married and raise a child. She was 18, and he was 19 and a college freshman. They were old enough to parent a baby, but they just weren't ready in their own minds. The pregnancy was accidental, and they didn't think abortion was a good choice. But they couldn't "give up their own flesh and blood" to strangers—could they? Despite the intense pressure to parent, the two decided on adoption.

Tom and Elizabeth were shocked to learn she was pregnant. Again. They already had four kids, and they had used precautions! And yet here it was, another baby on the way. They'd seen an ad in a newspaper about couples who couldn't have children and who wanted to adopt. Maybe they'd call the phone number in the ad and learn some more. But what would people think? After all, they were married people, not some 14-year-old kids who didn't know what was what.

These cases illustrate just a few of the many scenarios faced by birthparents when they consider adoption as an option for their babies. In this chapter, I'll discuss the issues birthparents face when they choose adoption.

Who Chooses Adoption?

Today, abortion or single parenting are the approved choices for many people with unplanned pregnancies. High school girls who "keep" their babies are admired. In fact, among some groups of teenage girls, having a baby is considered a rite of passage.

Still, despite the fact that adoption is a less-common choice for pregnant women, it's also true that some pregnant girls and women in the United States *are* still deciding on adoption. Adoption also now appears to be gaining more attention from pregnancy counselors, as both they and the general public have become aware of the enormous difficulties that teenage parents face in caring for infants.

Who are these people? Here is a profile of birthparents in the United States who choose adoption:

- Most are unmarried, but some are married or divorced. Some married birthmothers choose adoption as a solution to an unplanned pregnancy because they cannot cope with another child. Or they feel they aren't ready to be parents. In some cases, the child may have a disability that they find too difficult to handle.

- They are usually women over age 17 or 18, not 14-year-old unwed teens. (Most very young pregnant women decide to parent their babies instead of placing them for adoption.)

Of course, not all birthparents live in the United States. Many children adopted by Americans are from other countries—a category I also cover in this chapter.

Why Choose Adoption?

No single category of women and men choose to place their children for adoption—they are different people with different reasons for making the adoption decision. Some of the reasons birthparents place their children for adoption are …

- They feel they are unready to be parents.

- They don't plan to marry but want the child to be raised by two parents, as they were.

- They don't want to go on welfare but can't think of another way to support the child adequately.

- They want to continue or launch a career and want the child to have the attention they won't be able to provide.

- They have other children and feel they cannot support any more.

- The relationship has broken up, and they want the child to be raised by two parents.

- The birthmother is a single woman in another country, where single parenting is viewed extremely negatively.

Real Life Snapshots

What do birthmothers want? They want their children to be happy and loved. Here are some comments written by a birthmother:

"That day she was asleep when I told her goodbye. And that was also the day I had to sign the adoption papers. It was the hardest thing I have ever had to do. I had to remind myself that I was doing this for her, but I cried for days afterward.

I had told my social worker that if my child wasn't adopted by my next birthday, I would take her back. But 10 days before my birthday, she was placed in a home. I took that as God's sign that I had made the right choice. Six months later I received pictures and a 10-page typed letter from the adoptive parents, who agreed to send pictures of her every year.

When people see a picture of my daughter, I get different reactions when I tell them I put her up for adoption. Most want to know more about the adoption process, and I gladly share what I know. But some try to condemn me for my decision, saying I ran away from the problem. According to them, I'm cruel and don't deserve ever to have another child.

But I made my choice. It was the one that I thought would be best for my baby and for me."

(Written by Christa Jones, excerpted from the June 1995 issue of Essence.)

No matter why they place their children for adoption, most birthparents want to find adoptive parents who will be loving and kind and who will help the child achieve his or her potential. In addition to being loving individuals, birthparents want to make sure that the adoptive parents are financially secure. In addition, if the birthparents are deeply religious, they might want the adoptive parents to be religious, too.

The Difficulties of Choosing Adoption

It's not easy to be a pregnant woman choosing adoption today. Birthparents who choose adoption often have to endure many offensive comments from people who should know better. Here are some of the most common:

- How can you do that? That's your own flesh and blood!
- Why didn't you (or the pregnant woman) get an abortion?
- I could never give my baby to strangers!
- What if you can't ever have another child?
- Are you doing it for money? Selling your baby? That's disgusting!
- Why don't you at least *try* raising it? You could always have the kid adopted later.
- Why? Don't you care at all about your baby?
- You made your bed, now you should lie in it.

Birthparents deal with these comments in different ways. Some hide their adoption plan, while others don't talk about it much. Some argue with the people who make such comments, by asking whether *they* are willing to support the baby.

Birthparents who are married (or even divorced) and who choose adoption face even more vitriol, which can be very painful for them and divisive within their family. And yet they are nearly always trying to make a plan that they feel is best for their child.

What about *after* the baby is placed with the adopters? How does the birthmother feel then?

Most experts agree that birthmothers do grieve this loss. Although counseling can help them deal with the issues involved, it cannot make the grief disappear altogether, nor does an open adoption (in which the pregnant woman usually meets the prospective adoptive parents and may have a continuing relationship with them and her child) alleviate all the pain. Feelings of grief usually abate as time passes; however, birthmothers often feel sad on the child's birthday. The grief and sadness are usually mitigated by the birthmother's belief that adoption was the right choice for the child. Studies indicate that the birthmothers who are the most satisfied with the adoption decision are those who didn't feel that they were pressured into it but made the choice for adoption on their own.

Real Life Snapshots

Diane, a woman in her late twenties, learned she was pregnant even though she had used birth control. Because she decided against abortion, her co-workers assumed she'd become a single mom. But Diane assured them that adoption was her plan.

They didn't believe her. Diane was nice, smart, and had a great job! Of course she would raise the baby. Her co-workers threw a surprise baby shower and gave her many beautiful gifts for the child. They meant well, but they broke her heart. Diane went through with her adoption plan and gave the gifts to the adoptive parents.

Adoption Slanguage

Aside from direct criticism and questioning, birthparents who consider adoption often have to face implicit, unconscious put-downs in some of the terms used to describe adoption. You should avoid words that offend or annoy birthparents who are considering adoption. Consult the following for examples:

No	Yes
Gave up a baby	Placed a baby
Gave away a baby	Made an adoption plan
Put up for adoption	Chose adoption
Real parent	Birthparent
Real mother	Birthmother
Real father	Birthfather
Relinquished for adoption	Consented to adoption

It's His Baby, Too: The Birthfather's Role

In the fairly recent past, people didn't think much (if at all) about what a *biological father* thought when his unmarried girlfriend decided on adoption for their child. It was assumed that he didn't care or he was glad someone else would take care of "the problem." But this was not always a valid assumption in the past, and still isn't one now, particularly as the stigma of nonmarital childbearing has plummeted. More and more *birthfathers* are getting involved in the decisions that affect their children.

Laws on birthfathers' rights vary drastically from one state to the next, although all states address the issue in some manner:

- Some states have birthfather registries (also sometimes called *putative father* registries), where the birthfather must register his desire to parent the child if he wishes to assert his paternal rights. (Some states require that the biological father be notified of a pending adoption, whether he registers or not.)

- In addition, in many states, prospective fathers can register their "prebirth consent" to an adoption, even before the baby is born! This can make the situation much easier for the pregnant woman, who might otherwise fear that the birthfather will refuse to consent to the adoption after the baby is born and demand to raise the child himself. With the birthfather consent, she can feel freer to make her own decision about adoption. (Find out which states have prebirth consent options in Chapter 10.)

- In some states, birthfathers must take immediate and decisive action to claim paternity rights and block an adoption. In other states, the burden is laid on the agency or attorney to locate the birthfather and determine if he will consent to the adoption.

- If the birthmother is married, most states assume that the biological father is her husband, even if that's not true. Thus, his consent to the adoption is nearly always necessary. (Some exceptions might be if the husband was in prison or out of the country at the time of conception. In such cases, the birthmother might be able to convince a judge to terminate the *legal father's* rights without his consent. But this varies greatly from state to state.) Some adoption arrangers, if they believe the biological father is another person, will obtain the consent of the husband *and* the alleged father.

Adopterms

A **birthfather** is a man who, with a woman, conceives a child who is later adopted or for whom an adoption is planned. He may also be called the **biological father**.

A **putative father** is a man who is alleged to be the birthfather, usually by the birthmother. He may or may not verify that he is in fact the father.

Adopterms

A **legal father** is a man who is married to the birthmother at the time of conception or birth and who must consent to the adoption even if he isn't the biological father. If another man is the biological father, the adoption agency usually will provide notice to him about the adoption as well (although his consent may not be necessary, depending on state laws).

Confusing, isn't it? Read Chapter 10 for more information on state adoption laws and for a guide to the laws in your state.

Real Life Snapshots

In nearly all cases of adoption disputes, the highest court in each state is the court of last resort. However, the U.S. Supreme Court has stepped in to set some parameters on birthfather rights because constitutional issues of due process were involved.

In the case of *Stanley v. Illinois* (1972), for example, an unmarried father had lived with a woman for many years, and together they had parented their three children. After her death, the state removed the children from his custody solely because he had not been married to the mother. Stanley won custody of the children.

Several stepparent adoption cases have also made it to the Supreme Court. For example in *Quillon v. Walcott* (1978), Quillon, who was not married to his partner at any time, attempted to block the adoption of their child by the man she later married. He had never supported the child in any way, and he lost the case.

Finding the Birthfather

State laws vary a great deal on the responsibility of a putative (alleged) father in asserting his paternity. A few states rely on the assumption that if a man has intercourse with a woman, he should assume that he may have made her pregnant. If he wants to know whether he is to be a father, under this viewpoint, it's his responsibility to find out.

In many states, the adoption agency or attorney has an obligation to seek out the alleged father, either through phone calls, letters, or other means. If the father is unknown, the agency or attorney may publish a notice in the legal section of the newspaper (for example: "The child of Cheryl X, born on May 7, 2004, is to be adopted. If you think you may be the father of Cheryl X's child, then you must come forward within some time frame.")

The birthmother may be uncomfortable with such advertising, but if it is required by state law, she must agree if she wants the adoption to go forth.

In some states, such as Illinois, if the birthmother says she does not know who the birthfather is, she must provide a statement explaining why she cannot identify him.

As a result, how a birthfather is regarded and treated in one state may be (and often is) very different from how he would be treated in another state. Until and unless some uniformity is created in birthfather adoption laws, this situation will continue.

Many states have a putative father registry, where men who think they have fathered children can register to assert their paternity and their desire to parent the child. (See Chapter 10 for more information.) They may be notified of a pending adoption by this registration and, if they are opposed to the adoption, can take legal steps to attempt to block it.

Prebirth Consent

Most states allow unwed birthfathers to consent to an adoption before the baby is born. (See Chapter 10 for more information.) If the father has signed the prebirth consent, generally, after the child is born, the consent to the adoption is needed only from the birthmother.

Real Life Snapshots

In a very few isolated cases, birthfathers who have conceived children through rape are given control over the birthmother's adoption decision. In Wisconsin in 1992, a convicted rapist prevented a 14-year-old girl he had impregnated from placing her baby for adoption. He didn't want to give up his paternal rights. Outraged Wisconsin legislators subsequently changed the law so that the parental rights of rapists would be involuntarily terminated, and birthmothers would not need the consent of the birthfather to place a child of rape for adoption.

Consent to an adoption is not required in Virginia if the child is the result of a rape *and* the rapist was convicted of the crime. Other states are attempting to pass such laws. It seems only fair, though, that in these cases the adoption decision should be the birthmother's alone.

Note here that the consent of the biological father isn't always necessary, although notice to him is usually required. If the man who has been named by the birthmother signs a document denying paternity, the consent of the birthmother alone may be sufficient. Again, it's very important to remember that state laws vary drastically on this and other adoption matters.

The agency or attorney and prospective adoptive parents should be confident that the alleged father *is* the father (whether he admits to paternity or not) to avoid the problem of some other man stepping forward and attempting to assert paternal rights.

For this reason, many adoption social workers or attorneys seek either consent to an adoption or a denial of paternity from any man who might be the father of the child, including any men with whom the birthmother had sexual intercourse during the time frame that she became pregnant.

Proclaiming Paternity

Despite the heavy media coverage of birthfathers upsetting adoptions, most biological fathers do not protest or try to stop them. Here are a few reasons why a birthfather might assert his paternal rights:

- ♦ He wants to raise the child himself.

- ♦ He has parented the child in the past and wants a continuing relationship with the child.

- ♦ His parents want to raise the child and have convinced him to help them.

- ♦ He is angry with the birthmother and wants to exert power over her. He thinks this will force her to return to him.

- ♦ He wants to force the birthmother to raise the child. He assumes if he fights the adoption, she'll agree to parent.

- ♦ It's a macho thing—no one else should parent *his* child.

Of course, birthfathers aren't always opposed to adoption, and in some cases, they may help the birthmother to locate adoptive parents, attend counseling sessions, and participate fully in the process.

> **Familybuilding Tips**
>
> If a pregnant woman and a man both agree that he is the father of her child, this is usually assumed to be true; however, the only definitive proof is DNA paternity testing. The problem with paternity testing is timing: Testing cannot be performed safely until the baby is born, and then it takes about two weeks before results are received. Most birthmothers don't want to delay placement of the baby while waiting for paternity tests.
>
> Testing delays and hassles also mean that many adoptive families do not request paternity testing at all. As a result, paternity testing is usually done only if there is a challenge to paternity or there is some other legal reason for the test.

International Birthparents

Many people don't think about it much, but children who are adopted from other countries were conceived and born in the usual way. You'd be amazed at how many people tell me they want to adopt a child from another country so they don't have that "birthmother problem."

I know that what they really mean is they don't want to fear that the birthmother might change her mind about adoption, and they think that's less likely to happen outside of the United States. But sometimes I wonder if they realize that there *is* a mother in this equation and that at some point she will need to be acknowledged to the child.

Birthmothers from other countries choose adoption for their children for many of the same reasons as birthmothers in the United States: They aren't ready to be parents; they don't have the financial means to raise a child; and so on. Additionally, many countries still retain very strong cultural biases against nonmarital births; some birthmothers believe (rightly) that they and their children would be stigmatized if they became single parents.

For more information about adopting children from other countries, see Chapter 11.

The Least You Need to Know

- ◆ Society makes it hard for most birthparents to choose adoption for their babies.
- ◆ Most birthmothers who choose adoption are over 17 and unmarried, but some are younger, married, or divorced.
- ◆ Most pregnant women who consider adoption for their babies are looking for safe, stable, happy homes for their children.
- ◆ Birthfather rights vary from state to state.
- ◆ Birthmothers from other countries choose adoption for many of the same reasons as birthmothers in the United States.

Gathering Information

In This Chapter

◆ Joining an adoptive parent group

◆ Reading, writing, and researching about adoption

◆ Networking for adoption information

◆ Finding adoption information online

Diane and Jim wanted to adopt, but they had no idea where to begin. Then they read in the newspaper that a local adoptive parent group would be holding an information session. They called and were urged to attend—and they did. Speaking at this meeting were social workers from three different agencies, an adoption attorney, and also several parents who talked about adopting babies and older children. A birthmother talked about her decision to place her child for adoption. Even an adopted adult talked about growing up adopted! There was plenty to absorb and think about.

Louisa, a single woman, had many questions about adoption, but she didn't feel comfortable bringing them up in a group session. She found a "warmline" phone number sponsored by a parent group. The "warmline lady" was really helpful and nice. She couldn't answer a few questions but did direct Louisa to someone who could.

Tom wanted some information about adoption agencies, so he decided to search the Internet. He found five agencies that sounded like possible "candidates" for him and his wife, and he sent the agencies e-mail requests for more information.

Information sources, whether they are parent groups, specialized experts, or online sources, can provide you with the most current adoption and parenting information. In this chapter, I'll show you how to find the best local, regional, and national information sources available.

Been There, Done That: Adoptive Parent Groups

There are hundreds of active *adoptive parent groups* nationwide; some are new and some are well established. Some are very large and well organized, such as the Adoptive Parents Committee in New York, which has many chapters throughout the state and has a very popular annual conference. Others are small groups comprised of 20 or 30 people (or fewer) who enjoy getting together and sharing information.

Some adoptive parent groups concentrate on people adopting children from particular countries, such as China, Russia, or Guatemala. Others concentrate on older children or children with special problems. Some groups—particularly the large ones—provide information on all adoption options, including U.S. (also called *domestic*) adoption, international adoption, and children of all ages. Some groups are politically active and lobby for changes to state and federal adoption laws, and others don't see that as part of their mission.

For a listing of some adoptive parent groups, see Appendix E.

Adopterms

An **adoptive parent group** (sometimes called an **adoptive parent support group**) is a group of adoptive parents and prospective adoptive parents who meet to obtain information about adopting as well as to socialize and/or to discuss issues related to adoption. Often these groups can be very helpful to people who are trying to adopt a child.

Adoptinfo

Many people join more than one adoptive parent group. They may decide to become members of one group because of the great newsletter it produces even if they live too far away to attend meetings regularly. They join a local group to have face-to-face interaction.

Join the Group

Why re-invent the wheel? Believe it or not, almost any kind of adoption problem that you encounter has been faced by someone else. And almost any fear that looms paramount in your mind has been previously vanquished by another person. By joining an adoptive parent group, you stand to gain from the experience of others.

Here are just a few of the advantages of joining a group:

- A chance to learn the latest information

- An opportunity to meet people who have adopted—and to see their children

- A chance to meet social workers or attorneys and ask questions

- A feeling of camaraderie and support that you can't duplicate elsewhere

- Empathy and understanding for what you need

Of course, it's important to connect with a group that meets your needs—or is as close to what you need as possible. So, for example, if you want to adopt a child from China and a nearby parent group is made up solely of people who have adopted children in the United States, this group won't really be able to help you much. (They *can* empathize with your desire to adopt, the aggravation of waiting for your child, and so forth, so don't necessarily rule them out.) What you really need is to associate with others adopting children from other countries, especially from China.

However, if you want to adopt an infant through an agency or attorney in the United States and have no interest in intercountry adoption, a group focusing on adopting Chinese children wouldn't be of much help.

Finding a Group That's Right for You

So how do you find an adoptive parent group, anyway? And, when you've found one, how do you know whether it's right for you? Try these suggestions:

- Contact your state adoption office, usually based in the state capitol. (Check Appendix D for listings of adoption offices.)

- Ask local adoption agencies and/or adoption attorneys whether they are aware of any adoptive parent groups in the area. If any groups are within about 50 miles of where you live, consider traveling to a meeting to check out the group. It might be worth your time!

> **Familybuilding Tips**
>
> *Adoptive Families* magazine offers an annual Adoption Guide for wannabe adopters for $14.95 (including shipping and handling within the United States). To order, send $14.95 to *Adoptive Families* magazine at 42 West 38th St., Ste. 901, New York, NY 10019. You can also order the booklet online by going to www.adoptivefamilies.com.

◆ Ask your local RESOLVE group for recommendations. RESOLVE is a national group for people seeking help with infertility and also provides information on adoption. If you don't know of a local group, call RESOLVE at their main office, 617-623-0744, or write to them at RESOLVE, Inc., 1310 Broadway, Somerville, MA 02144-1731.

Adoption Alert _____

The downside of joining an adoptive parent group is that you might not always agree with other members' opinions. For example, one person might tell you that a particular adoption attorney should be avoided; others might like this attorney. It's also true that some groups are managed by an adoption agency or attorney, so their views prevail. As you gather information, don't be overly reliant on what any one person (or couple) says and don't assume that what another person thinks or feels is how you would or should think or feel.

◆ Ask your clergyperson.

◆ Ask your doctor.

◆ Call the nearest state adoption office and ask the state or county social workers whether they know of a group.

◆ Look in the Yellow Pages of your phone book under "Adoption." Some larger groups advertise there.

◆ Ask local adoption agencies for recommendations. (Note, however, that some agencies run their own parent groups for parents who have adopted through their agency. I recommend you start with a group of members who have adopted through a variety of sources instead.)

◆ Check the newspaper for listings of groups that meet regularly. (If you can't find such a list, call the newspaper and ask whether and when they include this information.)

◆ Ask hospital social workers at local hospitals (or within a 50-mile radius) whether they know of any parent groups. (Hospital social workers often become involved, if only peripherally, in infant adoptions.)

◆ Consult Appendix E in this book.

Networking Works

If you're seeking very basic how-to-adopt information, it's often best to ask local parent groups or adoption agencies rather than national groups. Part of the reason is that state laws differ so radically (and change so frequently) that it's very hard for any national group to advise you on the situation in your state.

Another reason is that it's a time-waster for experts within national groups to provide very basic information that you could obtain locally. However, if you have a specific question or problem—for example, related to a specific health problem or some other unique issue—then national experts are often a good resource. Just don't assume that someone who is an expert on one aspect of adoption (say, health or legal issues) also knows everything there is to know about other adoption topics.

Don't be afraid to ask friends and acquaintances whether they can recommend a local agency, group, or attorney—you never know who is knowledgeable about this topic. Other local sources to contact are your own physicians (and nurses) as well as social workers who work at local agencies or for the state or county public agency. Do keep in mind, however, that most government (public) social workers who work in the field of adoption concentrate on the placement of older children or children with special needs. So if you want to adopt a healthy infant, they may or may not be your best resource. By the same token, social workers and attorneys who concentrate on infant and international adoptions may be unable to advise you about adopting an older child from the foster care system.

Hot Type

If you want to learn even more about adoption, then read, read, read! Many good (and some mediocre) books on adoption are available. In addition, several adoption organizations distribute magazines and newsletters. I recommend that you read everything you can get your hands on, but that you read everything carefully and with a healthy dose of skepticism. Don't be afraid to discard positions that conflict with your values or don't pass the common-sense test.

Your local library is probably a good source for information; unfortunately many libraries keep books just about forever. A book that purports to tell you the latest about adoption—and was published in 1976—isn't going to help you. Stick with books published at least in this decade, if not this year or last year. For the absolutely newest books on adoption, check your bookstore or online bookstores, such as barnesandnoble.com or Amazon.com.

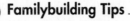

Familybuilding Tips

To learn about adoption, read about adoption. Let's say you've identified four or five books you need, but you can't afford them all, or you aren't really sure you want them all. Ask your librarian to order them for you through Interlibrary Loan.

Since you're talking to the librarian anyway, ask whether he or she is aware of any other information on adoption. Libraries often keep pamphlets, newspaper clippings, and other information on a number of topics, including adoption.

Organize the material you amass. It's far too easy to misplace something important. Put all your brochures, pamphlets, and so on in one or two big boxes so you know where they are when you need them.

Buy a notebook to keep track of information you obtain during phone calls. When you connect with an adoption professional, write down the date, who you talked to, and a summary of what was said. Make notes during the phone conversation, and afterwards jot down any questions you have or opinions you have formed about the agency.

Conference Calls

Some of the larger adoption support groups hold annual conferences where attendees have the opportunity to listen to speakers, peruse the latest adoption books, and meet other people seeking to adopt. For example, the ODS Adoption Community of New England, Inc., in Massachusetts holds an annual conference that's attended by several thousand people. These conferences are usually very uplifting and positive experiences. If a group in your area—or even in your state—offers an annual conference, I recommend that you attend.

Occasionally, hospitals or other organizations offer seminars on how to adopt a child. I attended such a seminar in my area several years ago and found it very well organized and informative. You might try contacting the major hospitals in your area and asking the public relations director whether they plan to offer any seminars on adopting a child. Who knows? You might inspire them to create such a program!

Cyberadoption: The Internet and Online Sources

Adoption is a very hot topic online, and you can find adoption-related material on the Internet in various ways. One way is to use a search engine (a program that browses for websites) such as www.google.com and try the keyword "adoption." This is not, however, the recommended way to search, because you'll end up with thousands of search results. You'll also find scads of sites related to the "adoption" of an interesting array of animals—dogs, cats, lemurs, and so forth. The animal sites are readily identifiable and can be easily ignored—unless you also want a pet!

Instead, use at least a couple of words, in quotations or parentheses (or both), such as ("adopting Chinese babies") or ("adopting infants") Chinese. Every search engine has its own vagaries, and you can try different options until you end up with a number of "hits" that seems worth looking at.

Here's a sampling of the kind of adoption-related sites you're likely to encounter:

◆ Websites maintained by individuals or organizations (adoption agencies or attorneys; adoptive parent support groups; or individual adoptive parents who want to share what they know; organizations that want to change state adoption laws; people who are trying to search for their birthparents)

◆ Subscription list services, chat rooms, and newsgroups maintained by special-interest groups on topics related to adoption, infertility, and parenting/family issues

◆ Actual photos of children who need families

◆ Advertisements from lawyers and other adoption groups

◆ Editorials and news articles related to adoption

◆ Self-help information for adoptive parents, adopted adults, or birthparents

In addition, consider checking out the following websites:

◆ The National Adoption Information Clearinghouse (NAIC) at www.calib.com/naic/ maintains a site that offers some helpful full-text articles.

◆ Adoption.com is a popular site that provides a great deal of information for adoptive parents and prospective adoptive parents (as well as adopted adults). Its address is www.adoption.com. This site covers both international and U.S. adoption.

◆ The State Department has a website for people interested in adopting foreign-born children. Check it out at http://travel.state.gov/adopt.html.

◆ Other sites with considerable information are www.adopting.org and www.comeunity.com. (You could spend hours surfing through this information and completely lose track of time. I know. I have.)

One amazing and exciting aspect of the Internet is that some sites, such as some adoption agencies, actually post photographs of adoptable children in the United States and other countries. So your computer can "show" you who your future child might be! Very heady stuff.

Mailing Lists

You can also subscribe to any number of adoption e-mail lists (also called mailing lists or "listservs") merely by sending the message "subscribe" to the appropriate address. For instance, Yahoo hosts a staggering number of lists on adoption; to learn more, go to http://groups.yahoo.com.

Some lists that focus on different types of children (older, younger, kids with particular problems, or kids from specific countries) and that are oriented to particular types of parents, such as single adopters or gay adopters. For instance, the Eastern European Adoption Coalition has 19 different listservs with more than 5,000 subscribers. To learn more, go to www.eeadopt.org. If you're single and want to adopt a child, obtain some help from a single adopter list at www.adopting.com/single-aparents/sap-faq.html. To learn more about a list for gay, bisexual, and lesbian parents, go to www.cyberhiway.com/aparent/faq.html.

Evaluating Sites

As you surf the Net, remember that all websites present a particular agenda or point of view, whether they are run by individuals, agencies, or organizations. Many people use the Internet to promote their own ideas about how adoption should be handled in their state or country.

Unfortunately, sometimes people state their own opinions as if they were facts or are clearly (or not-so-clearly) promoting a particular agenda. Read everything you read online with a healthy dose of skepticism. Here are a few questions to ask yourself as you cruise through websites or user newsgroups:

- ◆ What does the purpose of this site seem to be? To provide information, to sell you a product, to do something else? Be skeptical. Don't let your brains fall out just because a site has cute baby pictures everywhere.

- ◆ Can you determine how current the information is? It's a normal tendency to assume that anything posted on the Internet was placed there today, or maybe last week, at the latest. This is rarely true. Check at the bottom of the website page for notice of when the site was last updated.

- Who appear to be the target viewers? Adopted adults, adoptive parents, birth-parents, all of the above? This isn't good or bad, but you need to obtain a general idea of who the audience is.

- Who is providing this information? An agency, an attorney, an organization, an individual? The harder this is to determine, the more wary of the information you should be. Be especially skeptical if you can't find an address or phone number anywhere on the site, and when you click on a "contact us" icon, you simply get an email form to fill out. Sometimes it's just an oversight, but other times it's a sign that the organization isn't as legitimate as it wants you to think it is.

- If this site is linked to others, what are the other sites like? Remember "birds of a feather flock together." Good guys usually hang out with other good guys. And vice versa. Of course, there are exceptions. But in general, it's a reasonable assumption.

- Don't believe everything you read on the Internet. Keep your watchful eye and skeptical mind in high gear. There are plenty of people out there who are eager to part you from your hard-earned money. They don't care that you're a wonderful person who just wants a child to love. Such people see you as an easy mark. Even very smart people are taken in by adoption scammers.

Adoption Alert

If you do decide to post questions and opinions online, always remember that what you write in a public forum can be read by whomever logs on. Nor does it "scroll off": Material is often saved for years and is searchable. You don't want the child you adopt (or his friends!) to read years from now something embarrassing that you wrote.

Even with e-mail, be careful what you say about your family or private life. If you wouldn't mind reading what you said on the front page of your local newspaper, then go ahead and say it in an e-mail.

As long as you maintain some healthy skepticism about the material you come across on the Internet, you probably will be quite dazzled by the enormous wealth of information you find.

There's a great deal of information available out there for people who want to adopt and who are willing to do their homework. Information from people you know; magazines, newsletters, and books; adoption agency and attorney experts; and, of course, the ubiquitous cyberspace community is all available to you. You'll have to do some weeding and your own independent thinking, but there has never been a better time for gathering the information you need to adopt a child.

The Least You Need to Know

♦ Adoptive parent groups can offer information as well as support.

♦ Look for expert sources in your own "backyard."

♦ Many books, magazines, and newsletters specialize in adoption issues.

♦ Cyberspace is an exciting adoption resource, but be careful.

Part 2

What Are Your Options?

This part tells you about the "adoption arrangers"—the agencies and lawyers who can help you adopt a child. It explains the rules of U.S. and international adoptions and what you can do to afford an adoption. There's also an important chapter on screening out incompetent or unethical adoption arrangers. They're few and far between, but they're out there.

Don't be like some people and spend years "flying blind," wasting time and a lot of money. When it comes to adoption, knowledge is most definitely power.

Chapter **6**

The Adoption Arrangers

In This Chapter

♦ Distinguishing among adoption agencies

♦ Finding a good adoption agency

♦ Dealing with state agencies

♦ Locating a good adoption lawyer

♦ Considering open, semi-open, and confidential adoptions

Some people think the only acceptable way to adopt a child is to go through a traditional adoption agency. That's what Tom and Lisa did: They applied to a local agency that had been in business for a hundred years. The agency said the wait would be three years, but Tom and Lisa felt that was reasonable.

Sarah and Bill decided to adopt through an agency, too, but they felt that the New Age Agency, which just opened six months ago and promised very short waits, would be the right answer for them. They applied and were quickly accepted.

Lori wanted to adopt, but because she was single and under age 30, several agencies turned her down. She'd heard about private adoption and decided to hire a lawyer who handled adoptions instead.

This chapter is about the *adoption arrangers:* the agencies and attorneys that make adoptions a reality.

The Facts on Adoption Agencies

As I've mentioned in earlier chapters, there are both public and private adoption agencies. The *public agencies* are run by state or county governments; these agencies usually deal with foster children who were removed from the homes of their biological parents or who were abandoned by their birthparents. Most public agencies call themselves the Department of Children's Services or something similar.

In contrast, *private agencies* are licensed by the state to arrange adoptions. They are usually run by someone with an advanced degree in social work or psychology. After adoption agencies are licensed, they manage their own organizations. If a complaint is made, however, and the state licensing officials determine the agency has behaved improperly, the state may choose to take away the private agency's license, which means they're out of business.

State government social service agencies don't charge adoption fees because they are funded from federal and state tax dollars. Private agencies do charge fees, and sometimes these fees can be quite substantial—$25,000 or more. However, enormous differences exist among agencies in addition to fees they charge

Some agencies place children within only their county or state, and others actively engage in placing children in many areas of the country or even outside the United States. Some adoption arrangers place U.S.-born children, and others concentrate on placing children from other countries. Sometimes agencies handle both U.S. and intercountry adoption, although they usually specialize in one or the other.

Adopterms

Public agencies are run by state or county governments; these agencies usually deal with foster children. Private agencies are licensed by the state to arrange adoptions and usually are run by someone with an advanced degree in social work or psychology. They often place infants, but sometimes place older children for adoption.

If you're thinking about adopting a child from the United States, you can choose from hundreds of agencies. If you are interested in international adoption, many agencies concentrate on one country or one area; for example, as of this writing, adoptions from China and Russia are very popular, and some agencies are focusing on orphans from these countries. However, the laws surrounding international adoption can be very confusing and they also change frequently, so if you are interested in an international adoption, be sure to read Chapter 11.

There are religious-based (*sectarian*) agencies, such as Catholic Social Services, Jewish Social Services, LDS Social Services, and so on. There are also *nonsectarian* agencies for whom religion is not a key issue.

Some agencies specialize in placing children with special needs, and others concentrate on placing mostly infants who are healthy. (If an infant is born not healthy, these agencies may transfer the child to a state agency so the public agency can hopefully locate a family, unless one of the private agency's approved families will adopt the child.)

Adopterms

Sectarian agencies specialize in helping families with particular religious interests, although they may also work with families of other religions. **Nonsectarian** agencies do not have a particular religious orientation.

Why Use an Agency?

Many people believe that the right path to adoption starts when you walk through the door of an adoption agency. Here are some reasons why many people choose to adopt through agencies:

- They think agency adoptions are safer.

- They believe the only valid adoptions are performed by agencies. (In reality this is not true.)

- Their friends have adopted through agencies.

- They're worried that in a nonagency adoption, the birthmother might change her mind, and they'll lose all fees paid.

- They like the idea of the birthmother receiving counseling through the agency.

Adoption Alert

In the past, agency adoptions generally were safer because agencies didn't place children with families until and unless the birthparent rights were terminated and the agency had taken custody. Today, however, many agencies are involved in *direct placement* adoptions, in which a birthmother chooses the adoptive family. In these adoptions, if the birthmother changes her mind about adoption, the adoptive parents lose the child and might also lose some of the fees they've already paid.

For this reason, it's important to ask the agency what would happen if a direct adoption fell through. (Keep in mind that few birthmothers change their minds about adoption after a baby is placed with adoptive parents. If a birthmother is going to change her mind, it almost always takes place *before* placement.)

Finding an Agency

How do you locate a reputable and competent adoption agency? Many people merely pick up the Yellow Pages and start dialing every number listed under "Adoption." Not a good idea. The agency with the splashiest advertisement isn't necessarily the best one. (Although it might be.) Forget about making your agency choice solely by choosing the agency with the nicest website or the cutest photos of babies on the Internet. They might be the right agency for you, but you should check out other agencies, too. (Read more about using the Internet to help you in Chapter 5 and read about Internet scams in Chapter 9.)

> **Adoption Alert** _____
>
> Some people believe that if they pay very high fees—sometimes as high as $50,000 or more—they'll have a fast, problem-free adoption.
>
> Here's the thing: You don't get a better baby from the expensive agency. In fact, media reports over the past few years have documented that some very high-priced agencies skimped on many services and also withheld very important information on the birth-parents.
>
> This does not, of course, mean that the expensive agency is a bad guy. But you have to ask yourself what you're really getting for all the extra money.

How do you find a good adoption agency? That depends on what you're looking for. If you want to adopt a child from another country, the agency that mostly handles U.S. adoptions may not be good for you. And vice versa. It's also true that if you want to adopt a toddler or an older child, the agency that specializes in newborns is the wrong one for you.

You need to research what agencies are available in and out of your state and narrow them down to the organizations that you feel best suit your needs.

Here's how to track down reputable agencies:

1. Ask adoptive parent groups (see Chapter 5 and Appendix E) for names of reputable agencies that specialize in U.S. or international adoptions.

2. Ask your friends and relatives for names of good agencies.

3. Call up the state social services department and ask whether they have had any complaints about any agencies. Ask for names.

4. Ask your doctor for names of experienced agencies.

Scoping Out an Agency

After you've located a list of potential agencies, you should look into each one to find out whether it's a good match for you. First, check out the agencies' websites (most agencies have them), withholding judgment until you've considered at least five other agencies. (The first agency you find isn't always the best one.) If they have a website, you can read about their policies and procedures without making a single phone call. Then, if one or more agencies look like a good match, arrange to speak with social workers at the agencies. Ask them the following questions:

- Are they accepting applications?

- Do they place mostly infants or older children? From the United States or other countries?

- Can you have references of families with whom they have worked? Understand that only names of happy adopters will be provided, but at least you can obtain some inside information from such references.

- Do they offer a free orientation you can attend? If they do, go to it and ask questions.

- Do they have any brochures or literature they can send to you? Sometimes printed material the agency sends has information not available on their website, such as fees or policies.

Familybuilding Tips

One question to ask when choosing an adoption agency is whether or not the agency is affiliated with a larger "parent" organization, preferably one with a track record. Many newer, smaller adoption agencies have sprung up, and some are essentially "mom-and-pop" operations.

There's no guarantee that a large, established agency will be any better, but you should always find out what kind of organization you are dealing with before you sign up.

- How long has the agency has been in business? It need not be 50+ years, but if it opened last week, please be very careful. New agencies may need applicants; they also don't have track records and often charge higher fees. However, old agencies may be more stodgy and may have longer waits; established agencies are also more likely to still be in business if you encounter a problem later.

♦ Did the current agency director start the agency and, if so, why? Many agencies were launched by adoptive parents and some by adopted adults. Understanding the motivation for creating the agency may help you choose your agency.

♦ How many children did the agency place last year and the year before? Will the number of placements this year be roughly the same? People are often more willing to provide older statistics about their organization than current ones. However, after you have older statistics, it's generally easier to get newer ones.

♦ How long do most potential adoptive parents have to wait before their screening, usually called a home study, is done? Generally, most agencies like to place children with parents within about a year of doing the home study, although this isn't always true. After the agency tells you how long you would need to wait for your home study, ask them whether many people adopt within about a year of the home study. (For more on the home study process, see Chapter 12.)

♦ Does the agency have any limiting criteria for adopters: upper age limits, marital status, and so on? Keep in mind that if you want to adopt a child the agency defines as having "special needs" (such as a biracial child, a child with medical problems, or other definitions), it might waive its usual criteria.

♦ Does the agency have a program to let birthmothers choose parents? (Most of them do.) This may work to your advantage.

♦ Does the agency provide funds for food or shelter for the pregnant woman considering adoption? If so, will these costs or other expenses be passed on to you in addition to the fees charged by the agency? Or are these expenses included in the basic fees you will pay? If not, what if the pregnant woman needs financial help? Does the agency require her to apply for public assistance? Find out.

Familybuilding Tips

One way to estimate how long the wait will be at any given agency is to ask the agency when it could do your home study. Add about a year to the time frame you get. If the agency can do your home study in six months, then it could probably place a child with you in about a year and a half. Why? Because most agencies don't want to place a child with someone whose home study is more than a year old.

♦ Does the agency try to involve the pregnant woman's parents in the planning— even if she is over age 18? Studies have revealed that if the birthmother's parents are supportive, the outcome is better for all concerned. For example, they will not be shocked to learn that the newborn baby is to be adopted and make dramatic last-minute attempts to dissuade the birthmother from adoption. In addition, the birthparents' parents can provide medical information about themselves regarding possible inherited conditions.

◆ How does the agency obtain medical information on the children they place? Do they obtain it from the pregnant woman? From her doctor? Or in some other way?

◆ How does the agency define "special needs" in a child (refer to Chapter 3). You may find that you would be open to adopting a child that the agency regards as having special needs.

◆ If the agency specializes in U.S. adoptions, what is its policy on working with birthfathers? The agency must follow state law, but it might go above and beyond state laws.

◆ Does the agency arrange open adoptions (discussed later in this chapter), and how does it define open adoptions? Do birthmothers get to choose adoptive parents? Do birthmothers usually meet prospective adoptive parents? What does the agency staff think are the main benefits and disadvantages to open adoption? (See Chapter 6 for more information on open adoptions.) What constitutes an open adoption can vary considerably from agency to agency. At one agency, it might mean that pregnant women look at descriptions of adoptive parents or letters they write. At another agency, it might mean a one-time first-name-basis-only meeting occurs between pregnant women and prospective parents. It may also mean the agency expects continued contact for years. Find out by asking!

◆ If the agency arranges intercountry adoptions, has anyone on the staff traveled to the other country and visited the orphanages there? The more direct face-to-face experience they have with orphanage staff in the country, the better.

◆ What fees does the agency charge and when are they payable? Is there one home study fee and one placement fee, or are there a variety of separate fees for different services? If there are separate fees, at what points are they due? Try to determine at least a range of the *total* fees you might expect to pay, including everything (such as the expense involved in traveling to another country). If the agency doesn't provide this information, try to figure out a possible range yourself and then ask the social worker whether this range seems about right.

◆ What do they think is the most important thing to know about the agency? The answer to this question can sometimes be very revealing.

◆ Is there anything you haven't asked that is important to know? This is a question that is best asked in person or on the phone, rather than by e-mail, because you'll receive the most honest response that way.) Wait for the person to think and respond. Listen.

Screening an Agency

After you've picked one or two agencies that seem like a good fit, make sure that you screen them carefully. No matter what good things you may have heard about an agency, people change and policies change, and the agency that was aboveboard last year may now have financial problems—problems that it's now trying to bury with cash flow. Protect yourself.

This does not mean that I think most agencies are "bad." In my view, only a very small number of agencies will knowingly rip you off. A slightly greater number of agencies are incompetent at either adoption practice or at dealing in the business world. Because adoption represents a considerable investment of your time and money, as well as a major emotional investment, it's well worth it to be careful.

Here are some effective screening questions to ask the adoption agency:

◆ Does it have a board of directors? Ask for a list of the board members.

◆ Is it nonprofit? This is no guarantee of purity, but in adoption, a nonprofit adoption agency is preferable. Ask whether it is a 501(c)(3) corporation. This means it is registered with the state and also the IRS as a nonprofit organization.

◆ Does it produce an annual report? Ask to see the last one.

◆ Does its staff have child welfare training—degrees in social work, psychology, or counseling?

◆ Does it provide a contract to its adoptive family applicants? Ask to see a standard contract.

◆ How large is the staff? If there are only one or two people in the agency, this could mean that it is understaffed or that it is a startup agency. Find out.

◆ What will the agency do if a family adopts a child and the newly adopted child turns out to have unexpected problems? If the answer is "None of our children ever have problems," or "God helps all our families cope with any problem," they are probably in denial. Problems occasionally happen, and the agency should be willing to assist you within a reasonable time after the adoption. (If you adopt a baby and he then becomes a problem as a 16-year-old adolescent, the agency couldn't predict this!)

♦ Does the agency have a business manager or accountant who handles its financial affairs? Remember, an *adoption agency is a business*. Bills have to be paid or agencies go out of business.

Don't be afraid to ask these questions and others! You could save yourself thousands of dollars and untold heartache by just being a little careful. In addition, call the local Better Business Bureau and find out whether anyone has complained about the agency. Also call the state adoption office, usually located in the capital of your state. (See Appendix D for listings of public social services offices in each state.)

Signs of an A+ Agency

Although it's certainly not foolproof, some things indicate that an agency might be "good," meaning that it deals ethically with adopters and birthparents. Here are a few signs that an agency is one you should consider:

♦ The agency brings previous adopters and birthparents to a meeting where you can ask questions. They don't try to steer people away from asking questions they don't like.

♦ Social workers and staff seem to know and understand their roles and seem to feel that their jobs are important.

♦ No complaints have been made to the state or Better Business Bureaus against the agency. Keep in mind, however, that even a good agency may have been complained about for causes that the average person might find silly or unreasonable. So find out the nature of the complaint.

♦ The agency hasn't been sued more than once or twice. (Even a good agency can be sued. These are litigious times. Find out the reason for the lawsuit.) How do you know whether the agency has been sued? Believe it or not, in most cases you just ask them.

♦ The agency provides a clear and understandable explanation of its fees.

♦ The agency doesn't demand five figures ($10,000) or more right away, before you even have a home study.

Of course, you should also watch out for red flags indicating that an agency should not be trusted. For more on these, see Chapter 9.

State Government Agencies

As mentioned earlier, state agencies primarily place foster children for adoption when their biological parents' rights are terminated (or willingly given up). The children may have been physically or sexually abused, neglected, or abandoned. Their biological parents may have had problems with drug or alcohol abuse or mental illness.

As with private agencies, advantages and disadvantages exist to adopting through a government (public) agency. Here are some key advantages:

- The adoption should be free of charge or nearly free because it is supported by tax dollars.

- The biological parental rights are clearly terminated.

- The child may be able to retain public medical insurance, even after adoption (Medicaid).

- The child may be eligible for a monthly subsidy. (Don't factor that out. It might help a lot.)

- With many foster child adoptions, you will be eligible for a $10,160 income tax credit, even though the adoption is free. This is because the federal government wants to encourage people to adopt foster children. (Read more about the adoption tax credit in Chapter 8.)

The primary disadvantages are as follows:

- The wait might be very long.

- Extensive parental classes might be required. These classes can actually provide very helpful information, but they take extra time in your schedule.

- The child might need therapy someday to deal with the aftereffects of abuse.

- The child might need treatment for a medical condition.

- It might be difficult to obtain the adoption subsidy.

- You might need to deal with a lot of bureaucratic hassles and be very persistent. Government social workers are overburdened with details and paperwork. They need to know that you are very eager to adopt.

What You Need to Know

When a social worker is considering you for a particular child, she should give you general information about the child's background and problems. Most social workers are very forthcoming with this information, although it is illegal for them to violate the confidentiality of the biological family.

Adoption Alert _____

Studies have documented that many foster children receive abysmal medical care or no medical care at all. This may be because they get moved around a lot or because their medical records don't follow them.

Thus, the medical information on a child may be outdated or nonexistent. Find out when the child's last complete medical examination was and have the child checked before you adopt.

Confidentiality is not an excuse to prevent you from seeing state case files. Insist on seeing the child's records. Names of birthparents or other identifying data can be blanked out. Ask about any discrepancies, omissions, or problems that you see.

If you are considering adopting a child through the state or county agency, you should carefully weigh the pros and cons of this important decision that will affect not only you but also your partner, any other children you already have, and, of course, the child or children you adopt. This is a major life decision, after all. Remember, children who are in foster care have experienced at least one family disruption, therefore, they have some wounds. They are also in great need of a strong, committed, and loving family. Each child's personality and experience will be different, so it is important for you to consider all aspects and decide which child fits with your family and its strengths and weaknesses.

Adoptinfo

The federal government is actively recruiting adoptive parents nationwide in its Collaboration to AdoptUSKids program, managed by the Adoption Exchange Association in Baltimore, Maryland. Their website has photos and biographies of nearly 7,000 foster children in the United States needing families and will direct families to the state agency that can help them. For more information, go to www.AdoptUSKids.org or call 1-888-200-4005.

On the plus side …

 ◆ Foster children often have an intense desire for a family of their own. Possibly yours!

 ◆ Many foster children are very resilient, despite past adverse experiences.

 ◆ You can turn a child's life around. And change your own life, too.

On the negative side …

 ◆ Many foster children have received poor (or no) medical or dental care.

 ◆ Abuse isn't always documented. Some past incidents may not be in the child's record.

 ◆ It'll take time for the child to adjust to a new family—the older the child, the more time needed.

 ◆ The child might begin to act up when he or she starts to feel comfortable with you. (It's a test, only a test.)

Adopterms

An **independent adoption** refers to an adoption that is arranged through private individuals, attorneys, or adoption facilitators, rather than adoption agencies. It is a nonagency adoption, even though most states also require a home study.

While for some children the past traumas and other problems they have faced can be difficult to work with, most of the cons I've listed are "correctable" with patience, common sense, love, professional support, time, financial resources, and commitment.

Inside Info on Lawyers

When you arrange an adoption yourself or through an attorney (or through an adoption facilitator in some states), this is called an *independent adoption* or a *private adoption*. Some people also call it *direct placement* adoption.

Adopterms

A **black market adoption** refers to an adoption that is arranged outside the law and usually involves very large sums of money paid to an attorney, agency worker, or other individual. People sometimes use the term **gray market adoption** in association with nonagency adoptions to mean that the adoption isn't quite "on the level." But the reality is that an adoption is either legal, or it is illegal.

There are good lawyers and bad lawyers, just as there are good agencies and bad agencies. But for some reason, many people associate lawyers with the bad guys, and there are some who still think that attorney-arranged adoptions are *black market adoptions*. If the attorney is following the state law, an adoption is thoroughly legal.

Here are some reasons why people adopt independently:

- They think they can adopt faster.

- They want more control over the process than they think an agency will give.

- The adoption agencies won't accept them, or they think that they won't.

- Their friends have adopted independently.

- They want firsthand contact with birthparents (although adoptions through attorneys may be confidential in some states).

- No agencies exist in their area, and they don't wish to deal with an arranger outside of their area.

Adoption, Esq.

As with adoption agencies, many people seek adoption lawyers by looking in the Yellow Pages. Bad idea. Why? Because some attorneys advertise under "Adoption," even though they have little experience in this field, simply to drum up business. Or they handle mostly stepparent adoptions, which are very different (and much easier) than nonrelative adoptions. Some good adoption attorneys don't even believe in advertising, so you'll miss them if you dedicate yourself solely to a phonebook search.

So how do you find a good lawyer? I'm glad you asked.

- Ask local adoptive parent groups for names.

- Get a list of adoption attorneys from the American Academy of Adoption Attorneys or check their website directory at www.adoptionattorneys.org.

- Find out which judges finalize adoptions. Ask them (or their staff) for names of reputable adoption attorneys.

- Ask your family and friends for names of adoption attorneys. Make it clear that you want experienced adoption lawyers.

- Ask your physician (or a local gynecologist or pediatrician) for the names of adoption lawyers. Ask the nurses there, too. While you're at it, ask others in the health field, like your dentist and your pharmacist.

- Ask your friends to ask their doctors for names of adoption lawyers.

- Call all the possible candidates and find out how many adoptions each has handled. Fewer than 10 per year are not enough.

- Zero in on attorneys who specialize in adoption or who primarily work on adoptions.

Ask Questions!

Just as I urged you to check out adoption agencies, you should also check out adoption attorneys. You need an attorney who is experienced, ethical, and competent. You also need someone you can get along with. Follow your instincts and work with a lawyer with whom you feel comfortable.

> **Adoption Alert** _____
>
> What an attorney can do for wannabe adopters varies from state to state. In some states, people who wish to adopt must "find" the birthmother. They then notify the attorney, and she starts the adoption process. In other states, birthmothers go directly to lawyers and are matched with prospective parents.
>
> Some people live in one state and adopt a child from another state. In such cases, the Interstate Compact on the Placement of Children (a sort of treaty between states) is followed, and the social services department in each state signs off that their state laws have been complied with.

Here are some questions to ask an attorney with whom you are thinking of working:

◆ Do you specialize in adoptions or concentrate heavily on adoptions? What percentage of your business involves adoptions?

◆ Are you a member of any professional organizations related to adoption (such as the American Academy of Adoption Attorneys in Washington, D.C.)? Or a state adoption attorney organization or local adoptive parent groups?

◆ Have you participated in any state legislation on adoption? (Many times, experienced attorneys involve themselves in adoption law.)

◆ When you receive adoption fees, do you place them in escrow in the bank until a birthmother match has been made? (The wrong answer would be that the money is put in a Swiss bank account!)

◆ If paying birthmother expenses is lawful in your state, do you receive receipts from the birthmother for expenses she incurs, such as rent, electricity, doctor bills, and so on?

◆ Have you ever been sued by an adoptive parent or birthparent? If so, what happened?

◆ Have any of your adoptions been overturned? If so, what happened?

- Why do you do adoptions?

- What is the most important thing to know about you in relation to adoption?

- What services do you provide to birthparents?

- What services do you provide to adoptive parents?

- What are your fees? What does that include?

- What do you expect from me/us?

- What happens if an adoption has been arranged but the birthparents change their minds?

Familybuilding Tips

Can you adopt more quickly through a lawyer? Sometimes you can, especially if you are very active in identifying a birthmother or if it's legal for your attorney to arrange matches in your state. Pregnant women who seek adopting parents for their children are usually in their second or even third trimester, so the wait may be just a few months.

There is no guarantee that nonagency adoption is faster, however. A lot depends on you and how selective you are.

Checking Behind the Scenes

Here are some additional screening actions that you should take:

- Check with the local Better Business Bureau and see whether they have had any complaints about the attorney.

- Check with the adoption unit at the state social services department and ask if they have had any complaints against the attorney.

- Check with adoptive parent groups in the area to see if anyone has had any recent experiences with this attorney. If so, speak to the adopters directly. Don't get secondhand information.

- If possible, ask other attorneys this question: If they wanted to adopt, would they hire this person? (They may not wish to give you details, but a "no" or silence is revealing.)

For more information on adopting through attorneys, see Chapter 9.

"Open" or "Closed"?

When you decide to adopt, you'll also need to think about whether the adoption will be *confidential, semi-open,* or *open.* Everyone seems to have different definitions for these terms. For our purposes, I prefer the following definitions.

> **Familybuilding Tips** _____
>
> In an open adoption, the adoption arranger often creates a contract that spells out what is expected of each side; for example, how often photographs and letters will be exchanged, and how they will be exchanged (either directly or through the adoption arranger).
>
> If one side reneges on the agreement, the other may be able to take the matter to court, depending on which state the parties live in. However, in most cases, the contracts do not appear to be enforceable. But parties should be encouraged to act in good faith.

♦ In a **confidential adoption,** neither the adopter nor the birthparents know each other, nor do they ever meet. Instead, all the arrangements and paperwork occur through a middleman, usually an adoption agency or an attorney. Some people call this a *closed* adoption, although I prefer the terms *confidential* and *traditional* because they sound nonjudgmental. A confidential adoption doesn't mean that the adopters and birthparents know nothing about each other. What it means is they have no identifying information about each other.

♦ Usually, **semi-open** refers to an adoption in which the adopters and birthparents meet once or twice and on a first-name-only basis. In addition, they may agree to exchange pictures and letters on an annual or fairly infrequent basis through the adoption arranger. (If your adoption arranger advocates a semi-open adoption, be sure to ask for an exact definition of her terms.)

> **Adoption Alert** _____
>
> If you adopt your child from foster care, an open adoption may not be possible, either because the agency has a policy of not releasing identifying information for any reason or because doing so in your situation isn't in the best interests of the child. Most international adoptions are confidential as well.

♦ In an **open adoption,** as I define it, the adopters and the birthparents both know each other's full names, both first and last names. (It is not open if only one side has identifying information about the other.) They may agree to exchange photos and letters directly, without using the agency or attorney as a middleman. Sometimes a semi-open adoption later becomes an open adoption, if both parties decide that they want it that way.

Many wannabe adopters don't realize that they have more choices than they know. For example, if they want an open adoption, but their agency does not advocate open adoptions, they can choose another agency.

Conversely, if they want a confidential adoption, they should not feel unduly pressured into agreeing to an open adoption. Adopters who agree to an open adoption against their wishes may later find it difficult to fulfill their side of the agreement (for example, sending the birthmother letters and photos). This is terribly unfair to both the birthmother and the child. Agreeing to an open adoption when they don't want one is also unfair to the adopters themselves.

The exact definition of open adoption varies from agency to agency, as well as between attorneys. So you need to ask the agency or attorney how *they* define open adoption.

Familybuilding Tips

Some studies indicate that open adoption is a better choice for everyone involved, while others point away from that conclusion.

A 1996 study reported in *Child Development* found that all the children studied "reported positive levels of self-esteem, curiosity about their birthparents, and satisfaction with the openness situation" regardless of whether their adoptions were closed, semi-open, or open. What this seems to mean is that the child's sense of security in his adoptive family is more important than contact with the birth family.

For many agencies, open adoption means that the birthmothers choose pre-approved families from five or six resumés or autobiographies.

Some (not many) agencies encourage a complete disclosure of identities between birthparents and adopting parents, as well as an ongoing close relationship. Agencies that support fully open disclosures believe that an open adoption is a better way for both adoptive parents and birthparents—as well as the children. Agencies that don't support open adoption feel just as strongly that continued contact is not a good idea for any of the parties.

The pros and cons of open adoption have been endlessly debated by social workers and attorneys. It appears that those who support open adoptions are completely committed to them; those who believe in confidential adoptions seem equally convinced that open adoptions are catastrophic. Adopters need to deal with an adoption arranger that they feel comfortable with. The following table presents some classic differences between the two styles of adoption.

Open Adoption Pros and Cons

Pros	Cons
Your child will never have to search for birthparents.	Your child may never wish to search for birthparents.
The adopted adult can easily establish a relationship with birthparents.	The birthparents may want more or less contact than the adopted adult wants.
The minor child may be able to have a positive relationship with birthparents.	An unstable birthparent could cause problems.
You may feel more relaxed about the adoption knowing exactly who the birthmother is.	You may feel less of a sense of entitlement and see yourself as not a "real mother."
You gain more "extended family."	Do you really want more extended family?
The birthmother may be less likely to change her mind about the adoption because she knows you.	Open adoption may attract birth mothers who don't really want their babies adopted, and see open adoption as "halfway."
The birthmother may be less likely to change her mind about the adoption because it would hurt you too much.	The birthmother might feel she should have more input into childrearing than you'd like.
As time passes, if the birthmother has a change in her health status, she can notify you about conditions that could later affect your child.	Often people lose track of each other and the birthmother may not tell you about health changes.

Bottom line: Make sure you completely understand what level of openness is expected of you, and that you're comfortable with any future obligations you agree to before committing to an adoption.

Familybuilding Tips

In a U.S. adoption, it's very important that adoptive parents and birthparents agree to terms that they feel they can comply with. Some adoptive parents agree to anything, just so they can "get the baby." Then they don't follow through. Others make sincere agreements but find that what they agreed to is too difficult with raising a new family—such as weekly letters to the birthmother. (Do *you* write weekly letters to anyone? E-mail doesn't count.) This mistreatment has led to heartbreak and anger among birthparents.

The Least You Need to Know

♦ It's essential that you screen agencies and attorneys before you sign on the dotted line.

♦ Don't assume that the cost of the adoption necessarily reflects the quality of the services.

♦ Adoption is a business for adoption arrangers. Agencies and attorneys should be kindhearted, but they should also be able to manage a business.

♦ Don't be afraid to ask questions!

♦ Understand the differences between open, semi-open, and confidential adoptions so you can decide which is best for you.

Chapter 7

Going Your Own Way

In This Chapter

- Finding a child to adopt on your own
- Asking friends, family, healthcare professionals, and others for assistance
- Advertising for adoption
- Finding your child online

Passivity is no virtue when it comes to adoption, especially if you want to adopt an infant in the United States. (Not that it works well with adopting an older child, either!) It can often be tremendously helpful to mobilize your very own *people assets*—your circle of friends and relatives. And in turn, you could also ask them to get the word out to *their* friends and relatives. This tactic can help you amass a great deal of information, as well as possible leads on a pregnant woman considering adoption for her baby. In this chapter, I'll show you how you can do a lot of the legwork on your own. (Although you'll still need an agency and/or an attorney to make the adoption legal.)

Networking

Not everyone among your family and friends will think that adopting a child is the greatest idea they've ever heard. You will need to learn to deflect criticism and intrusive questions in order to gain their moral support and any important information they have. You'll also need to expand your informational search outward, to parent support groups and local experts (see Chapter 5). Increasing numbers of wannabe adopters are also using the Internet's vast capabilities, which I discuss later in this chapter.

Real Life Snapshots

Several years ago, I led an adoptive parent group that included a couple in their 50s. They had learned that their son and daughter-in-law (who lived in another state) wanted to adopt a child, and they decided they were going to help.

They asked me what books to read and how to obtain information on agencies and attorneys, and they came to our meetings and asked lots of questions. Did their son adopt? He sure did! It's safe to say he succeeded a lot faster than he would have on his own, because he was fortunate to have his parents' tremendous informational and moral support.

Warning: If you're in the "I don't know whether I want to adopt yet" stage—or even in the "I guess I sorta/kinda/maybe want to adopt" stage, I recommend you consider holding off telling your friends and relatives. If you've made up your mind that you really do want to adopt a child, networking can pay off in informational dividends.

Familybuilding Tips

Even if you don't want to find your "own" birthmother, spreading the word about your interest in adoption can generate information about agencies and attorneys—who's good, who's not so good, and so forth. It's an extremely valuable way to get information fast, whether you want to adopt your baby from Indiana or India.

What Do You Say?

If you plan to network with your family and friends, you need to keep your message clear and short. Tell people in writing, whenever possible, so they have something to refer to. It's easy to forget when it's not *you* who wants to adopt.

Here are the basics your friends and family need to know—and remember to keep it simple! Tell them:

- ◆ Whether you want to adopt an infant, toddler, or older child.

- ◆ Whether you want to adopt in the United States or another country. (If another country, which one?)

- ◆ How they can contact you.

Real Life Snapshots

Here's an anecdote provided to me by Los Angeles attorney David J. Radis:

> I was contacted by a birthmother living in Ireland who was an American citizen. She asked my office to put her in touch with prospective adopting families and indicated that she wanted to come to California to deliver and place the baby. I had a family I felt would be a perfect match for her and tried to contact them. I was advised that they were out of the country—in Ireland. I was put in touch with them in Ireland the day before they were scheduled to return to the U.S. and discovered that they were a few miles from the birthmother's home and, in fact, knew her father. They met, agreed to the terms of the placement, and the birthmother placed her baby with them. In fact, she later placed another child—a biological sibling— with the same family.

(Printed with permission of David J. Radis, Attorney, Los Angeles, California.)

What about deflecting annoying questions about *why you can't have children* (which, at a family gathering, probably sounds to you as if it were being announced at ear-shattering levels with a bullhorn to the world at large)? If pressed for details, say that it's just not possible. You do *not* owe everyone the innermost details of what works and doesn't work, plumbing-wise. If people continue to press you, you can smile mysteriously, play deaf, and change the subject or wander off.

What if others doubt aloud whether you should adopt a child who falls into a certain category, say a Russian child or a foster child? Assure the questioner that you're thoroughly researching all the issues (you can tell them that you've read this book!) and thank them for their concern. Then if they persist, use the same tactics I recommended for handling intrusive questions about your infertility.

What if they *do* find a potential lead for you?

Let's say that your networking pays off, and Auntie Em and Uncle Henry call you excitedly. They've heard of a young woman, age 19, who belongs to a neighboring church and who wants her baby adopted! She's due in about a month. She wants her baby adopted by a childless couple in another state, someone of her religion. And you fit! Is this a done deal or what?

Before you decide to rush your relatives into getting all the info on this young woman and then seeing whether they can sign her up for you, step back a moment and think about this. It's far better for you to enlist the aid of an adoption agency or an adoption attorney, who can kindly but detachedly work on obtaining the information on the young woman. If you haven't had a home study (required in most states) but think there's a good chance this adoption could work, now is a very good time to find out how to obtain one.

Real Life Snapshots

Sometimes the people doing your networking can surprise you. In one case, it was a six-year-old boy!

The Gladney Center, an adoption agency in Fort Worth, Texas, reprinted an article by an adoptive mother in their newsletter, *Bright Futures*. The mom had been shopping in the supermarket with her little boy, who was wearing his "I'm a big brother" tee shirt. When a lady in the vegetable aisle commented on his shirt, he told her all about his adopted baby sister. The mom walked away thinking how the poor lady had been bored silly by her enthusiastic little son.

But she was wrong. Several weeks later, the lady saw them again and thanked the child. Why? Because a woman in her family was agonizing over what to do about an unplanned pregnancy. The lady was so impressed with this little boy's explanation about adoption and his positive attitude that she conveyed the information to the niece, who decided to place her baby for adoption.

Said the mother, "Who would have ever guessed that in the vegetable aisle at a grocery store, a six-year-old could make such an impact!"

I also recommend that you take an additional action, and this can be very hard: Very sweetly ask your relatives to step back and let the adoption experts (and you) make the next moves. They might be resistant because they want to help you, and they "know" this is just meant to be. But hang tough. Also, realize that the woman should not be pressured in any way. It's probably okay for others to tell her how wonderful you are—once. It's natural for your relatives to want to follow this thing through, but it's better if they don't.

Also, be sure to read Chapter 12, for more information on the home study and what social workers do during the course of the home study.

Taking Out a Classified Ad

Another route to get the word out is advertising in the classified ads section of the newspaper. In the classifieds, people place ads if they want to hire workers, if they want to sell a car, if they want to know if someone found their dog, and sometimes they advertise if they want to adopt a baby.

You'll see these ads in some national and some local newspapers (that is, if adoption ads are legal in your state). "Happy loving couple longs to adopt a child. Please call us at ..." They might give their first names. They might mention that they are a Christian couple, or vegetarians, or even talk briefly about their pets. They'll include whatever they think might work to attract someone who'll consider adoption.

Adoption Alert

Advertising your desire to adopt in the classified ads isn't legal in every state: California, Florida, Massachusetts, and other states ban all advertising by people seeking to adopt. And even if states do allow adoption ads, some newspapers refuse to accept them (they have the right to do so).

Does It Pay to Advertise?

Do classified ads work? Yes, they do, although not for everyone.

Here are the major benefits to advertising in classified ads:

- You spread the word that you want to adopt far beyond your own neighborhood or even your own city.

- You can screen any responses to the ad yourself or have them referred to your attorney or agency. (Some states don't allow attorneys to screen such calls.)

- Your waiting period to adopt may be cut down considerably.

But there are also disadvantages to advertising in the classifieds:

- People who want to scam you may see you as an easy mark.

- Annoying people may call you with prank calls.

- You may have trouble knowing what to say—and not say—when someone calls.

- Classifieds can be expensive, depending on where you advertise. In addition, some people choose to put in an 800 line or a separate "adoption" phone line to handle the phone calls, which adds to the cost.

Writing an Effective Ad

If you do opt to advertise, take some time to think about what your ad will say. Read the ads written by others. Consider paying extra for a box around your ad or some other way to make your ad stand out. Here are some items to mention:

- If your religious orientation is important to you, then list it.

- If you love pets, say so. (If you have a dog, state what breed it is, otherwise pregnant women considering adoption might be afraid it's a dangerous breed. So if you have a friendly collie or beagle, say so.)

- If you love sports, say so.

- Think about what is generally appealing about your environment: safe neighborhood, good schools, and so on.

- If you're married, stress your joint commitment. One birthmother told me that it was the husband and adoptive father-to-be who was important to her. He was the element she couldn't provide her child.

- If your entire family is excited about your adopting, this is a plus to mention.

- It's also a good idea to make some reference to your intense desire/longing to adopt a child as well as your eagerness and excitement.

Do *not* however, state your gross or net income. Do not state your profession if you could be easily identified in your area—for example, you're a neurosurgeon in Somewhere, New Hampshire. Some adoption agencies and attorneys instruct prospective adopters on how, where, and when to place ads, so don't be afraid to ask them for advice.

 Familybuilding Tips

> Should you include an 800 number in your ad? Some people believe it will encourage people to call, and others say that birthmothers believe all 800 numbers are really numbers for agencies or attorneys. Some people include a toll-call number in their ad and encourage pregnant women to call them collect. However, some birthmothers might feel funny about leaving their name when they call collect. It's up to you to weigh the advantages and disadvantages.

I read a note on America Online from someone who recommended saying in your ad that you're looking forward to 2 A.M. wakeups and changing diapers. That's good advice; when writing your ad, think about what might appeal to a pregnant woman who is considering adoption.

Keep in mind that some people will think advertising your desire to adopt is bad or seedy. You probably won't be able to convince them of your sincerity and honesty, so don't waste a lot of time worrying about it. After telling the person that it's legal to advertise in your state (if it is), if the person continues to make negative comments, just say you disagree and walk away.

Taking Calls

How do you handle a call from a birthparent who answers your ad? I'll cover what you need to know about birthparents in Chapter 16. For now, though, I want to offer you tips on setting up your phone service so you are fully prepared to act on any calls that come in.

When you're in the process of adopting, your primary link to a possible birthmother or to the agency itself is often your telephone. What normally works with your home and work phone might need to be re-evaluated during the pre-adopt stages. Here are a few tips:

- If you are having your phone calls forwarded to your cell phone, make sure you have it turned on and fully charged at all times!

- If you are having calls forwarded to a work phone, tell your assistant or anyone who shares your line what you are doing, if you feel comfortable with that. If not, alert them you might be receiving an important but private phone call and that the caller might not want to leave a message. You don't have to elaborate. Either way, you want to make sure that your co-workers will rush to find you if a call comes through.

> **Familybuilding Tips**
>
> Are there any times during the year that are better to advertise than other times? Experts say yes; pregnancies among young women are especially likely after social occasions, such as spring break, summer vacation, and the winter holidays. Remember, most pregnant women don't seriously consider adoption until their second or third trimester.

- Should you get two phone lines? Opinion is mixed on this one. Consider your own situation. If someone in your family (maybe you!) is a phone-aholic, then you probably should get two phones. Also, if you have two lines, use the second line exclusively for adoption calls.

- Should you get a toll-free (800 or 888) number? Again, opinion is mixed. If you get an 800 phone line, then birthmothers not in your local dialing area can call you at no charge. However, you will have to pay an extra fee. And some birthmothers assume that only attorneys and agencies have toll-free phone numbers.

◆ If annoying calls become a problem (if you place an ad about adopting a child, you might receive calls from people who want to tell you just how you and they can make a baby together in rather blunt terms), you can contact your phone company about a "call blocking" option, which allows you to block either a specific number or the number of the last person who called you. (You can get full details from a telephone company representative.)

Real Life Snapshots

One woman who successfully adopted several children always asks the birthparents who call for their phone number and address. She then asks permission to send them a brief list of questions. She says her questions are not what's really important—what's more important is that only people seriously considering adoption are willing to give their name and address and to return her questionnaire.

If you want to use this tactic, but not give your own address, you might think about getting a post office box in your city or a nearby city.

Creative Advertising

Some wannabe adopters create business card–sized ads that say things like "Please help us adopt" and include a phone number. They staple them to bulletin boards, hand them out to people, and send them in holiday greeting or birthday cards. The same advice applies here as in the classifieds: Be careful and screen anyone who calls you. Alternatively, include the name of your attorney or adoption agency on the card.

Adoption Alert

Before you advertise on a website, find out who owns it, what organization sponsors it, and what its primary goals are.

In addition, keep in mind that any information you provide can be read by people worldwide. Be careful about offering information about your personal income or other data that could leave you open to scammers.

Advertising on the Internet

Some websites will let you advertise yourself as prospective parents, either for free or for a fee. For example, www.adoption.com posts photos and information on people wanting to adopt.

Let's say you've placed an ad on the Internet and a birthmother contacts you by e-mail. She's favorably impressed with your Internet ad and says that you seem like you might be perfect for her baby. Let's say she's in New Mexico, and you're in New York. Do you book a ticket on the next flight to New Mexico? I don't recommend this. Instead, get basic information, such as when she is due, how old she is, how long she's been thinking about adoption, and whether she's working with a particular agency or attorney. Don't expect to get all this information in one burst! Give her a chance to talk. It's scary for her to contact you, even though you probably never thought about that.

If this is her first adoption contact, it's a good idea to refer her to your adoption agency or attorney. Or tell her you'd like to give her e-mail address to your adoption arranger. Then the arranger can work on obtaining details, making contacts with an arranger in the other state, and so forth.

Do You Have to Advertise?

Let's say advertising is legal in your state, but you don't feel comfortable about doing it. Does this mean you should abandon all hope for adopting a child? Not at all! Instead, use the other networking tips described at the beginning of this chapter to work on identifying a birthmother in the United States.

Finally, some adoption arrangers will identify birthmothers and make matches between them and you—basically handling the adoption for you in the traditional and confidential manner. If this is what you truly want, then locate an agency or attorney with this service (see Chapter 6 on adoption arrangers).

Straight Talk About Adoption Facilitators

Some states, including California, allow people who are not agency social workers or attorneys to help people find birthmothers (for a fee). These people are called *adoption facilitators* or *adoption consultants*.

> **Adoption Alert**
>
> Incidentally, when you are in the process of adopting, it's also a very good idea to muzzle yourself with regard to telling your friends and relatives everything you know about the birthmother and the child. Sadly, people tend to remember the negative, and it's really not necessary for everyone to know that the birthmother's uncle was an alcoholic. If you tell them this, they will remember it. Forever.

> **Adopterms**
>
> In some states, **adoption facilitators** or **adoption consultants** act as adoption "middlemen," and help people identify pregnant women considering adoption, assist prospective adoptive parents to compose adoption resumés, and arrange birthmother meetings. Some people use the term "facilitator" for anyone who is a nonsocial worker engaged in arranging adoptions and include adoption attorneys in this definition. However, I do not include lawyers in my own definition.

> **Adoption Alert**
>
> If you identify a birthmother through advertising, you often will find that she confides many of her problems to you. Experts say it's common to feel you should give her advice or counseling. Even if you are a trained and very skilled counselor, you should *not* counsel the pregnant woman, because of your very personal interest in this case and your lack of professional detachment. Instead, let the agency, attorney, or other adoption arranger help the birthmother sort out her personal problems.

They may coach people seeking to adopt, assist them with writing or placing ads or adoption resumés (see Chapter 12), tell them what to say when a call comes in, and so forth. They are usually not licensed (although some facilitators may be licensed social workers) and, thus, might not be policed or overseen by any governmental authority. However, after a birthmother says she wants to place her child, the adoption must be turned over to an adoption agency or an attorney.

As with just about everything else, there are good and bad facilitators. Personally, I strongly recommend that you work with an agency or an attorney; however, if you believe a facilitator is the right path to your child (and if using such a middleman is legal in your state), then be sure to ask plenty of questions. Here are just a few questions you might ask:

◆ Do you have one fee or several fees? What are they and how much are they? Some consultants charge a flat rate; others charge by the hour, or charge different fees for different services. Also, find out whether you will be billed for miscellaneous expenses like phone calls.

◆ What services are included in your fee?

◆ What are your credentials? (Some adoption consultants are social workers; some are not licensed in any capacity. Be sure to ask.)

◆ How many adoptions have you helped arrange?

◆ How many adoptions that you helped arrange fell through? If the number is more than 20 or 30 percent, the facilitator might not be a very effective screener of birthmothers. But neither is it normal for a facilitator to claim that none of her adoptions have fallen through. If the facilitator says that she has arranged 500 adoptions and not a single birthmother has ever changed her mind before the baby was placed with a family, she's probably lying. Go to someone else.

◆ How do birthparents find you, and what services do you provide them?

♦ Can you give me some references? Although it's true that many adoptive parents do *not* want their names released to anyone, it's also true that some people are willing to talk to hopeful adopters. The facilitator should be able to provide the names of some people who are willing to talk to you about their adoption.

The facilitator might even bring people who are references to a seminar or other group meeting. That's okay, but you should also try to talk to the people privately, either in person or for just a brief chat on the phone. Why? If you talk to them by yourself, you might get more candid responses to your questions.

♦ May I see a sample contract? It should spell out what the facilitator is expected to do, how much you will pay, and other conditions of the service to be rendered. A contract isn't an assurance that you will adopt a baby or that you'll be happy with the service, but at least it will give you an idea of who is supposed to do what, for how much, and when.

In addition to talking to the facilitator, checking references, and reviewing a contract, you should ask outside organizations about the facilitator. Do local adoptive parent groups know about this individual, and if so, what do they think? Does the state social services office have any experience with this person?

You can also ask local adoption agencies and attorneys for their opinions; however, expect that many will be disdainful and negative. After all, the facilitator is doing something they believe is really *their* job, and there's bound to be some professional jealousy. And don't forget that in some states, it is unlawful to pay anyone other than a licensed agency or an attorney to assist with a child placement.

The Least You Need to Know

♦ With some guidance, your family and friends can help you adopt a child.

♦ Advertising works for many people, as long as you know the pitfalls.

♦ The Internet is an amazing informational source that can facilitate your adoption.

♦ Adoption facilitators might be another route to your child. Make sure you screen a facilitator carefully before hiring him or her.

Chapter 8

Affording Adoption

In This Chapter

- Dealing with the costs of adoption
- Making an adoption financial plan
- Investigating state and federal options
- Considering benefits your employer may offer

In an earlier chapter, I discussed whether it's "fair" that adoption usually costs a substantial amount of money, so I won't beat that drum again. (Read Chapter 2 if you missed it.) The good news is that Uncle Sam now offers major tax benefits to adopters. In addition, if you adopt a foster child, even if it costs you nothing, you can take a tax credit of more than $10,000 as of 2003.

In this chapter, I'll explain these benefits and help you figure out other ways you can afford the fees associated with adoption, whether you adopt through an adoption agency or privately. Keep reading!

How Much Does It Cost?

Adopting a healthy infant could cause you to incur costs of $25,000 to $30,000 or more, depending on the situation. It's very difficult, however, to give flat figures or averages because of variations in state laws, differences in agency and attorney policies, and a myriad of other factors.

Having said that, however, if I were pressed up against a wall and compelled by a manic wannabe adopter to state an average fee to adopt a child not in the state social services system—stand and deliver—I'd reluctantly say that average fees to adopt a healthy infant are about $20,000, whether U.S. or international.

> ### Adoptinfo
>
> If you are matched to a particular pregnant women who is planning adoption for her baby, some agencies (and most attorneys) may be willing to reduce their fees if the birthmother is on Medicaid or a private insurance plan—because that insurance will cover the prenatal care and the delivery of the child. This could lower your costs by thousands of dollars.
>
> Ask the agency or attorney whether fees are changed in any way if the birthmother has private insurance or is on Medicaid.
>
> Also, keep in mind that sometimes birthmothers choose to place their babies for adoption *after* the birth, when the child is a few months old or older. In that case, there should be no medical fees. Ask the agency or attorney what the fees are when that happens.

In the case of an adoption through the state or county, there should be either no fees or minimal fees. (The adoption is often an older child adoption.) The costs of a public adoption are borne by the taxpayers. In fact, the federal government offers financial incentives to states to terminate the parental rights of parents in the case of children who have been in foster care for several years. In the past, many children entered foster care as small children, and they often stayed in foster care until they "aged out" at the age of 18. Finally, the federal government realized this was a bad plan for children and changed their policies, as did the states.

Adoption Alert

Some agencies charge on a sliding scale. That means that they tag the fees to your income, with a minimum and maximum fee. Thus, affluent people are charged at the uppermost levels, and less-affluent people pay fees on the lower end of the scale. Be sure to ask the agency whether they use the sliding-scale system.

If an adoption arranger gives you a flat fee on the expenses to adopt, ask what it includes! The fee could (but might not) cover these expenses:

- Application fee (which may be several hundred dollars or more)
- Lawyer's fees and court costs

- ◆ Travel expenses, in the case of international adoption or the adoption of a child from another state

- ◆ Home study fee (this could be several thousand dollars)

- ◆ Living expenses for the birthmother, if legal in that state

- ◆ Medical expenses of the birthmother, if legal in that state

- ◆ Placement fee of the adoption agency, which could be $5,000 or more and is paid upon placement of the child)

A good agency or attorney will give you a breakdown of the approximate costs. Of course, expenses may change. For example, if the birthmother must have a C-section instead of a vaginal delivery, the surgery and hospital bills will be greater. Attorneys and agencies should give you a range of high to low and that includes most contingencies when birthmother expenses are involved. (Although no one can predict everything that might happen, experienced adoption arrangers should be able to give you a very good idea of the range, in most cases.)

Some agencies charge adopters flat rates, regardless of whether or not the birthmother has her own insurance.

> **Familybuilding Tips**
>
> If Agency A tells you that their adoption expenses are about $15,000, and Agency B says their fees are about $20,000, then the smart thing is to go with Agency A, right? Not so fast! First, you need to find out what Agency A includes in its fees.
>
> In our example, let's say Agency A doesn't include living expenses for the birthmother (estimated at about $3,000) or lawyer fees. You might find out that the total fees for Agency A are equal to (or even greater than) what Agency B charges. Get the information on total costs, and then you can make a sound financial comparison.

Standard Payment Terms

If no pregnant woman or child is immediately matched to you, you usually will pay an application fee (if you're working with an agency) or a retainer (if you're working with an attorney). The amount of this fee varies. You'll also usually have to pay for a home study because most states require one, whether you adopt through an agency or privately. Expect this to cost at least several thousand dollars, depending on the agency.

After a birthmother or child is identified and if living or medical expenses are involved, you will pay estimated expenses to the arranger. You may also need to pay court costs and other fees in advance. The largest sums usually are due just before or at the time of placement.

If you're adopting your child from another country, you'll need to travel to that country to finalize the adoption, which means that you will have to buy plane tickets and pay for a hotel room, meals, and so on. Some agencies also encourage you to bring gifts and toys for the orphanage.

Making a Financial Plan

When you've got an estimate of all the expenses involved, you can start to make a financial plan. That is, unless you have 20 grand or more in the bank.

CAUTION

Adoption Alert

Most of us groan over having to pay thousands of dollars to adopt. Although adoption arrangers may sympathize, I advise you to *not* groan endlessly about your financial agony to them. They've heard it all before and don't need to hear it again. If you continue to make a big deal about it, they may wonder whether you can truly afford the adoption and/or you really want to adopt.

This does *not* mean, however, that you shouldn't ask about where your money is going or question it if you don't understand a fee or something doesn't seem quite right. You should! Find out when payments will be due and what they are for; and if there are any changes, get an explanation. But zip your lip on general complaints. If arrangers think you've taken a vow of poverty, they may see others as more suitable parents.

If you don't have enough money in the bank to cover the cost of adoption—most of us don't—how the heck do you come up with the cash? Here are some ways you may be able to afford adoption fees:

- ◆ Ask family members for a loan. (They may even offer you money as a gift.) Sure, it can be a little embarrassing to be 35 or 40 years old (or older) and asking your parents for money. But the truth is, the adoption fees may be beyond your current means, even though you do have the financial ability to support a child.

  The "up" side of asking your parents or relatives for a loan is that you just might get it. The downside is that they might not ever let you forget it. You know your own family. Take into account the pros and cons.

◆ Ask someone in your family to co-sign for you on a loan application. Again, consider the pros and cons of asking your parents, a sibling, or another family member for financial help.

◆ If you have a 401(k) plan with your employer, find out whether you can borrow on it.

◆ Find out whether your employer offers adoption benefits. Many corporations provide adoption benefits of $3,000 or more, and they might also offer loans at reduced rates to adopting parents. They see this as a way of granting adoptive parents similar benefits to biological parents, who often receive benefits for prenatal care and childbirth. Others offer paid or unpaid leave beyond what is required by the *Family Medical and Leave Act.*

◆ Find out whether your employer or your spouse's employer offers low-interest loans.

◆ Check with your credit union or bank. You may be able to borrow a considerable sum and have it gradually deducted from your paycheck until it's paid off.

◆ Consider a home equity loan.

◆ Find out whether you can borrow on your insurance policy.

◆ In a pinch, put some expenses on plastic. You may be able to charge some fees on your credit card.

> **Adopterms** _____
>
> The **Family Medical and Leave Act** (FMLA) of 1993 is a federal law that requires employers of more than 50 workers to give full-time employees up to 12 weeks of *unpaid* leave for the birth or adoption of a child. (Adopted children are specifically included in the law.) Check with your Human Resources department for more details.

> **Adoption Alert** _____
>
> What if an adoption falls through? In an agency adoption, the agency usually won't charge its full fees. The most you should lose is money paid for applying to the agency, the home study fees, and any money directly associated with the birthmother's expenses. Many attorneys will also be willing to work with you if an adoption falls through—but assume nothing. Ask up front what would happen if an adoption doesn't work out and you want to "try again."

Government Funding

As I mentioned at the beginning of this chapter, the federal and some state governments now offer a number of benefits or reimbursements for some adoption costs.

Federal laws also require employers that provide health insurance to give the same insurance to newly-adopted children.

Thanks, Uncle Sam!

The federal government gives adopters a big break in the form of an income tax credit of $10,160 for adoption expenses. If you adopt two children, then you can take double the adoption expenses as a credit, or up to $20,320. (Assuming you spend at least that amount to adopt the children, if they are not foster children.) And if you adopt three children … well, you do the math. The adoption tax credit can be applied to all allowable expenses, which include agency fees, attorney fees, court costs, travel (including meals and lodging), medical expenses for the birthmother, and other fees related to the adoption. Expenses that are *not* allowed under this law are expenses for stepparent adoptions or surrogate parent arrangements. The adoption must also comply with federal and state laws.

> **Familybuilding Tips**
>
> Don't forget to ask local adoptive parent groups for suggestions for covering adoption expenses. They may have devised good ways to finance adoptions. In addition, they are probably aware of state adoption benefits as well as benefits offered by many employers in the area.

Not everyone is eligible for the tax credit. If your adjusted income is over about $152,000, it disappears altogether. For more information, ask the IRS for Publication 968, "Tax Benefits for Adoption."

The adoption tax credit may be taken the year before the adoption becomes final, the year it becomes final, or the year after, depending on various circumstances. (Read the IRS pamphlet!)

To apply for an income tax credit, be sure to keep records of all your adoption expenses—save all your receipts!—so that you can document them. You may have to give the IRS information such as the name of the adoption arranger and other details.

> **Adoptinfo**
>
> If you adopt a child from foster care and your adjusted earnings don't exceed $152,000, you're entitled to a $10,160 tax credit, even if you don't incur any expenses. Congress enacted this credit to encourage people to adopt foster children.
>
> In addition, you may also be eligible for a monthly subsidy payment and Medicaid medical benefits for the child. Subsidy programs have increased considerably in the past several years, as states have worked hard to place children for adoption. State social workers can provide more information on subsidy programs.

State of Adoption

Be sure to check whether your own state offers adoption deductions. For example, in 2003, Oklahoma passed legislation to increase to $20,000 (it was $10,000) the state income tax deduction for nonrecurring adoption expenses. Maybe your state has a similar deduction! Additionally, if you adopt a child from the state or county public social services department, the child may be eligible for Medicaid (free medical care). The child may also be eligible for a monthly payment from the state social services department (for which you would be the payee), particularly if the child has serious health or psychiatric problems.

> **Familybuilding Tips**
>
> If your employer gives you adoption money, you must subtract that before taking the federal income tax credit. Here are two simple examples: Let's say your expenses were an incredibly low $3,000, and your employer gave you a grant of $2,000. Because you only spent $1,000 of your own money, you only qualify for a $1,000 tax credit. (Unless you adopted your child from foster care, in which case you can take the credit of $10,160, regardless of what expenses you incurred, as long as you are within the income limitations.)

Federal Laws on Health Insurance

If you work for an employer that provides health insurance for your children, any children you adopt must also be covered, based on provisions of the federal Health Insurance Portability and Accountability Act (HIPAA) of 1996 as well as the Omnibus Budget Reconciliation Act (OBRA) of 1993. Whatever your insurance company would cover for a nonadopted child (with the exception of prenatal care and the delivery of your infant), they must also cover for an adopted child. Ask your attorney or social worker for further information.

Be sure to let your insurance company know as soon as possible when you adopt your child. They can't exclude any pre-existing medical conditions the child has, but it may take time to get a child into their bureaucratic system. If you have any problems with an insurance company refusing to cover your adopted child, contact the state insurance commissioner for help.

If you have individual insurance rather than insurance provided by your employer, the federal law does not apply, but state laws may mandate that your adopted child is covered. Check with your attorney or social worker.

It would be great if adoption were free, but thousands of families have figured out ways to cover the cost of bringing a new child into their families. Isn't your family worth the expense?

The Least You Need to Know

- Most people can afford to adopt, but it takes good financial planning.

- Your employer may have an adoption benefit—the average is about $3,000.

- Some birthmothers may have private insurance or Medicaid, which might reduce your expenses.

- Companies that provide health insurance for employees' children must also cover adopted children, with no pre-existing condition clauses.

- The federal government now provides a substantial adoption income tax credit. Some states also have adoption income tax credit.

Chapter 9

Who Can You Really Trust?

In This Chapter

- ◆ Signs of an unethical adoption agency
- ◆ Common adoption scams
- ◆ Internet scams
- ◆ What to do if you get ripped off

Sometimes it seems that even very intelligent people lose at least 20 IQ points when they enter the adoption arena. They are bedazzled by the dream of adopting a child to love, and they will agree to anything, anyhow, any way.

Don't let your brains fall out just because you want to adopt! Remember: If it sounds too good to be true, it probably is. This chapter will show you how to avoid some common adoption scams.

What to Watch Out For

Most of the people involved in arranging adoptions are good, honest, sincere, hardworking people whose primary goal is to help children be placed with good families. Others have goals that are not so honorable, and still others are well intentioned but incompetent. And, unfortunately, you can't always tell who's good or bad by how they look or sound. (After all, if they looked evil and scary, they wouldn't be very effective at ripping people off, right?)

Scammers can be agencies, attorneys, adoption facilitators, or anyone else even peripherally involved in adoption. Do not presume that an agency license or bar association membership necessarily infuses its holder with honesty and good intentions!

I promised you back in Chapter 6 that I'd describe situations you should view as red flags when dealing with adoption agencies. Here they are:

- The adoption arranger asks for all or most of the adoption fees up front, before a birthmother has been matched with you or has chosen you.

- The agency keeps asking you for money for "special funds," implying that if you don't pay, you might have to wait considerably longer for a child.

- The agency promises you a child within three to six months before doing a home study on you. No one should make promises unless or until you've at least been interviewed in person. (Not even then, really. They should wait until your home study is completed before talking about particular children or birthmothers.)

- The adoption arranger seems to be withholding information.

- The agency resists answering your questions or is evasive.

- The agency tells you that they've never had a child with a serious medical problem. If they've been in business more than a few years, they probably have seen at least one child with a problem.

Common Adoption Scams

What kinds of bad things do scammers do to people who want to adopt? You want specifics? Okay. I warn you about major scams to avoid in the following sections.

Money Manipulators

Beware of any agency that asks for a *lot* of money up front, even though there is no birthmother or child matched to you. (By "a lot," I mean $25,000 or more). Instead, if you decide to sign up with an agency, you should pay an application fee and a home study fee (which together may cost several thousand dollars but should *not* run into five figures.) Often, fraudulent agencies who receive big bucks up front will spend your money, rather than putting it in an escrow account. They'll use any excuse to ask for more money—"birthmother funds" or special fees or anything else they can think of.

Moral: Don't pay more than several thousand dollars up front to cover the cost of your application and home study unless the agency can tell you the details about a specific pregnant woman or a specific child. Also, make sure you have a contract in writing (see Chapter 6). A contract doesn't ensure you won't get ripped off, but it does spell out the terms and conditions of your agreement and what you should be able to expect. Be sure to also check with your state licensing authorities to find out whether the agency is in good standing and whether any complaints have been made against them.

International adopters are especially vulnerable to financial scams. I've heard of agencies charging up to $40,000 (not including airfare!) or more to place children from Russian orphanages. The child is already born, no prenatal care or hospital costs need to be paid, no birthmother needs support money, and the child is living in a state institution. There's no reason why the agency should be charging so much money! Of course, people adopting a baby from the United States have been cheated, too, paying huge sums of money to unscrupulous individuals.

Moral: It's best to deal with only reputable adoption agencies that have been in business for at least three or four years *and* that have a track record. In general, newer is not better, especially when it comes to international adoption agencies. Even if you're adopting a child from a country that has only recently begun to allow international adoptions, stick with well-established and experienced international adoption agencies. They are best equipped to anticipate potential problems.

> **⚠ CAUTION**
>
> **Adoption Alert**
>
> Experienced agencies that handle international or U.S. adoptions may tell you that the total fees, including travel, range from about $20,000–$30,000 and sometimes a few thousand more. Be wary if an inexperienced agency asks for a lot more. Anyone who asks you for more than $50,000 should be immediately suspect.

> **⚠ CAUTION**
>
> **Adoption Alert**
>
> One adoption applicant I know cried bitterly when her very high-priced adoption agency went under. She and her husband had given them their life savings. The agency had repeatedly asked for more money—once, supposedly, to help the birthmother—and had implied that if she gave money faster, they would find a child for her faster. But the agency didn't find her a child. They went out of business instead.

Another scam I've witnessed (infrequently) goes like this: The adoption arranger gets an application fee and home study fee from Family Number One. They later offer Family Number One a child, but warn them it will be a very expensive adoption. Family Number One says they want to think about it for a few days, and the arranger agrees. However, in the meantime, the double-dealing arranger finds Family Number Two, who is willing to pay the very high fees right away. The arranger tells Family Number Two that they can have the child, even before Family Number One has had a chance to give their answer. The arranger makes up a story to pacify Family Number One if they have decided they want to adopt the child, but he also keeps their fee.

This arranger may do the same thing over and over to some families, never giving them a child and driving them crazy. Sometimes the emotional abuse caused by the unethical behavior can be even worse than the financial abuse.

Moral: If an arranger tells you that an adoption is going to cost "more than usual," find out why. If it's high medical bills because the birthmother or child was ill, or for some other rational reason, that may be okay. Ask to see the bills. If the reasons for the high fees don't make sense, don't agree.

Guilt Trips

Guilt is a very effective way to scam people. "If you don't adopt this poor little sick infant," some adoption arrangers might say, "she'll have to go to foster care!" Or, if she's a newborn child from another country who needs a family, she'll go to the orphanage! She might die! It may sound heartless, but it's not your responsibility to save all the world's sick orphans. You simply cannot. If you don't want to adopt a child with medical problems, you don't have to.

> **CAUTION**
>
> **Adoption Alert** _____
>
> Be skeptical if an international adoption arranger assures you that a foreign child is completely healthy; these people are rarely doctors, and by giving you a medical opinion, they are setting themselves up for a possible lawsuit if you adopt the child and later find out that the child is ill.
>
> By the same token, adoption arrangers cannot and should not guarantee lifelong physical and psychiatric health for every child they place. Instead, they should provide you with all the medical and psychiatric information they have. Then you should ask a physician to evaluate it and also to advise you about the information provided, especially if it doesn't seem to be reliable.

In addition, don't let an agency guilt you into adopting an older child if you really want a baby or toddler, especially if the older child has been in foster care or an orphanage for years. Some families have adopted children who were as old as 11 or 12 from an orphanage, assuming that their love will conquer all and that their newly adopted child will be just like the 11-year-old child who lives next door, who has always had a stable and happy life. They are shocked when the older child they adopt has a lot of emotional problems. Adoption is a wonderful way to create families, and many older children from the United States and other countries urgently need families. But go into adoption with your eyes wide open.

Scammers who work these angles know that most prospective adoptive parents are very soft-hearted. (Look at the huge surge of Americans who adopted Romanian children back in 1990 and 1991, after the news media documented the horrible conditions in Romanian orphanages.) Compassion is good but should always be tempered with old-fashioned common sense.

The guilt tactic can be combined with the expensive-adoption tactic. For example, the agency might tell you that this poor little sick child incurred horrendous medical bills and ask you to pay for them.

First of all, you should demand medical information for any child you are thinking about adopting (see Chapter 15). If the child is indeed sick, make sure the agency can document any and all medical expenses that the child has incurred. Does a doctor in another country really need the equivalent of $2,500 to do a physical examination?

In yet another version of the international adoption scam, inadequate or no medical information is provided, and the agency refuses to try to obtain additional information, saying they can't (which usually means they won't). Although they may not be able to provide information about prenatal conditions and what kind of shape the child was in at birth, they should be able to provide a health status of the child since he or she arrived in the orphanage. If you are thinking about adopting a four-year-old child, and all you are given is a paragraph or two, this isn't enough information. Ask for more. (See Chapter 15 for more on medical information and Chapter 11 for more information on international adoptions.)

Birthmother Scams

Most women who say they're considering adoption really *are* considering adoption. It's only natural that they sometimes change their minds after the baby is born, but it's usually a sincere change of heart.

Very infrequently, though, a pregnant woman or her friends will scam one or more couples, by convincing each couple that they want the couple to adopt the child. The reason? Greed. If they can get several thousand dollars from one family, then they may be able to get even more from another family, and another, and another. Sometimes the woman involved in this scam isn't even pregnant!

Moral: Don't give any money to any pregnant woman directly. And don't give any money to an intermediary until it has been verified that the woman is actually pregnant. If you talk to the pregnant woman directly and she's far more interested in your bottom line than your parenting capabilities, that's a bad sign. (For more information on birthmothers, see Chapter 16.)

Instead, make sure all financial arrangements are handled by a professional, either an agency worker or an attorney. It's very difficult for most adopting parents to say no to the birthmother of their child—but some financial requests may be inappropriate or even illegal.

Real Life Snapshots

A 1997 *Washington Post* article chronicled the story of Barbara and Andrew Ship, a doctor and her graduate-student husband who lost nearly $28,000 in an adoption that went sour.

First, the couple found out that the attorney for their adoption agency had been suspended from practicing law for three years in another state. Then the agency apparently failed to find information on the birthfather. Next, the couple learned that the birthmother wasn't receiving support money they had paid to the agency. Finally, they read a scathing article about their agency in a national magazine. Still the couple convinced themselves that everything would be all right.

It wasn't. Just before the baby was born, the birthmother contacted the birthfather to tell him about the adoption. He subsequently hired an attorney to fight for custody. The agency told the couple not to worry. They took the baby home.

They should have worried. They contacted a reputable attorney, who told them they could fight for custody in court, but they would probably lose. When the child was one month old, the birthmother revoked her consent to the adoption.

The good news is that the couple *did* subsequently adopt a baby through another adoption agency.

Keep in mind that thousands of adoptions sail through the courts every year. Luckily, stories like these are the exception, not the rule.

The Wrong Child for You

In some cases, the arranger may not have the kind of child you want to adopt, but they don't tell you this. One family stayed with an agency for an astounding 10 years. They told the agency they wanted to adopt a healthy infant, but the agency offered them one child after another with severe disabilities. The agency actively urged them to stay on, because "their child" would surely appear at any time. And, after all, they had so much time invested … Moral: Find out what kind of children (age, race, and so on) the adoption arranger places. If they never (or almost never) place the type of child you want, don't sign up. If you have already signed up, and you have any qualms about it, bail out. Now.

A few arrangers will try to insist that you adopt a child they do have, whether or not the child is right for you. In this scam, the adoption arranger may tell you that there are *no* children available like the kind you want to adopt. Instead, you should adopt a child from the group that they have.

Moral: Adoption arrangers want to place the children they have experience with placing. But it's immoral and unethical for them to tell you that you can't adopt a child merely because they don't place the sort of child you wish to adopt. Maybe it really would be harder to adopt the child you seek. But if you have your heart set on adopting a particular child, don't go for what would be "second best" in your mind and heart—unless you have a change of mind and heart. You are not doing the child any favors if you really cannot handle his special needs. Seek out other adoption arrangers.

False Promises

If an adoption arranger promises to give you a baby within a few months the first time you talk to her, watch out! No reputable arranger would make such a promise, even if they think they could probably fulfill it. They certainly wouldn't make such a promise before you have completed the home study process.

CAUTION Adoption Alert _____

If something about your adoption seems wrong and alarm bells are clanging in your head, don't ignore them. Many victims of adoption scams later said they felt that something was wrong at the time but that they ignored their gut feelings.

Talk to others about your fears, such as people in adoptive parent groups or even other agencies or attorneys. They can help you sort out valid fears from silly ones.

Moral: Many arrangers may be able to place children within a relatively short time, but they usually warn you that situations can change and won't make guarantees. If they don't give you this kind of caveat, don't deal with them.

Internet Scams

In 2000, an adoption facilitator offered biracial twins for adoption on the Internet. Several families wanted to adopt the twins. The story is far too complicated to describe in all its details here, but basically, the twins were given to one family, then were taken away from them and given to another family. The babies were later removed from the second family and placed in the foster care system before they were finally adopted, three years later.

Each of an unknown number of families (except for the family who finally adopted the children) paid the adoption facilitator money to adopt the twins, and none of the families got any of their money back. In fact, they spent even more money on legal fees. In 2004, the birthmother sought to overturn the adoption and regain legal custody of the twins. Because this case is so confusing (and I'm no attorney), it's impossible to know how it'll turn out. One hopes, however, that whatever is best for the twins will be the outcome.

This is just one of the adoption scams that have been orchestrated via the Internet. No one knows how many occur or how often they happen. Many people are embarrassed to tell others that they've been scammed and, consequently, it's never reported.

To avoid finding yourself a victim of such a scam, watch out for these warning signs:

- The organization openly promises babies can be adopted very easily and quickly (legitimate adoption organizations rarely make such promises).

- The organization requires a significant up-front payment, such as $25,000 or more, before a home study is done.

- The website indicates that you must act NOW or this particular infant or child will not be available.

Quick and Fast Adoption

Although adoption need not take five years or longer, any website or organization that heavily emphasizes the speediness of their adoptions is suspect. Even if they place children quickly (for instance, if they work with foreign orphanages that have a lot of babies) that fact should not be the main "selling point" to their services. If it is, you should be skeptical.

Requiring Big Money Up Front

If you find a site on the Internet that promises you a baby fast, on the condition that you plunk down thousands of dollars, be suspicious. Most agencies charge up front for an application fee and a home study. Only when a child is available to be adopted should you be asked to pay large sums of money (five figures) to make the adoption happen. And you should not be offered a child until *after* you've had your home study. After all, how does the agency know whether you're suitable to adopt a child until the home study is done? If they don't care about that issue, they're not for you.

Attorneys shouldn't require large sums up front either, unless they know a pregnant woman or birthmother who is ready to place her child soon. Also, reputable attorneys won't take your money until they have a chance to talk to you directly.

Quick! Act Now or Baby Will Be Gone!

People on any Internet site—or in any e-mails that you get from the organization running the site—who urge you to act now or someone else is going to adopt this baby right away, are acting unethically and are highly suspicious. Never allow yourself to be rushed into an adoption. If it feels wrong to you, in your gut, it probably is wrong. You'll be sorry later on if you agree to highly questionable demands.

How Do They Get Away with It?

Unfortunately, adoption scams often go unprosecuted. Even if they have been mistreated, people often think that the agency or arranger didn't really *mean* to scam them. And even if they know they've been scammed, prospective adopters may feel stupid for having fallen for the scam and be too embarrassed to complain to anyone. Furthermore, they might think there's no way to get their money back, and so there's no point in doing anything.

A failed adoption can be an emotionally and financially draining event. Just because you are upset and disappointed doesn't mean that you shouldn't seek recourse if you are the victim of a scam. Even if it's a matter of incompetence and not malevolence, the person should be stopped.

If You Get Ripped Off

I hope you digest this information in time to avoid any adoption scammers. However, if you fear you've already been trapped and squeezed by one, don't give up hope. Here are your options:

♦ If it's an adoption agency that ripped you off, report the problem to the state licensing bureau, the state adoption coordinator's office, the Attorney General's office, the Better Business Bureau (www.bbb.org), local adoptive parent groups, and any other group that might be able to take action against the offending agency.

♦ If it's an attorney, contact the state bar association, the Attorney General's office, the Better Business Bureau, local adoptive parent groups, and any county or other attorney groups. You can also contact the American Academy of Adoption Attorneys in Washington, D.C.

♦ If it's a private social worker or adoption facilitator, inform the state adoption coordinator, the National Association of Social Workers (if a social worker), the Attorney General, the Better Business Bureau, and local adoptive parent groups.

♦ If it's a pregnant woman (or a person pretending to be a pregnant woman) who scammed you, contact the Attorney General's office and any other organizations your attorney or agency recommend. If she gets away with it once, she might try it again. Try to stop her from inflicting this financial and emotional pain on others. You could also consider alerting the media.

♦ If you want to complain about an organization online, you can contact the Better Business Bureau, the National Adoption Information Clearinghouse (http:/naic/acf.hhs.gov), your state Attorney General (www.theadoptionguide.com/ag.shtml) or the National Fraud Information Center (www.fraud.com).

♦ Some people choose the courts and file lawsuits against the attorney, the agency, or even the birthmother.

> **Adoption Alert**
>
> I've said this before (in Chapter 6), but I'll say it again: Don't trust an arranger just because you like him or her. Get references, talk to people who have used the arranger before, talk to licensing boards, and follow all of the screening tactics I laid out for you. Don't fool yourself that this background work isn't important or that it's too hard.

This chapter isn't intended to scare you away from adoption. Instead, it's meant to encourage you to enter the process with your eyes wide open. Don't forget that most adoptions go through without a hitch. Not all adoptions that fall through are due to fraud. However, if you suspect that an agency or individual you're working with is trying to scam you, steer clear of them and report them to the appropriate authorities.

The Least You Need to Know

- Most adoption arrangers are ethical and efficient, but you should be aware of possible adoption scams.

- Carefully screen any adoption arranger with whom you are thinking about dealing.

- Never release a large amount of money to an adoption arranger without knowing that they have a birthparent or child for you.

- Don't assume that organizations that advertise adoption services on the Internet are always good. Most *are* good, but some are con artists.

- If you are scammed, contact the Better Business Bureau, state bar association, and local adoptive parent groups.

Chapter 10

State to State

In This Chapter

- ◆ How adoption laws differ from state to state
- ◆ The rights and responsibilities of birthparents
- ◆ The rights and responsibilities of adoptive parents

Do you remember that old legal drama *L.A. Law?* Maybe you saw the storyline when Ann and her husband Stuart adopted a baby in a private adoption. Several months later, the birthmother showed up and demanded her baby back. A courtroom battle ensued, and the birthmother won. After that, many people nationwide worried about adopting a baby because the birthmother might change her mind.

What many people didn't know then (and still don't know now) is that adoption is governed by state law, and the law in California was (and is now) very different from laws in other states.

In this chapter, I will show you how state laws affect the adoption of children from the United States (for details on international adoption, see Chapter 11). Please, don't be scared away from adopting in the United States by watching some made-for-TV movie on a women-as-victims channel or by reading a melodramatic story in a magazine article about an adoption gone bad. Here's an insider secret: Most adoptions are extremely exciting to the people involved but (although the child is great!) the details are a little boring to everyone else. This is one of those times when boring is good!

Birthparent Rights

The laws governing birthparents' rights and responsibilities differ widely from state to state. Birthfather rights, in particular, are all over the map, although a few highly public court battles in the late twentieth century caused states to recognize the rights of birthfathers.

Here is a small sampling of birthparent issues that different states handle differently:

◆ Whether a birthmother or birthfather might revoke consent (change their minds)

◆ Whether the state has a birthfather registry for alleged unmarried fathers to assert paternity

◆ Whether a state allows prebirth consent by the birthfather

◆ Procedures if the birthmother doesn't know (or refuses to name) the biological father

We'll look at each of these issues in turn over the next few pages.

Revoking Consent

In Chapter 16, I'll talk about certain signs that you can use to help determine whether a birthmother might be likely to change her mind about adoption. In this section, I discuss how *long* birthmothers have to change their minds. A few hours, a day, a week, months? Or no time at all?

Adopterms

Consent to an adoption means the birthmother (and, hopefully, the birthfather) voluntarily agree that their child may be adopted. To **revoke consent** means that they take back consent. If consent is **irrevocable**, it may not be taken back.

Well, it depends. Most people assume that birthparents automatically have until the day the adoption is finalized to take back (revoke) their consent to the adoption. But in most cases, this is not true. Unless a fraud has been committed, many states allow no time after signing adoption *consent* papers to change one's mind. Other states give birthparents a brief window of time—say, 72 hours—after the consent documents are signed to *revoke* it, although a few allow for much longer revocation periods. It's also true that some states impose a waiting period after the child is born before birthparents may consent to the adoption. See the adoption law chart at the end of this chapter for specific time frame information in each state.

So, you might say, how come we had that 1993 Baby Richard case in Illinois, in which the three-year-old boy, placed with his adoptive parents as an infant, was given to his birthparents? That was a highly unusual case. It occurred because the birthfather claimed his rights had been violated, and the court agreed, because the birthmother had lied to the birthfather about what happened to the child. The ruling caused a furor, however, and because of it, Illinois adoption laws were changed.

Adoptinfo

Even in states where consent is irrevocable, there is usually some provision for cases of fraud or duress (if the birthparents were deceived by the adoptive parents or the adoption arranger, for example).

In some states, consent can be revoked for any reason. In others, a birthparent who wants to revoke consent must request a hearing so a judge can decide whether consent may be revoked. Usually if any significant amount of time has passed, the court will be asked to consider the best interests of the child.

Getting Registered

Many states have *birthfather registries* (also known as putative father registries) where unmarried men who believe they have fathered a child can register their paternity. (Check the adoption law chart at the end of this chapter to see which states have such registries.)

In some states, if the birthfather fails to register, then the birthmother may place the child for adoption without taking any further action with regard to the birthfather. In other states, additional efforts must be made to serve notice about the child's birth to the birthfather. If he has registered, a birthfather usually can block (or at least delay) an attempt by the birthmother to place the child for adoption.

Whether it's fair or unfair to require an unmarried father to register his paternity can be debated endlessly. Supporters of registries say that it is a man's responsibility to find out whether or not a woman he has had sex with has become pregnant and whether or not he wants to assert paternal rights. The registry protects the birthfather by notifying the court of his paternity in cases where the birthmother chooses to withhold the information.

Opponents say that fathers should not have to guess whether a pregnancy has occurred and that a man should not be separated from his genetic child without his knowledge or permission. Some say the birthfather's right to his child should be equal to the birthmother's right. It's likely this debate will continue.

Prebirth Consent

A relatively new "animal" for many states, *prebirth consent*, means that a birthfather who is not married to the birthmother can agree to an adoption while a woman is pregnant. In other words, he doesn't have to wait until the child is born to sign his consent to the adoption.

Adoptinfo

Colorado is unique in that it has three different ways in which children can be adopted by nonrelatives, according to W. Thomas Beltz, a prominent adoption attorney in Colorado Springs who has handled all three types of adoption for clients.

In the first way, the child is placed with the family, the birthmother is counseled by an agency, and she petitions the court for the termination of her parental rights to be accepted after the child's birth. Her presence is required at a court hearing. The birthfather is served notice of the adoption plan, and if he doesn't respond, then his rights can be terminated.

In an expedited relinquishment, the pregnant woman actually can sign the paperwork for the baby to be adopted before the child's birth. In this method, the birthmother may petition for the baby to be adopted four days after birth, and the judge must decide whether to accept the petition and terminate her rights or require the court hearing within seven days. In addition, the birthfather is served notice of the adoption plan. If he fails to respond, his parental rights may be terminated.

A third way to adopt in Colorado is called a custodial adoption and was enacted into Colorado law in 1999. In this form of adoption, which starts out as a guardianship, the family can apply to adopt after the child has lived with them a year. They won't need to hire an agency, and the birthmother isn't required to receive any counseling under state law. As a result, the family will save thousands of dollars (as much as $7,500) and will need to pay only a few thousand dollars in legal fees; however, the major drawback is that the birthmother could decide to take her child back during that one-year time frame.

Alabama, Arkansas, Delaware, Florida, Hawaii, Illinois, Indiana, Kansas, Louisiana, Michigan, Missouri, Nevada, North Carolina, New Mexico, New York, North Carolina, North Dakota, Oklahoma, Oregon, Pennsylvania, Tennessee, Utah, Vermont, and Washington all have prebirth consent laws. Usually the consent is irrevocable after the birth, although sometimes it may be revoked for a brief period, depending on the state.

Birthmothers, however, almost always sign consent after the child is born, usually within a specified time frame of hours or days.

Prebirth consent is a hotly contested issue. Is it fair? Some people wonder why the birthfather can sign before the child is born when the birthmother can't sign until the child is born. One response is that the birthmother who is considering adoption must take action soon after the child is born. Most birthmothers don't want the child placed in foster care while a birthfather is sought or while he makes up his mind. Remember that prebirth consents are allowed in some states, and they are not required. They are generally used for birthfathers who want to end their involvement prior to the child's birth.

Birthfather Unknown

State laws vary in cases where the birthmother doesn't know—or refuses to disclose—the name of the biological father. In some states, she must swear before a judge that she doesn't know who the birthfather is, or she must provide a reason why she can't (or won't) name him. In other states, the responsibility lies with the birthfather—he's expected to come forward if he wants to assert his paternal rights.

It's a good idea, however, for the adoption arranger to try to determine who the biological father is before birth whenever possible. The arranger then can try to legally terminate his paternal rights and also obtain genetic and medical background information from him to provide to the adoptive parents.

Adoptive Parent Rights

There are also several other adoption issues affecting adoptive parents that are handled differently by different states. Here are a few of them:

- When an adoption can be *finalized* in court
- What medical and genetic information should be provided to the adopting parents
- Whether a home study is required, and if so, when it must be done
- Whether prospective adopters may advertise for birthparents

> **Adopterms** ___
>
> To **finalize** an adoption means to go to court before a judge to receive legal permission and recognition that the child is yours.

Again, I'll explain each issue in more detail in the following pages.

Are We There Yet? Finalizing Adoption

When an adoption is finalized, the child is recognized as the adoptive parents' legal child. I'll explain the process of finalization more in Chapter 18. For now, you should know that finalization times vary from state to state. In some states, it takes just a few months; in others, finalization may not occur for eight months or more. But in most states, finalization will occur at around six months after placement.

I can't emphasize enough that in most states this does *not* mean the birthparents can claim the child any time up until finalization in every state. Not at all. As explained earlier, many states make the consent to an adoption irrevocable upon signing, although others allow certain time periods during which consent can be revoked. (One exception is if the birthmother has been defrauded—in that case, she may be allowed to revoke consent, within a reasonable period of time from placement.) Very few states allow the birthmother to revoke consent until finalization.

Medical History

Many states also require that the agency or attorney collect medical or genetic information, although most states don't specify exactly what information should be gathered. There are several reasons for collecting this data. One is that such information is valuable to the adoptive parent and later will be valuable to the adopted child.

Another is that in some rare cases, medical or psychiatric information that was known by an adoption arranger was withheld. A new tort called *wrongful adoption* has sprung up as a result. (A *tort* is a civil action for damages resulting from wrongdoing.)

Adopterms

Wrongful adoption refers to an adoption that would theoretically not have taken place had the adopters been given information that was known to the adoption arranger. The information was purposely withheld or misrepresented.

Wrongful adoption claims may not be upheld if the agency didn't have access to information or couldn't have known information because the birthparents or others didn't provide it or if the contract between the agency and the adopters limited their liability. Adoption arrangers should not be expected to be guarantors that the child is perfectly healthy, now and forever. They should, however, disclose all information that they do have. The first such case of wrongful adoption was *Burr vs. Board of County Commissioners of Stark County* in Ohio, in 1986. In 1964, the Burrs adopted a child. They were told his birthmother was a healthy young woman. In fact, she was a psychiatric inpatient, and other important information about the child himself had been withheld. After years of difficulty with the child, the information came to light when the Burrs obtained permission to open sealed adoption records.

Adoptinfo

Gibbs v. Ernst was a wrongful adoption case that occurred in Pennsylvania. After the Gibb family adopted a five-year-old boy in 1985, they began having serious problems: The child was extremely violent and dangerous. In 1989, they were told that the child had experienced severe physical and sexual abuse before he was adopted. This information was in the record but had never been disclosed, despite the family's requests for complete information.

The adopters sued and won their case. The court said, "Providing full and complete information is crucial because the consequences of nondisclosure can be catastrophic; ignorance of medical or psychological history can prevent the adopting parents and their doctors from providing effective treatment, or any treatment at all. Moreover, full and accurate disclosure ensures that the adopting parents are emotionally and financially equipped to raise a child with special needs. Failure to provide adequate background information can result in the placement of children with families unable or unwilling to cope with physical or mental problems, leading to failed adoptions."

It's important to note that wrongful adoption cases are rare, and the overwhelming majority of adoption arrangers provide prospective parents with all the nonidentifying information to which they have access. Still, there may well be a few misguided arrangers who fail to provide information, believing it will not matter to the child and will only upset the parents.

Adopting parents should always insist that they obtain all medical and psychiatric information about the birthparents and the child that is available to the arranger. I suggest that adoptive parents send a letter to the arranger stating that they assume they have received all medical, psychiatric, and social information and that if that is not true, they need to know right away. When adopting an older child, parents should find out the child's abuse and placement history.

Remember, if the agency does not have access to information, then they can't give it to you. Nor should you expect your child to be perfect because the agency didn't find any serious medical or psychiatric problems in the information provided.

Home Study

Although it has long been standard practice in agency adoptions, many state laws now require *preplacement home studies*. This means the child cannot be placed until the family has been deemed suitable. (See Chapter 12 for detailed information on what is involved in the home study.)

Okay to Advertise?

State adoption laws differ on whether people who wish to adopt may advertise for birthparents in newspapers or other media. Some states ban such advertisements outright; others allow it. In a few states, the hopeful adopters must first have an approved home study.

As discussed in Chapter 7, advertising works well for some people and not for others. Many adopters believe that they should have the right to advertise for birthparents. They argue that there are advertisements for strip clubs and all sorts of unsavory activities—how could advertising the desire to adopt be any worse?

Others believe that advertising reduces adoption and even children to the level of a commodity. This debate is likely to continue.

> **Adopterms**
>
> A **preplacement home study** is a background investigation and interview of the adopting parents, accomplished before a child is placed with the family.
>
> A **postplacement home study** is a background investigation and interview of the adopting parents after the child has already been placed with the family.

Changing Laws

It's important to understand that states are constantly changing their adoption laws (which is quite frustrating for an adoption writer!).

> **Familybuilding Tips**
>
> If you aren't happy with the adoption laws in your state—for example, if you think your state *should* have a birthfather registry—then you should contact your state legislators and let them know.

Why can't they just get it right and leave it alone? Because states are constantly reacting to new situations, to pressures from constituents, and to many other factors. The aforementioned Baby Richard case, for example, caused many states to change their laws regarding the rights of biological fathers. Other cases and situations are also likely to inspire legislators to try to fine-tune the law more—or radically revise it, in some cases.

Laws are also subject to the interpretation of judges, and even judges within the same state or county might differ in their interpretation.

Cross-Country: Interstate Adoption

Although many people adopt children from the state where they reside, it's also possible to adopt children from other states. The Interstate Compact on the Placement of Children (ICPC) is a sort of treaty that governs how interstate adoptions are managed. It's up to the ICPC administrators to ensure that laws of both states are complied with. If those laws conflict, the administrators, who are based at the state social services office headquarters, work it out.

Interstate adoptions aren't always smooth sailing. Potential adopters who don't know anything about interstate adoption may arrange their own adoption with a birthmother from another state but fail to contact an adoption agency or attorney in either state. This is a huge mistake.

Familybuilding Tips

I advise most people to try to adopt a child in their home state first. It can be more complicated when you are involved with the laws of several states, although good attorneys should be able to smooth over any rough edges.

Sometimes people adopt a child from another state because they don't want the birthmother to live nearby, whether it's an open adoption or a confidential one. However, there is no guarantee that she will always live in that faraway state.

To arrange an interstate adoption correctly and lawfully, you probably will have to hire an agency or attorney in both states to ensure that the laws are complied with. This adds to your financial costs.

Do You Need a Law Degree?

If you're not an attorney—and even if you are—you shouldn't expect to handle all or even most of the details of your child's adoption. Still, you should obtain some basic adoption law education. Here's how:

1. Check with local adoptive parent groups. They may have summarized the basics of adoption law in your state.

2. Ask your attorney. He or she might have encapsulated key adoption issues in a pamphlet or handout.

3. Read the law yourself. Contact the reference librarian in your public library and ask to see a copy of the state laws (specifically, the adoption statutes). Some state adoption statutes are well written and easy to understand; others are full of legalese.

   If your public library doesn't have a copy, contact the nearest law library. (Law libraries are usually located at the courthouse.) Ask the law librarian where the state adoption statutes can be found.

Do keep in mind that you will not become an instant expert after reading the adoption law. There are limits as to what you can expect to understand and achieve on your own, especially since case law affects interpretation. My opinion is that, with the possible exception of a stepparent adoption, it's a very bad idea to try to manage the legal paperwork yourself.

The best defense is to hire the best attorney you can find to handle all the legal details surrounding the adoption of your child. Make sure that the attorney is an adoption attorney—not your mother's cousin Fred, who is a great tax attorney but knows nothing about adoption. Well-meaning Fred could unintentionally cause you terrible legal problems and might even ruin your child's adoption by making a major mistake. Courts can be very unbending sometimes. Better to be safe by hiring an experienced and competent attorney up front. You can hire Fred to do your taxes, an area with which he's familiar. (You wouldn't ask your adoption attorney to do your taxes, would you?)

State Adoption Law Chart

I have created a state-by-state adoption law chart so you can compare and contrast laws in your state with the laws in other states. To obtain the data for the chart, I recruited prominent adoption attorneys throughout the country and requested that they respond to my questions about state laws.

Although this chart reflects the most recent information I could find, remember that adoption laws are subject to change—and *do* change frequently. Be sure to consult with an attorney in your own state (or the state from which you wish to adopt a child). The chart should be used as a general guide *only*.

Summary of U.S. State Adoption Laws

State	When May Consent Be Signed?	Time to Revoke Consent?*	Bfather Registry?	Ads Okay?	Father Prebirth Consent?	Time to Finalize?	Med. Exp/ BMom May Be Paid?	Liv. Exp/ BMom May Be Paid?
AL	Birthfather: anytime before or after child born. Birthmother: Before birth, before a Probate Court Judge; anytime after birth	5–14 days 5 days, no questions. An additional 9 days for best interest of child	Yes	Yes	Yes	90 days	Yes, with court approval	Yes
AK	Anytime after birth	10 days	No	Yes	No	Usually takes 60 days	Yes	Yes
AR	Anytime after birth	10 days	Yes	Yes	Yes	11 days	Yes	Yes
AZ	72 hours after birth	Irrevocable	Yes	Yes	No	3–6 months	Yes	Yes. Court approval required for expenses over $1,000
CA	Anytime after birth, usually after hospital release	Agency: Until accepted by state, usually 3–4 days after signing Private: 30 days after signing, unless waiver executed. With waiver, consent is irrevocable	No	No	No	Usually 6 months	Yes.	Yes
CO	After birth: court terminates to agency	Irrevocable	No	Yes	In some cases	6 months	Yes, with court approval	Yes, with court approval
CT	48 hours after birth	Anytime before court hearing terminating parental rights	No	Yes	No	About 6 months	Yes	Yes, up to $1,200
DE	Anytime after birth	14 days	No	No	Yes	At least 6 months	Yes, but pymts. are made into escrow account, not directly to BMom	Yes, but pymts. are made into escrow account, not directly to BMom

continues

Summary of U.S. State Adoption Laws (continued)

State	When May Consent Be Signed?	Time to Revoke Consent?*	Bfather Registry?	Ads Okay?	Father Prebirth Consent?	Time to Finalize?	Med. Exp/BMom May Be Paid?	Liv. Exp/BMom May Be Paid?
DC	Anytime after birth	Irrevocable once filed with court	No	Yes	No	6 months	Yes	No
FL	48 hours after birth	Irrevocable if child under 6 months. If child 6 months or older, 3 days to revoke.	Yes	Yes, but only through an agency or attorney	Yes	4–6 months	Yes, up to $5,000 living & medical exp. w/o court review. All expenses must be disclosed to the court.	Yes, up to $5,000 living & medical exp. w/o court review. All expenses must be disclosed to the court.
GA	Agency: 24 hours after birth. Independent: Anytime after birth	10 days	Yes	No	No	45–60 days from filing petition	Yes	No
HI	Anytime after birth	Irrevocable	No	Yes	Yes	About	Yes 2–3 months	Yes
ID	Anytime after birth, but it must be witnessed by a judge	Irrevocable	Yes	No	No	Agency: 8–10 mos. Private: 3–5 months	Yes	Yes, $2,000 limit.
IL	72 hours after birth	Irrevocable	Yes	Yes	Yes	About 6 months	Yes	Yes. In agency adoption, expenses must be preapproved by agency. In private adoption, expenses must be preapproved by court.
IN	Anytime after birth	Irrevocable	Yes	Yes	Yes	At least 1 month	Yes	Yes, up to $3,000

State	When May Consent Be Signed?	Time to Revoke Consent?*	Bfather Registry?	Ads Okay?	Father Prebirth Consent?	Time to Finalize?	Med. Exp/ BMom May Be Paid?	Liv. Exp/ BMom May Be Paid?
IA	72 hours after birth	96 hours	Yes	Yes	No	6 months	Yes	Yes
KS	12 hours after birth	Birthparent may petition the court prior to finalization (30–60 days after signing) but has burden of proof	No	No	Yes	30–60 days	Yes	Yes
KY	72 hours after birth	20 days	No	No	No	3 months	Yes	Yes
LA	5 days after birth	Irrevocable	Yes	No	Yes	Private: 1 year Agency: 6 months	Yes	Yes, rent and food and, if possible, paid directly to provider
ME	Anytime after birth, if a judge is available	3 days	No	No	No	About 1 mo.	Yes	Yes
MA	4 days after birth	Irrevocable	Yes	No	No	6 months	Yes	Yes. Monthly payments up to $980/month, limited to lodging, food, utilities, and clothing.
MD	Anytime after birth	30 days	No	Yes	No	30 days	Yes	No
MI	Anytime after birth when court hearing can be scheduled	Only until order terminating rights is entered, which usually happens when consent is given	Yes	Yes	Yes	6 months	Yes, if not otherwise covered by insurance or public assistance	Yes, if reasonable and necessary
MN	72 hours after birth	10 days	Yes	Yes	No	More than 90 days	Yes	Yes
MS	72 hours after birth	Irrevocable	No	Yes	No	Right away to 6 months	Yes	No, unless through a MS agency

continues

Summary of U.S. State Adoption Laws (continued)

State	When May Consent Be Signed?	Time to Revoke Consent?*	Bfather Registry?	Ads Okay?	Father Prebirth Consent?	Time to Finalize?	Med. Exp/ BMom May Be Paid?	Liv. Exp/ BMom May Be Paid?
MO	48 hours after birth	Until filed with court. After filing, court must act within 3 days.	Yes	Yes	Yes	6 months	Yes	Yes
NE	48 hours after birth	Irrevocable	Yes	Yes	No	6 months	Yes	Yes
NV	72 hours after birth	Irrevocable	No	Yes	Yes	6 months	Yes	Yes
NH	72 hours after birth	Irrevocable	Yes	Yes	No	6 months	Yes	Yes
NM	48 hours after birth	Irrevocable	Yes	Yes	No	4–7 months	Yes	Yes. Payments must be to third party, not to birthmother
NJ	72 hours after birth	Agency: irrevocable Private: can be withdrawn prior to court action	No	Yes	No	Agency: 8 months Private: 10–11 months	Yes	Yes
NY	Anytime after birth	Agency: 30 days Private: 45 days	Yes	Yes	No	3–6 months	Yes	Yes
NC	Anytime after birth	7 days	No	Yes, with home study	Yes	6 months in most cases	Yes	Yes
ND	Agency: anytime after birth Identified adoption: 48 hours after birth	Irrevocable in most cases	No	Yes	Yes	6 months	Yes	Yes
OH	72 hours after birth	Irrevocable	Yes	No	No	7 months	Yes	No
OK	Anytime after birth	Irrevocable in most cases	Yes	Yes	Yes	2–3 months	Yes	Yes, up to $500 w/o court approval
OR	Anytime after birth	Agency: irrevocable after placement Private: usually irrevocable 1–3 days after adoption petition filed	No	Yes, with home study	Yes	3–6 months	Yes	Yes

State	When May Consent Be Signed?	Time to Revoke Consent?*	Bfather Registry?	Ads Okay?	Father Prebirth Consent?	Time to Finalize?	Med. Exp/ BMom May Be Paid?	Liv. Exp/ BMom May Be Paid?
PA	72 hours after birth	Revocable until court terminates parental rights: 2–4 months	Yes	Yes	Yes	About 6 months	Yes	No
SC	Anytime after birth	Irrevocable	No	Yes	No	3–6 months	Yes	Yes
SD	Cannot be filed with court until 5 days after birth	Irrevocable	No	Yes	No	6 months	Yes	Yes, if reasonable and court approved
TN	72 hours after birth	10 days	Yes	Yes	Yes	6 months	Yes	Yes
TX	48 hours after birth	Agency: irrevocable Private: 10 days to revoke	Yes	Yes, with home study	No	6 months	Yes	No
UT	24 hours after birth	Irrevocable	Yes	Yes	Yes	6 months	Yes	Yes
VT	36 hours after birth	21 days	Yes	Yes	Yes	6 months	Yes	Yes
VA	10 days after birth	15 days	No	Yes	No	8 months	Yes	Yes
WA	48 hours after birth	Until court approval	No	Yes, with home study	Yes	1–6 months	Yes	Yes, if disclosed to and approved by court and deemed proper
WV	72 hours after birth	Irrevocable	No	Yes	No	6 months	Yes	Yes
WI	Anytime after birth	Until termination of parental rights signed by judge	No	Yes, with home study	No	6 months	Yes	Yes, up to $1,000
WY	Anytime after birth	Irrevocable	Yes	Yes	No	6 months	Yes	Yes

Note: The State-By-State Adoption Law Chart is based on information I compiled from attorneys who are expert in state adoption law. (I was unable to obtain updated information from Montana and Rhode Island, so those states are not included on the chart.) I am not an attorney myself; thus, there could be some errors of interpretation. It's also true that state laws change, so do not assume the laws described on this chart are etched in granite for all time. They aren't. Instead, use the chart as a guide only, and consult with your adoption arranger on the current laws as of the time that you adopt.

The Least You Need to Know

- ◆ State laws affect the rights and responsibilities of both birthparents and adoptive parents.

- ◆ State adoption laws are subject to change.

- ◆ Adopters who wish to arrange interstate adoption must comply with the laws of both states.

- ◆ Although it's important to educate yourself about state adoption law, you must leave the legal work to an attorney.

Chapter 11

Going International

In This Chapter

- ◆ Trends in international adoption
- ◆ Pros and cons of international adoption
- ◆ How to arrange an international adoption
- ◆ Bringing your child home

Single mom Donna Sanford spent about 18 months preparing herself to adopt a child from China. She read everything she could and learned as much as possible. When she was matched with her daughter, she felt very prepared and was tremendously excited. In fact, Sanford, the publisher of the trade magazine *EXPO, The Magazine for Exposition Management*, wrote about her adoption in her publisher's column! Here's a brief excerpt:

> The two-week trip to pick up my daughter was exhilarating, exhausting, awe-inspiring and humbling—much like labor and delivery has been described to me. There were about 10 families traveling together, and the first three days were spent sight-seeing at such wonders as the Forbidden City and the Great Wall. On the fourth day we received our babies from the orphanage, and Nia took one look at me and literally screamed for five solid hours. After crying

herself to sleep, she awoke the next morning happy to see me and we've been best friends ever since. The next nine days were a mixture of official business—notarizations, registrations, medical exams, visa photos, embassy interviews—sight-seeing and bonding time.

Sanford says one thing she was *not* prepared for was the five-hour-straight crying jag, and she cautions people about it. She believes that Nia had probably never seen a blue-eyed blonde-haired woman before, and it scared her! But Donna Sanford is definitely "Mom" now.

It's tough enough to actually decide that you want to adopt a child—but, as Donna Sanford's story shows, it can be even tougher if you want to adopt a child from overseas—especially if you aren't prepared for most contingencies. This chapter discusses the issues you need to know about how to prepare yourself for an international adoption.

Adopting Abroad

International adoption has become a very popular option in the United States. Americans adopted 21,616 children from other countries in 2003—double the numbers of children adopted internationally in 1996, and almost triple from the numbers adopted in 1992! This number will probably continue to grow, because there are plenty more children around the globe who need families.

Adoptinfo

The Hague Convention on Intercountry Adoption is an international treaty between many countries worldwide on how international adoption should be handled. The United States signed the agreement in 1994, and in 2000 the Intercountry Adoption Act became a U.S. law. As of 2004, the regulations are being finalized. The U.S. State Department will be the regulating agency of the Hague Convention in the United States.

In fact, orphanages worldwide are filled with children who need parents. Dr. Jerri Ann Jenista, an Ann Arbor, Michigan, pediatrician and adoptive parent who is experienced in international adoption medicine, says that there are huge numbers of children in Russia and China, as well as other countries, who need families. She says that although no one knows for sure how many children live in orphanages, there may be as many as 500,000 infants and children in Russian institutions alone, and an estimated 1 million Chinese children are in orphanages. These numbers do not include the children living on the streets.

Countries open their doors to international adoption for different and complex reasons. As of this writing, the largest regions from which children are adopted by Americans are China and the former Communist countries of Eastern Europe, particularly the countries that formed the former Soviet Union, such as Russia, Kazakhstan, Ukraine, and Belarus. Countries "close" and "open" to adoption periodically, but international adoptions as a whole continue.

Trends in international adoption are strongly affected by changes in the adoption laws of foreign countries. For example, within the past decade, China has "opened" as a country from which Americans may adopt children. Due to a national policy in China of strict population control, a cultural preference for male children, and the fact that Chinese parents can't legally make an adoption plan for their children, many Chinese parents have abandoned their female children to orphanages. As a consequence, many Chinese girls are available for adoption.

It's important to be aware going into the international adoption process, however, that countries "open" and "close" their doors to adoption for many reasons, including economic, political, social, and others. For example, the country may wish for only its citizens to adopt their orphaned children, rather than for people in other countries to adopt them—a reason for closing the door. Or it may be facing serious economic problems that have created a situation in which there are many orphans—a reason for opening the door. Sometimes the reasons for openings and closings are not apparent.

In addition, different countries have different rules on who may adopt their children. For example, Korea is largely unavailable to single adopters or to individuals over age 40, and China bans adoptions by gays and lesbians.

How do families choose the country from where they adopt their child? Often they choose a particular country because someone they know successfully adopted from that country. They may choose a country based on what an adoption agency advises. Sometimes they select a particular country because they have relatives there or because they have lived in or visited the country and had a positive experience. In some cases, a country is chosen because the family believes they can adopt quickly and without much difficulty. These are only a few of the reasons, which range from emotional to carefully reasoned, why families choose particular countries from which to adopt.

Should You Adopt Internationally?

Because you are dealing with two countries and usually have to travel overseas to go and get the child, international adoptions are by their very nature more complicated than U.S. adoptions. In addition to the fact that U.S. adoptions are usually less complicated, here are some of the reasons some people cite for not wanting to adopt internationally:

♦ They are concerned about the health of a child raised in an orphanage.

♦ They are worried about the high cost of many international adoptions, including the cost associated with foreign travel.

♦ They don't like the idea of traveling to a foreign country and staying for days or weeks in another culture while waiting for the paperwork to be processed.

Other adopters have equally strong views about why international adoptions are preferable:

♦ They believe their waiting time to adopt a child will be very short.

♦ They feel they can't adopt a same-race child in the United States but can do so from another country.

♦ They are opposed to open adoptions involving contact with birthparents (most intercountry adoptions are not open).

♦ They think that birthparents from other countries will be less likely to change their minds about an adoption.

♦ They think children living in overseas orphanages will not have been exposed to abuse and neglect.

I'll examine many of these opinions over the next few pages. For now, take a look at the number of adoptions in the top 10 countries in the world from 1999 to 2003, based on immigrant visas issued to children adopted by Americans. As you can see, China has been the number-one country from 2000 to 2003.

International Adoption Statistics, Top 10 Countries, Based on Immigrant Visas Issued to Orphans Coming to the United States, FY 1999–2003

2003	2002	2001	2000	1999
China 6,859	China 5,053	China 4,681	China 5,053	Russia 4,348
Russia 5,209	Russia 4,939	Russia 4,279	Russia 4,269	China 4,101
Guatemala 2,328	Guatemala 2,219	S. Korea 1,870	S. Korea 1,794	S. Korea 2,008
S. Korea 1,790	S. Korea 1,779	Guatemala 1,609	Guatemala 1,518	Guatemala 1,002
Kazakhstan 825	Ukraine 1,106	Ukraine 1,246	Romania 1,122	Romania 895
Ukraine 702	Kazakhstan 819	Romania 782	Vietnam 724	Vietnam 709
India 472	Vietnam 766	Vietnam 737	Ukraine 659	India 500
Vietnam 382	India 466	Kazakhstan 672	India 503	Ukraine 323
Colombia 272	Colombia 334	India 543	Cambodia 402	Cambodia 248
Haiti 250	Bulgaria 260	Colombia 407	Kazakhstan 399	Colombia 231

Source: U.S. State Department (http://travel.state.gov/orphan_numbers.html)

In the following sections, I examine whether people's perceptions match the reality.

Are International Adoptions More Difficult?

Is it easier to adopt a child in the United States than in another country? With a few exceptions, I don't think adoption is easy no matter what, whether your child comes from the United States or anywhere else. Children don't drop into your lap from the sky (which is good—it would be pretty painful if they did!).

In some ways, U.S. adoptions are easier. For example, there's no language barrier with most U.S. adoptions. (You are not allowed to consider a Southern drawl or

New England accent as another language!) But language barriers are frequent with international adoptions, in which you must rely on your agency and their interpreters for a lot of information.

U.S. adoptions also seem easier to people who want to avoid the expense and difficulties of foreign travel, which is mandatory in most cases. In some countries, including China, Russia, and many others, you actually adopt the child in the country itself; thus, your presence there is required. In the case of a married couple, sometimes one person can travel; however, it's best if both go and provide moral support to each other. Also, some countries may require that both parents be there prior to the finalization of the adoption. If only one parent travels overseas, then you need to do a readoption, or complete the adoption again in the state in which you live.

> **Adoption Alert**
>
> In many countries, the adoption is considered final after a court proceeding in the country the child is from; and as a result, if there are any problems after you leave the country—such as undetected medical problems or other issues—the child is still your legal responsibility. You can't return the child.

> **Adoption Alert**
>
> If you are considering using an international adoption agency, find out whether the director or any of the staff has ever traveled to the countries with which they arrange adoptions. It's not a good sign if no one in the agency has ever traveled to the country from which they make placements. How do you find out? You ask!

Are International Adoptions Faster?

The time it takes to successfully adopt a child in the United States can be measured in months or years, depending on the speed of your adoption agency or your own efforts.

Whether the wait to adopt a child from another country is shorter than adopting a child in the United States depends on a lot of variables: which country you choose to adopt from, the age of the child you want, how fast you can put together your application, and other factors. It might be six months, several years, or longer (which is also true with U.S. adoptions). Or you might apply for a child from a particular country, and then the country decides to put all international adoptions on hold. If that happens, you'll have to wait until your agency gets the word that adoptions may resume again.

Will You Get Accurate and Complete Medical Information?

The medical and genetic information that you receive on a U.S.–born child usually will be more comprehensive than the medical information you can obtain on many orphans from other countries. There are exceptions, however, and some countries, such as Korea, provide very good medical information on the children.

Often there is very little health information available on children living in overseas orphanages, particularly health data about their lives before they entered the orphanage. To complicate matters further, if a child does have medical records, the records may be in a foreign language and may use medical terminology with which U.S. physicians are unfamiliar.

As a result, children may have undisclosed illnesses or infections—some of which may be serious—when the child is adopted. With good medical care, many of the children thrive; however, some do not. Still, the overwhelming majority of intercountry adopters report that they are happy with their children and are glad that they adopted.

For those reasons, experts strongly recommend that you find a pediatrician or nurse practitioner who will advise you on the health issues that may be present in a child you are thinking about adopting. The person you choose to review medical information should be able to review screening information provided by the country for infectious diseases (including tuberculosis, hepatitis B, HIV, and intestinal parasites), blood disorders (anemia and lead poisoning), and growth problems such as rickets and growth delays. (Appendix G lists some medical experts who specialize in international adoption for you to consider. Additional names are available online from the American Academy of Pediatrics at www.aap.org/sections/adoption/adopt-states/adoption-map.html).

It's best to have a local pediatrician lined up before you adopt your child. She should be someone who's willing to work with a child who may have illnesses that are not common in the United States.

Adopt International has developed forms to help prospective parents understand the possible health problems that a child adopted from another country might have. I've reprinted those forms here so you can see the health issues involved.

Medical Risks in International Adoption.

(Reprinted with permission of Adopt International, Redwood City, California. The agency is waived from any liability from the use of information in this form. Each agency must seek legal counsel in its own state to determine specifics to be included or excluded in their own forms.)

Lynne Jacobs, Executive Director
A Non-Profit Agency
Licensed by the State of California and Hawaii

Medical Risks in International Adoption

I/We_____and_____,
have been given information about various medical conditions and about the medical risks in foreign adoptions, including but not limited to the following conditions:

Salmonella	Tuberculosis	Hepatitis A, B, C, and D
Milk Intolerance	Scabies/Lice	Parasites
Pneumonia	Chronic infections	Depression
Developmental delays	Vision problems	Hearing problems
Decayed teeth	Learning disabilities	Malnutrition
HIV positive	Physical Abuse	Sexual Abuse
Undiagnosed Genetic Problems	Retardation	Chronic ear/sinus infection
Fetal Alcohol Syndrome or Effects	Mental Deficiency	Premature Birth
Complications of Prematurely	Attachment Disorder	Hernias
Post Traumatic Stress Disorder	Post Institutional Care Symptoms	

I/We have been fully informed about the risks inherent in international adoption due to unknown birth parents, lack of information, and/or unreliable testing. I/We understand that I/we will receive all information and medical diagnosis that has been provided by the foreign country for the child/ren referred to me/us. I/We have the opportunity to discuss medical, emotional and psychological risks with a physician of our choice and have the right to have the child/ren examined and tested by a physician of our choice should I/we choose to do so. I/We acknowledge, understand and accept the medical policy of Adopt International and hold them harmless for diseases and conditions that cannot be diagnosed with reliability.

_____   _____   _____
Signature   Signature   Date

STATE OF _____
COUNTY OF _____

On this _____ day of _____in the year of 19__, before me, the undersigned, a Notary Public in and for said State, personally appeared_____, personally known to me (or proved on the basis of satisfactory evidence) to be the person(s) whose name(s) is/are subscribed to the within instrument and acknowledged to me that he/she/they executed the same in his/her/their authorized capacity(ies), and that by his/her/their signature(s) on the instrument the person(s), or the entity upon behalf of which the person(s) acted, executed the instrument.
WITNESS my hand and official seal.

_____
Signature of Notary

MEDICAL RISK 4/24/97

121 Springdale Way, Redwood City, California 94062
Fax: (415) 369-7400   Tel: (415) 369-7300

900 Fort Street Mall, Pioneer Plaza, Suite 1700, Honolulu, Hawaii 96813
(808) 523-1400   (800) 969-6665

Internet: 74734.3044@COMPUSERVE.COM

international

Lynne Jacobs, Executive Director
A Non-Profit Agency
Licensed by the State of California and Hawaii

CHILD ACCEPTANCE AND MEDICAL RELEASE

I/We, acknowledge that I/we accept the following named child for adoption placement:

_____   _____
Child's Name   Date of Birth

The attached medical diagnosis has been made in the child's country of origin:

I/We, acknowledge that I/we have received from Adopt International all information made available to them about the medical, emotional, and psychological status of this child. I/We also understand that every attempt has been made, by Adopt International, to gather complete medical information regarding this child.

I/We have fully read and confirm our understanding of the "Risks Which May Occur in International Adoptions."

I/We understand that the above named child may arrive in the United States with previously undiagnosed medical, physiological, emotional, or psychological problems.

I/We understand that accurate testing procedures for Hepatitis B and HIV may not be possible. I/We accept the risks that this child may test positive after entry into the U.S.

Further, I/We voluntarily release Adopt International and its staff of any liability for any such problems.

_____   _____
Adoptive Mother   Adoptive Father

STATE OF CALIFORNIA
COUNTY OF _____

On this_____day of _____in the year of 19__, before me, the undersigned, a Notary Public in and for said State, personally appeared_____, personally known to me (or proved on the basis of satisfactory evidence) to be the person(s) whose name(s) is/are subscribed to the within instrument and acknowledged to me that he/she/they executed the same in his/her/their authorized capacity(ies), and that by his/her/their signature(s) on the instrument the person(s), or the entity upon behalf of which the person(s) acted, executed the instrument.

WITNESS my hand and official seal.

_____
Signature of Notary

121 Springdale Way, Redwood City, California 94062
Fax: (415) 369-7400   Tel: (415) 369-7300

900 Fort Street Mall, Pioneer Plaza, Suite 1700, Honolulu, Hawaii 96813
(808) 523-1400   (800) 969-6665

Internet: 74734.3044@COMPUSERVE.COM

Child Acceptance and Medical Release.

(Reprinted with permission of Adopt International, Redwood City, California. The agency is waived from any liability from the use of information in this form. Each agency must seek legal counsel in its own state to determine specifics to be included or excluded in their own forms.)

How Important Is Race?

Many Americans who adopt children from Eastern Europe do so because they are white. Many Caucasian people in the United States state quite openly that they want to adopt a white child and they don't want to wait years to adopt—so they'll adopt a child from a European orphanage or hospital. What they might not realize is that the wait is *not* always years and years for healthy white infants in the United States. It's also true that thousands of Americans are adopting children of other races—and for them, race is not an issue.

> **CAUTION**
>
> **Adoption Alert**
>
> Just because a child is from Eastern Europe doesn't mean that she'll be a blue-eyed blonde child. People of all races live in Eastern Europe.

Can Overseas Birthparents Change Their Minds?

Another reason why people adopt from other countries is they don't like the idea of an open adoption—an adoption in which the adoptive parents and birthparents are in contact. In an international adoption, the child's custody usually has been transferred to the orphanage, and the birthmother and adoptive parents will *not*. Nor will she have any choice in the selection of the parents of her child.

Most foreign birthmothers don't change their minds about adoption because their rights have been terminated already by the time the child is adopted. However, it does happen occasionally, even in intercountry adoptions, that a birthmother has a change of heart and struggles to gain her child back.

Adoptinfo

According to many medical experts on international adoption, infants in orphanages lose one month of development and physical growth for every three to four months in the institution. Some studies, such as those done by Dr. Michael Rutter on 111 children adopted before age two from Romania, have shown that many children have significant "catch-up" growth. According to Rutter's study, reported in a 1998 issue of the *Journal of Child Psychology and Psychiatry and Allied Disciplines,* when they were first adopted, many children (51 percent) were below the third percentile in weight. This means that 97 percent of other children of the same age weighed more than them. However, when the children were re-evaluated at the age of 4, only 2 percent of them were at this low weight.

Are Children in Overseas Orphanages Less Likely to Be Abused?

Some Americans believe that children don't get abused or neglected in overseas orphanages. Actually, abuse—both physical and sexual—and neglect do occur to children in many orphanages worldwide. Furthermore, the deprivation inherent in orphanage life is enough to be harmful to some children. It's hard to know which children are resilient enough to recover from early problems. It's also true that the longer a child lives in an orphanage, the higher the probability she will experience health or psychological problems later on.

Experts such as Dr. Dana Johnson of the International Adoption Clinic at the University of Minnesota consider institutionalized children to be a high-risk group. According to Johnson, "Over 50 percent of institutionalized children in Eastern Europe are low birth weight infants, many were born prematurely, and some have been exposed to alcohol *in utero*." Dr. Johnson says that the effects may be lifelong.

Real Life Snapshots

Back in 1990–1991, when the media broke the story of thousands of Romanian children languishing in orphanages, many Americans rushed to Romania to adopt. Roughly 3,500 Romanian children were adopted by Americans. Many adopters assumed that with enough love and care, the children would recover.

Canadian physicians found that three to four years after the adoption, the children adopted after the age of two were at least two and a half years behind in development, and none had achieved an average intelligence level.

In another study of Romanian children adopted by Americans, approximately 20 percent of the parents said the experience was harder than they anticipated; however, only 7 percent said they had considered disrupting the adoption, and 91 percent felt positive about the adoption.

The moral: Be prepared for the unexpected. Children adopted internationally will certainly do much better with an adoptive family than in an orphanage, but families need to be committed to meeting the child's physical, developmental, and psychological needs.

Arranging an International Adoption

Americans wanting to adopt children from other countries must comply with the rules of the U.S. Citizenship and Immigration Services, which has requirements for adoptive parents and also for the children they adopt. The set of documents that is required varies from country to country.

If you want to adopt a child from another country, the U.S. Citizenship and Immigration Services requires the following:

◆ A preplacement home study (somewhat comparable to a background investigation) to be done by a licensed adoption agency (whether your state law requires one or not).

◆ Your dossier, which is a set of documents, including your birth certificate, marriage certificate, and other documents, depending on the country.

◆ Your fingerprints.

◆ Proof of citizenship. If you're married, either you or your spouse must be a U.S. citizen in order to adopt a child from another country. If you're not married, then you must be a U.S. citizen to adopt.

◆ Copies of your income tax statements.

◆ Your signature on a statement of financial responsibility, stating that should the child have to enter the foster care system, you will reimburse the state or county.

◆ A completed application for an orphan visa, the document that will enable your child to enter the United States.

Finding Your Child

Although a home study by an adoption agency is mandatory when adopting internationally, some families choose to do some of the legwork of actually finding a child themselves. I think that this is an extremely risky proposition, especially with implementation of the Hague Convention adoption requirements, which can be quite complex. Agencies understand what needs to be done, but few individuals can wade their way through the morass of rules and regulations. Except in very rare cases, it's best to leave it up to the experts.

When an agency does find a potential child for you, obtain as much background information as you can. Here are some questions to ask:

◆ How much time has the child spent in the orphanage? (The longer, the worse.)

> **Adoptinfo**
>
> If you plan to adopt your child from Guatemala, consider downloading a free booklet published in 1994 and written by adoptive parents Marcy McKay and Richard Stollberg with Bea Evans: "Guatemala Travel and Etiquette: A Guide for Adoptive Parents" is packed with helpful hints. Download this guide at www.guatadopt.com/documents/travelguide.pdf.

◆ What is the child's birth history, including birth weight, head size, length of pregnancy, and any birth complications?

◆ How has the child's development been, particularly speech and language? Does the child hear? See? Does she interact with other children and the caregivers?

◆ How does the child compare to other children of the same age?

◆ Does the child have any medical problems or allergies? Has she had any surgeries or been on any medications? Has there been any history of hospitalization?

◆ Is a videotape of the child available? Can you receive this tape along with medical records?

◆ Why is the child available for adoption? Were the parental rights terminated voluntarily or involuntarily?

◆ Is there any history of mental illness or physical illness in family members?

◆ Does the child have any siblings? If so, where are they?

> **Adoptinfo**
>
> If you're adopting a baby inter-nationally, bring diapers and baby bottles when you go to pick him or her up. If possible, find out the child's weight and height ahead of time and bring along clothes as well. For infants and smaller children, a Snugli carrier is helpful for carrying the child around, while also ena-bling the child to be close to you and helping you both develop a closer bond.

When a child is assigned to you, contact the State Department to request a visa for the child. Of course, you should have your own passport ready as well. Don't wait until the last minute to apply for your passport!

Whenever possible, travel with other couples or singles who are also adopting. You may find each other's help invaluable! Also, contact other couples who have traveled recently. Find out whether there are any travel services they used that were particu-larly helpful—or that should be avoided. Get the latest information you can find.

Before you leave, be sure to find out whether any shots are a good idea. Often you may need injections for tetanus and hepatitis A and B. You might also need shots for cholera or other diseases. Anyone who accompanies you should be injected as well; for example, excited grandparents who will be traveling with you should definitely get their shots, too. Other household members should consider being immunized for hepatitis B, in case the child turns out to be a hepatitis carrier. (Hepatitis is conta-gious by blood and body fluids.)

Bring any medications you need and bring at least an extra week's supply in case you are delayed. Be sure to bring clothes for the child, and if she's an infant or toddler, bring bottles and diapers!

> **CAUTION**
>
> **Adoption Alert** _____
>
> Citizenship rules for adopted children changed (for the dramatically better!) with the Child Citizenship Act, passed in 2000 and first implemented in 2001. In the past, it was extremely cumbersome for adoptive parents to obtain citizenship for their newly adopted children—it involved lots of paperwork, phone calls, and worry. Now the government has apparently decided international adoption is a good thing and that child citizenship should be expedited.
>
> With the newest part of the program, effective January 20, 2004, children under age 18 adopted under the IR-3 entrant program (the main way in which children adopted from other countries enter the United States) automatically will become citizens, and their families should receive certificates of citizenship for their children within about 45 days of the child's entry into the United States. In the past, families had to wait 12 to 18 months or longer to obtain citizenship documents. Contact your adoption agency or attorney for further information.

Making Your Child Comfortable

What can you do to help your child make the transition to your culture and your life easier? Here are a few suggestions:

◆ If the child is an infant on formula, buy a few cans or a case of formula in the other country. Gradually switch over to U.S. formula by mixing the foreign formula and U.S. formula $^1/_2$ and $^1/_2$ for a few weeks, as an addition to other foods you provide. Don't be in a hurry to wean your baby off the bottle. It may be a source of comfort to her.

◆ If she's an older child, try to get a few recipes from the child's culture, understanding you'll never get it just right. But do *not* continue an inadequate diet! Just don't rush the child off to the nearest fast food place when you get off the plane. She'll have time for that later. Instead, keep it simple at first: rice, bread, noodles, cereal, and fruit are good choices.

◆ Don't swamp the child with toys and gifts. He's probably not used to it, and it could cause a "systems overload." Start with one or two toys and introduce more toys gradually. Even if it's Christmas!

◆ Give the child a chance to get used to your family and maybe the grandparents. Wait a few weeks before throwing a party. Household members need to be your new child's main source of care and nurturing for a while after you bring her home.

◆ Find out what fabrics the child is used to wearing. If cotton, buy some cotton clothes. Ask the agency to ask the orphanage for this information.

◆ Learn some words from the other country, such as "Hello" and "I like you." You don't have to become an expert overnight. Children pick up language rapidly. But knowing some basic words in the beginning can help.

◆ Don't force eye contact. Look at your child, but don't move the baby or child's head to look directly at you. That can be very stressful. Give him a chance to get used to you.

Getting Physical

Within about two to four weeks of arrival, your child should be given a comprehensive physical examination. Be sure to let your pediatrician know that *The Red Book*, a source available to all pediatricians from the American Academy of Pediatrics, lists the medical tests that should be performed on children adopted from other countries. For very specific medical problems, the AAP offers an online list of pediatricians who are expert in international and foster care medicine at www.aap.org/sections/adoption/adopt-states/adoption-map.html. You might also wish to consult with one of the international adoption medical experts listed in Appendix G.

For More Information

It's impossible to encapsulate everything you need to know about international adoption in one chapter. For a comprehensive step-by-step guide, read *How to Adopt Internationally: A Guide for Agency-Directed and Independent Adoptions* by Jean Nelson-Erichsen and Heino R. Erichsen (Fort Worth, Texas: Mesa House Publishing, 2003).

The Least You Need to Know

◆ International adoptions are an increasingly popular choice for American adopters.

◆ International adoption is affected by trends in other countries.

◆ International adoptions are not necessarily faster or easier than U.S. adoptions.

◆ Children adopted from orphanages should be given full health and medical checkups, because they are at risk for developmental delays, growth delays, infectious diseases, and other medical problems.

Part

Finding Your Child

It's meant to be! That's how most people feel when they've adopted a child. That doesn't mean they expected a child to fall into their laps. They learned as much as they could about their child before making a commitment. This part will show you what you need to know about birthparents and their children.

The home study evaluation and the wait for approval can drive the average person into fits of fear. Don't let that happen to you. In this part, you'll find out what the home study involves and how to survive it—and the waiting afterward.

This part also includes issues faced by adoptive singles, gays and lesbians, disabled people, and older nontraditional adopters. They certainly can and do adopt!

12

Getting to Know You: The Home Study

In This Chapter

◆ Surviving your home study

◆ Dealing with your social worker

◆ Handling interviews and tests

◆ Getting great references

Amy cleaned the dust bunnies from underneath the bed, scrubbed the floors, and polished items that hadn't seen Lemon Pledge in months—or maybe longer. And yet she still thought it wasn't good enough. Then she had an idea: She'd pretend she was her mother, doing an inspection. And she went back to work.

Amy was preparing for a *home study*, a process in which potential adoptive parents are evaluated for their fitness as parents. Many people mistakenly think that a home study is primarily an inspection of their home (and so, it had better be so clean it could pass a military inspection). But a home study is far more than that.

The home study can include interviews, visits to the home, checking references, and reviewing medical, financial, and other relevant information. It's a scary idea to many people, who balk at having to "prove their worthiness" to a total stranger. But remember: If perfection were required to adopt a child, there would be no adoptive parents and no adoption!

This chapter covers the basics of why home studies are done, what they are like, and how to survive your own home study.

Why Have a Home Study?

Why do agencies perform home studies? For one thing, home studies are required by law in most states, whether you adopt your child through an adoption agency or with the assistance of an adoption attorney (and are always required in international adoptions). Home studies are performed for several other primary reasons:

♦ To evaluate the prospective adopter's desire and commitment to adopt. This is particularly important when a couple is applying to adopt; both people must want a child. If one partner is just going along with the adoption plan to make the other partner happy, the resulting adoption will not be fair to the child, who needs a complete, committed family.

♦ To explore the reasons why the prospective adopter wants to adopt. Some adopters may still be grieving over an infertility problem. Others have lost young children—an agonizing loss—and are seeking a replacement child. The adopters need sound reasons for wanting to adopt: They have accepted their infertility and are eager to become parents. Or they want to give a child who's "already here" a happy home life. There are lots of other good reasons, too.

♦ To evaluate the prospective adopter as a possible parent. How can a social worker know if you'd be a good parent if you've never had a child before? She can't. She has to go by the information you provide and the information she obtains from your references. (I'll talk more about references later in this chapter.)

Adopterms

The **home study** is a process that includes interviewing prospective parents, talking to them in their homes, checking their references and reviewing medical, financial, and other relevant information. Criminal records checks and child abuse clearances are also usually performed. The home study might take a day, a week, a month, or longer, depending on the agency.

◆ To educate the prospective adopter about adoption (and possibly about the child he or she is seeking to adopt). With some agencies, this aspect may be small or nonexistent; other agencies provide reading lists, arrange meetings with birthparents and adopted adults, and do more to help the prospective adopter understand adoption.

◆ To give the prospective adopter a chance for self-evaluation. The home study practically forces prospective adopters to evaluate themselves as future parents. They engage in a learning process that can be scary, but also personally fulfilling.

◆ To check background, criminal records, and financial resources.

Real Life Snapshots

The social worker walked around slowly, frowning hard at the grass. What was wrong, the prospective adoptive mom thought? Was there something wrong with the grass? It was mowed; it was green. What could it be? The wannabe mom sighed and restrained herself from blurting out to the social worker, "You don't like the grass? We'll change it!"

That prospective adoptive mom was *me*. I would have redone the grass if I thought the social worker wanted me and my husband to do that. But she didn't. Instead, she was probably lost in thought, thinking about some other problem. Who knows? We passed the home study investigation. Nearly everyone "makes it through." And others who decide they probably don't fit the criteria drop out of the process before they can be turned down.

Get Your Application In

After you've selected an adoption agency or your adoption attorney (see Chapter 6), you don't just jump into the home study the next day. First, most agencies require you to fill out an application and pay a fee (about $250–$500, although some agencies charge less or more) to process it.

What's involved with the application? The agency needs to know basic information: who you are, where you work, if you have kids already and how old they are, and so forth.

Familybuilding Tips

During the home study process, if a pregnant woman has been identified who's considering you as a possible parent for her child, she'll also be asked numerous questions about her circumstances. In addition, if the birthfather is available, social workers will contact him to find out how he feels about adoption and obtain medical and social information on him.

If you work with an adoption attorney, she will also have many questions for you and may request a retainer in the beginning of the process. (The amounts that are requested vary greatly.) The following pages contain an Adoption Information Sheet used by The Gladney Center in Fort Worth, Texas.

Getting On Your Case

After the application stage, the agency can move you into the more involved home study phase. And if you work with an attorney (assuming that your state requires a home study, as most do), the attorney should recommend agencies that can perform your home study. The home study will be performed by a social worker or case-worker assigned to your case.

One sad truth is that social workers rarely receive much, if any, training on adoption and related issues in graduate school. As a result, sometimes the social worker doing your home study may know *less* about adoption than you do. Generally, a new social worker in this situation will be supervised by a more experienced social worker, and you will both learn the process together. If, however, you have some concerns about your social worker, you can always ask her for a joint meeting with her supervisor. However, it's better to try to work with her before going over her head, so as not to alienate her.

Home Sweet Home

Although the check of your residence isn't the most critical issue in a home study, a social worker will (or should) examine your home to see whether it is reasonably clean and safe and whether there is a place (or a plan for a place) for the child to live. Social workers normally don't look inside your kitchen cabinets to see whether your pots and pans are neatly arrayed, nor will they check your medicine cabinet in the bathroom to see whether you have any interesting drugs in there.

Social workers also want to see you in your home to get a feel for how you and your family members interact with each other in the comfort of your own home.

Although your home doesn't have to be picture perfect for the visit, it should appear to be a safe place for a child. Here are a few things you should check before the social worker comes to your home:

◆ Fix any safety hazards, such as cords lying around. If you have stairs, make sure you have a plan to gate them off so they are safe for a young infant or toddler.

◆ Make sure you have at least one smoke detector on every floor.

◆ Make sure you have a plan to lock up poisonous household chemicals and other hazards.

◆ If you have a swimming pool, make sure you have a plan to have it fenced and gated for controlled access (if it isn't already).

Real Life Snapshots

One couple told me a funny story about their first home study: There were strange noises coming from another room, and the social worker wondered aloud what was going on. The couple assured him that the sounds were coming from their cat, who liked to climb in and out of paper bags and make weird noises. The worker wasn't convinced—he said the noises sounded like a child to him—and he demanded to take a look. Result: one cat and one red-faced social worker!

Visiting Hour

When the social worker comes to your home, keep in mind that she or he is a professional who is on the job. This is not the time to invite a friend or family member to stop by. (If they come over unannounced, tell them it's not a good time and arrange to see them later.) Should you offer the social worker any refreshments? Sure, offer something to drink, like coffee or ice water. However, don't spend a great deal of time beforehand creating fancy appetizers or elaborate dessert creations. The social worker is there to do a job.

What can you expect to be asked about? Usually the questions fall into the categories of why you want to adopt (and if you're infertile, the worker will probably want to explore this issue), what you do for a living, what your hobbies are, and any other questions that might give the social worker a picture of who you are. Here are some questions that you may be asked (and not in this order!):

◆ When did you start thinking about adoption? Why?

◆ Are you infertile? How do you know?

◆ How did you and your spouse (if you're married) meet each other? What drew you together then? How has your relationship changed?

◆ Have you gathered any information about adoption? What have you learned?

◆ Do you both (if a couple) want to adopt?

◆ How do you think a child would change your career? Your marriage? Your life in general?

◆ What do you have to offer a child?

◆ Do you know anything about birthparents? If so, what do you know?

◆ How do you feel about birthparents in general?

◆ Do your parents and other relatives know you want to adopt? Why or why not? If they know, how do they feel about it?

◆ Do you think adopted children should be told about being adopted? Why or why not?

◆ How will you afford the adoption fees?

◆ What is the greatest advantage to adopting a child? What is the greatest disadvantage?

◆ What are your hobbies and interests? Will you need to adapt them in some way after you adopt? If so, how?

◆ How will you feel if the adopted child turns out to be very different from you?

◆ What would be a "perfect" adoption experience for you?

◆ Do you think you will continue fertility treatments at the same time you seek to adopt? If so, why?

Be friendly and polite but remember that this is an evaluation process. Answer questions honestly—many adoption professionals say they hate it when applicants lie to them, and sometimes this can be a reason to turn an applicant down.

Familybuilding Tips

During the social worker's visit, don't assume that any one tiny detail will derail you. Here's one way to look at it. If *you* were a social worker and you visited a potential adopter, and she had a few dirty dishes in the sink, would you turn her down just because of that? Now, be fair!

This doesn't mean you should bare your most personal secrets (for example, you tried marijuana once when you were 16). You should, however, be forthright about matters that can be checked (for example, if you were arrested and charged with drug use as an adult 10 years ago) or that continue to cause you problems.

The biggest "enemy" in the home study process is probably your own fear. Tracy and Steve, an adoptive couple I know, remember that they didn't have milk in the house when the social worker came over: He thought she had bought milk and she thought he had. But neither did. So when the social worker asked for milk with her tea, oops!

Both were convinced they had failed. Tracy thought that this lapse would be seen as a failure to communicate in her marriage and a lack of competence at running a household. "We actually agonized about this for days and didn't relax until we got the okay weeks later!" says Tracy. "Now we joke about it, and the social worker, who we still know, claims she didn't even remember asking for milk—she prefers lemon!"

Your Other Children

If you already have other children, expect the social worker to ask about them and also to interview them, if they are old enough (usually over age five). If you have adult children, the social worker might want to talk to them, too.

The best way to prepare your children is to *tell* them that you want to adopt and why you want to adopt. Also assure them that you will still love them and not provide exclusive attention to the adopted child. (Note: Adult children need to know this, too!)

Your Pets

I'm not kidding here: The social worker will want to see any pets you have to determine their compatibility with children. This is probably a good time to take a hard look at whether you really want to keep Brutus, your pet pit bull. (I know I am risking the wrath of pit bull lovers everywhere, who swear they are the nicest, kindest creatures on God's green earth. But you'll have to ask yourself: How badly do you want to adopt?)

Don't worry that the social worker is a dog person and you love cats or hamsters or whatever. If your pets look well cared for, relatively clean and happy, that should be enough. Just keep them from jumping all over the social worker when she visits.

Familybuilding Tips

Many pet-owning adoptive parents have told me that their social workers wanted proof that their pets had had their shots. One prospective parent complained that she kept her cats indoors all the time, so she hadn't got them any shots. Too bad, the social worker said; if she wanted to adopt, the cats would get their injections. Not surprisingly, the cats received a quick trip to the vet to be immunized.

Testing, Testing

Some agencies and attorneys require hopeful adopters to take a psychological test. This test is usually given by a psychologist, and its purpose is to rule out any serious psychological problems. (Presumably, if you have any, you already know about them.)

I have heard some prospective adopters say they won't go to agencies or lawyers who require psychological testing or even just an interview with a psychologist. Why? They fear that some imaginary problem could be attributed to them, forever destroying their chance at adoption.

CAUTION

Adoption Alert _____

What if you don't pass a psychological evaluation? Does this go on some permanent record somewhere? No—at least not one that an adoption agency can access. The therapist will keep a record. If your insurance company paid for the evaluation, it will also have a written record. What information is released by the therapist to the insurance company varies considerably. Your insurance company should not release this confidential information without your permission. Keep in mind that states have laws regarding confidentiality of medical and psychological records. In addition, a federal law about medical confidentiality, the Health Insurance Portability and Accountability Act (HIPAA) Privacy Rule, also protects the privacy of your medical records.

Let's look at the *forever* angle for a moment, because I have heard this fear voiced many times by people who want to adopt. Too often, they think they have one chance and one chance only to adopt a child. If they are turned down in their home study, they reason, they'll never ever adopt a child.

But that depends so much on *why* you were turned down. Unfortunately, denials occasionally are based on personality conflicts between a social worker and prospective adopters. Where one social worker will see how wonderful you would be for a child, another might see problems.

If you were turned down to adopt because you recently—within the past three to five years—used illegal drugs, for example, then other agencies will usually also turn you down. Drug abuse is a serious problem, and the agency needs to approve only parents they feel confident are responsible adults. However, if the turn-down was because the social worker's not sure you've "worked through" your feelings about infertility, that's an opinion, and another social worker at another agency might disagree with that opinion. (Although Social Worker Number One might be right, and you should consider that possibility.)

I have known people who did some serious introspection and soul-searching after being turned down by an adoption agency. They couldn't understand why they were turned down, and their desire to adopt was still intense. They applied to another agency and later they did successfully adopt a child. So don't think in terms of "never" or "one and only." These are negative and self-defeating modes of thinking.

This Is Your Life

Many agencies and some attorneys will ask you to write a few pages about yourself. They want to know who you are as a person, according to you. This exercise also forces you to think about yourself in different ways: as a parent, as a provider, as a spouse. You may have taken these roles for granted; now you must explore them. This information is often shared with birthmothers as they select the family they want for their child. In a confidential adoption, identifying information will be deleted.

The autobiography (which is sometimes prepared in a resumé format) doesn't have to reveal your deepest, darkest secrets. You can reveal them if you want to, but remember, this isn't the soap channel, and you don't get extra points for agonizing. Here are a few pointers for preparing an autobiography:

- ◆ Write it yourself. Some people ask others (spouses or friends) to write their autobiography for them. This is a bad idea. Even a professional writer would have great difficulty capturing the spirit of who *you* are, why you want to adopt, and so forth. Also, this document should not be overly polished and slick—somehow, it's less believable that way.

- ◆ Type it. Do not hand in a sloppy, handwritten document.

- ◆ Add photos, if you want. Some agencies request a photo of you and your family to attach to the autobiography. If you think open adoption is okay (see Chapter 16), then this shouldn't be a problem. However, if you want a confidential adoption, it doesn't make sense to submit a photo, and I advise against it. It might inadvertently be provided to birthmothers. If the agency insists on a photo—and I don't know why they would, in a confidential adoption—make it clear the photo is for "agency staff eyes only."

Familybuilding Tips

If you submit a photo of your family to the adoption arranger, make sure you are smiling! Grim features have no place here. If you have a pet, try to get it in the picture, too. (Yes, I *know* it's hard to get pets to sit still! But it's worth it.)

◆ If you do decide to attach photos, you can use a candid snapshot. Some people have a professional photographer take their pictures, but this is not necessary or expected.

Surviving Your Social Worker

Most adopters are at least a little afraid of their social worker—whether they admit it or not. Most social workers are compassionate people who want adopters to succeed. But they are human, and they have human flaws. Here are a few do's and don'ts on dealing with your social worker as you wait:

◆ Don't call the social worker daily or even weekly unless you have a specific problem or issue to discuss.

◆ Don't call the social worker early on Monday morning or late on Friday afternoon. (Actually, try to avoid calling anyone at these times—most people are not at their best then.)

◆ Don't expect the social worker to be the supreme authority on adoption. Hopefully, she'll have read a few books and know something. But don't depend on her for all information.

◆ Do treat the social worker with respect and courtesy at all times.

◆ Do try to see the process from the social worker's view—she's in charge of placing children and wants them to go to the best family.

Most social workers are very nice people, but once in a while a social worker can get heady with power and jerk you around a little. Here's an example of minor "jerking around," although the social worker might not see it that way: It's Thursday and you have an appointment for her to come for a visit next Thursday. She calls you and says her schedule is a mess next week but she has some free time tomorrow (or worse—this afternoon!). So can she come then instead of next week? This means you don't have much time to clean—and you might have thought a week wasn't enough!

So what do you do? If you have a valid reason (needing extra cleaning time doesn't count) for her to *not* come, then tell her so. If you have an appointment with your dentist for a root canal and don't feel well, that is a good excuse. (Do not suddenly arrange for a root canal to avoid the social worker. Not worth it.) If you have an important business or family event already scheduled, explain this. Otherwise, get out the mop and broom now!

Here's an example of major jerking around: Terri was talking to the social worker at a follow-up visit and holding and hugging the baby. Suddenly, the worker said, "You know, she's not your baby until *I* say that she's your baby!" Terri burst into tears. The worker then said, "Well, I didn't say I wouldn't approve you," and Terri cried more. What happened? The social worker approved the family. Either she was having a bad day, or she was on a power trip (or both), but she was unfair to the new mom. Terri told the agency director about it later, and the worker was reprimanded.

Sometimes it's personal. Dana says when the social worker found out that her father was an alcoholic, she insisted that Dana agree to have nothing to do with him after the adoption. The social worker was estranged and unforgiving of her own father's alcoholism. Said Dana, "She had a hard time accepting I had come to terms with my father's problem and argued with me about whether he should be in my life at all." Dana wasn't about to disown her father, although she'd always make sure her child was safe around him, and she stuck to her guns. The adoption went through.

Generally, you can put up with minor annoyances. But if things get bad, and you truly believe that a social worker isn't being fair to you, take action. Ask the social worker whether he or she has a problem with your application or if you have caused offense in any way. Tell him or her that you truly want to adopt and you are genuinely committed to being a good parent.

If that doesn't work, you have the option of talking to the social worker's supervisor or the agency director. You may be able to get someone else assigned to your case.

Adoption Alert

Rarely, a social worker may be a perfectionist who turns down applicants for no good reason. If she does this too much, her adoption agency would go out of business. For this reason, problem social workers usually don't last long with any agency.

Despite the lapses of judgment I just referred to, most social workers are very nice and normal people! Hold that thought in your mind, because it's the truth.

Even the best adoption agency or attorney finds that sometimes people get angry or feel like they're being left out of decisions. For the large part, this is because the process of adoption is incredibly anxiety-inducing.

Remember, your adoption arranger can't share every minute detail with you. However, if you've heard nothing for weeks or months, it's probably time to give your adoption arranger a friendly call to find out how things are going. Glitches and oversights do take place. Don't expect everything to zoom through, problem-free.

If you feel like nothing is going right and there are far too many errors or omissions in the process, you might be right. See Chapter 9 for information on dealing with adoption scammers.

> ### Familybuilding Tips
>
> The most important thing you should convey in an adoption resumé is why you want to adopt (beyond being infertile, if that's the case) and why you think you would make good parents. Any past experience with children is good to mention.
>
> It's also good to mention anyone in your extended family (don't name actual names) who is favorable to adoption. It's nice to think of people who are eager to become grandparents through adoption. Some pregnant women considering adoption fear that the child will not be accepted by the adoptive family, so if your family is pro-adoption, mention it!

Your Adoption Resumé

The resumé-like write-up is part of the home study for many adoption arrangers. This is often a one- or two-page account of your family, sometimes including a photograph.

Beyond the basic format, however, an adoption resumé should not sound like a job resumé. The adoption resumé should convey the idea that you are a healthy, happy family and would make good adoptive parents. Of course, it should also be clear that you and/or your spouse are employed and can financially support a child.

The adoption resumé may be given to an adoption agency or adoption attorney to show to pregnant women considering adoption. Some people also post their own adoption resumés on websites on the Internet.

> ### Adoptinfo
>
> If you hope to adopt an infant in the United States, some agencies will ask you to write a "Dear Birthmother" letter in addition to an autobiography or adoption resumé. This is a heartfelt letter that is shown to pregnant women who are considering adoption for their babies. Basically, the letter explains why you fervently hope to adopt and why you believe that you'll be a very good parent. The social worker should explain this type of letter to you and show you letters that others have written, although you need to compose your own letter. Read more about birthmother letters in Chapter 16.

How much detail you include is up to you; however, I suggest avoiding including things like your annual income, or your beach home in Bermuda, if you are so fortunate!

If you have other children, you could mention their ages and how they feel about having a new sibling. You could even talk about the family dog or cat! A lot of birth-mothers are attracted to families with pets.

Backup Material

As part of the home study, you'll need to amass lots of information—both personal and financial—for your social worker. The specific documents you need to gather may be determined by state law. (If you are adopting a child from another country, the U.S. Citizenship and Immigration Services requires very specific information; see Chapter 11.)

Here are some of the financial materials you may be asked to provide:

- Income tax statements for the past three years
- Pay stubs to verify your current wages
- Savings account passbooks or statements
- 401k information
- Debt information (balances on your credit cards, loans, and so on)

Here are some of the personal materials you may be asked to provide. (You may need originals or certified copies of some documents.)

- Your marriage certificate
- Certificate of divorce, if you are divorced
- The results of a physical examination performed by your doctor
- Names of references the social worker can contact

Let's look more closely at some of these personal requirements.

Getting Physical

The adoption arranger wants you to get a physical exam because she wants to know whether your life expectancy is normal and whether you have any known (or un-known) serious medical problems. At your physical, your doctor probably will check your main body systems: heart, lungs, and so forth. You will probably also need to get some lab work, such as a complete blood count or a urinalysis. Often the social worker or agency will specify which medical tests they want performed at your physical. You may be checked for specific illnesses, such as hepatitis or HIV. You do *not* have to be a perfect specimen of manhood or womanhood, but you should be healthy enough to parent a child.

Your physical exam might not be covered by insurance because, theoretically, it might not be necessary. So find out ahead of time if it will or will not be covered. If not, pay for it yourself and add the expense of the physical exam to your other adoption expenses that you'll be applying toward the adoption tax credit. (Chapter 8 offers more details on the $10,160 income tax credit for adoption.)

Checking Your References

Most agencies and attorneys will ask you for the names of personal references. They want people who will vouch for your good character and the likelihood that you'll make a good parent. Often, they will ask your references to write letters on your behalf. Here are a few do's and don'ts when dealing with references:

- ◆ Don't give out anyone's name without checking with the person first. Some people don't like the idea of writing adoption references, for a number of reasons: They don't like the idea of adoption. They don't like the idea of *you* adopting. They might feel uncomfortable writing a reference in the fear that what they say will get you turned down. So always ask first.

- ◆ Do try to give the names of people who are parents themselves. They don't have to be adoptive parents, but it's easier for parents to write about child care than it is for people who don't have kids.

- ◆ Do try to give references that can be reached locally. (Or at least who live somewhere in your state.) If you've lived in the area a few years and you can't think of anyone local who is willing to give you a personal reference, your social worker will wonder why.

- ◆ Do let potential references know how important these letters are to you. Tell your chosen references that they should consider this as serious as if they were giving you a reference for a prospective employer or for a bank loan. I don't think too many people would joke around to a bank official. Nor should they to a social worker.

- ◆ Do make sure your references understand what's expected of them: to verify that they think you're good parent material. Toward that end, any child care experience you've had that they can discuss is good. Your nurturing qualities should be emphasized. Your good upstanding character is important to note.

Real Life Snapshots

Kelly, an adoptive parent I know, decided to read her reference letters before they were mailed to the adoption agency. Good thing she did: "One letter was from my oldest friend, but she wrote about her mother's death, then her own divorce, and then her father's illness and subsequent death. The gist was that I had always been there for her. But the letter was really depressing and of course entirely irrelevant to our needs."

She explained to her friend what was needed, and her friend rewrote the letter. "She wrote a lovely letter about our friendship through the years and our positive relationship with her son."

The other reference was mean-spirited. "It said how cynical and jaded we were and that our real salvation would be in having someone to call us Mommy and Daddy." Kelly found someone to replace this reference. Later, the writer said she wrote the letter as a gag; she thought Kelly was joking about adoption.

Does this mean that you should read what people write before they mail their letters? That's up to you. Many people might not want you to read what they've written, even if it's very positive. Also, the agency might disapprove of your screening your references. However, Kelly is convinced that those initial references could have caused problems and certainly would have delayed her home study process.

What to Do If You Are Turned Down

Rejection doesn't happen much in adoption, because most families who think they might get rejected by an agency drop out of the home study process before it ends. But once in a while, a family is surprised by their rejection. Here are a few reasons why prospective adopters might not be approved for adoption:

♦ The social worker is being unreasonable. (See "Surviving Your Social Worker" earlier in this chapter.)

♦ The social worker feels you are still yearning for a biological child.

Few people completely lose their sadness about not being able to have a biological child. But they should work through the issue when they apply to adopt. If the prospective parents have lost a pregnancy or a child, they need time to grieve this loss. Adopted kids should never be "replacement kids."

If your social worker believes that you still need to work on grief issues, at least consider the possibility that she might be right. If you still think she's wrong, talk to her about it. Realize that the social worker may not change her mind; you might need to apply to another agency or attorney. The good news is that you will be prepared to deal with issues of infertility, grief, and loss, should the new social worker bring them up.

Real Life Snapshots

Noreen and Tom applied to their local adoption agency and were very excited about finally having a child. Noreen had suffered four miscarriages; that's why she and Tom applied to adopt.

Unfortunately, the agency turned them down. They were not given a reason why. For several years, they felt like something was wrong with them.

Then they moved to another state and decided to try again. They applied to a new adoption agency, were approved, and brought home their baby son about a year later.

Were Tom and Noreen better people later? Was the first social worker wrong? I don't know. What I do know is that if Tom and Noreen had given up, they wouldn't have their son today.

◆ You lied to the social worker about something serious—such as a previous drug offense.

Lying really aggravates most social workers. This does not, however, mean that you must confess every minor infraction that you've ever made. The social worker is not there to give you absolution. She's a person evaluating you as a prospective parent. So when it comes to important issues that would reflect on your ability to raise a child, don't lie.

◆ Your references weren't strong—or they were negative.

I discussed the importance of references in Chapter 12. A bad reference might not completely derail your adoption, but it could delay you for months. So don't underestimate their importance.

In nearly all cases, your references will be so glowing you'd be embarrassed to read them. But if you've given someone's name as a reference without his knowledge, or if you've given the name of someone who (unbeknownst to you) believes adoption is a bad institution, you could be asking for trouble.

◆ You have a serious or life-threatening medical problem.

If you have a serious medical problem, you might get turned down. This does not (or should not) include disabilities such as being wheelchair-bound or other chronic problems that will not radically shorten your life span.

Is this fair? After all, thanks to medical progress, many serious illnesses can be controlled. The problem is that social workers are supposed to consider the best interests of a child. All other things being equal, they would rather place a child with a healthy family than with one who is not.

If you are rejected for health reasons, you might want to reapply to the agency or another agency in a year or two, with a letter from your physician describing your state of health and the prognosis.

I guess the bottom line here is, throughout the entire home study process, sincerity should shine through. You, your family, and your references should always strive to be positive but truthful. Accentuate the positive, eliminate the negative. And don't mess with Mr. In-between.

The Least You Need to Know

- Home studies are more than a check of your house.

- Be prepared for the home visit: Make sure your house is clean, safe, and welcoming to a child—or you have a plan to make it that way.

- If you write an autobiography or resumé, be sure to emphasize why and how much you want to adopt, rather than how rich or smart you are.

- Make sure you know, and provide, all of the documentation your social worker asks for.

- Choose your references carefully and make sure they know what's expected of them.

- If your home study is disapproved (which rarely happens), ask why. It might be a problem you can resolve.

Chapter **13**

Special Interests: The Nontraditional Adopter

In This Chapter

- ◆ Adopting if you're single
- ◆ Adopting if you're gay or lesbian
- ◆ Adopting if you're disabled
- ◆ Adopting if you're over 45

Lana and Ted, in their late 40s, wanted to adopt a child but figured they were "too old." Then they read a story about other latter-day Baby Boomers adopting from China. They investigated and found out it *was* possible for them to adopt. Today, Lana and Ted are the proud parents of a Chinese baby girl.

At age 39, Lucy's biological clock was screaming for a baby. Unfortunately, because of a medical problem, Lucy couldn't have children. She was single, so she figured adoption was out of the question. But everything clicked into place one day when Lucy overheard a single adoptive mom talking about how singles *could* adopt. Lucy took in the beaming face of the mother and her cute little boy and wondered if maybe she really *could* be a parent. Today, Lucy is the mom of an adorable biracial daughter.

When many people think of new adoptive parents, they envision Mom and Dad, a healthy heterosexual married couple, probably in their thirties, with their same-race adopted child. The fact is that adopters don't always fit this profile.

This chapter covers the nontraditional parent, whether single, gay, lesbian, or bi-sexual, disabled, or older than average.

Single with Children

Every state in the United States allows single people to adopt. As a result, marital status isn't a legal barrier to adopting a child anywhere. At least, not officially. Many adoption agencies and attorneys, however, still perceive the married couple as the ideal choice for the children they place. So sometimes the single man or woman drops to the end of the adoption line when it comes to priorities—depending on who the adoption arranger is. However, this is much less true today than in past years, especially if you're interested in adopting your child from another country. Smart singles do their homework!

Let's back up for a moment and address one issue that seems to baffle some people: why singles choose to adopt kids.

CAUTION

Adoption Alert _____

Sometimes ill children are offered to nontraditional adopters (as well as traditional adopters), because it's hard for the agency to find parents for the child.

A nontraditional parent usually has less of a tough time adopting a child with special needs, so if you hope to adopt such a child, you shouldn't hesitate to try—after carefully considering each child's individual medical problems. However, if you don't want to adopt a child with special needs, be sure to be upfront about this with your social worker and stick to your position. Don't be guilted into adopting a child with needs that you think might be too hard for you to cope with.

Single Adoptions: Pros and Cons

Single men and women want to adopt a child for many of the same reasons that married people want to (wanting a child to love, wanting to give a child a family, not being able to get pregnant, and so on). But why, you might be wondering, don't they wait until they're married? Here are some reasons:

◆ They have no desire to marry, but don't want to forego parenthood.

◆ They might like to marry but they haven't yet married, and they're afraid they might not ever find the right man or woman. However, they do know that they want to become parents.

◆ They may be gay or lesbian, and marriage isn't an available option for them.

◆ They are divorced and don't believe they will remarry—yet they don't want to forego parenting.

◆ They are infertile and want to become parents.

◆ They want to provide families for children who need them now.

Real Life Snapshots

Dr. Jerri Ann Jenista, a pediatrician and mother of five adopted children, offered readers some helpful and humorous hints to single parenting in *The Handbook for Single Adoptive Parents* (published by The National Council for Single Adoptive Parents). Here are just a few:

"Good friends, especially other single parents, are a must. These are the people who will bail you out when you need to go Christmas shopping without children or you are in the hospital with pneumonia."

"Reliable day care is the key to survival. Approval for additional children should be sought from your day care provider, not your adoption agency or your family."

"The plumbing, electrical and heating systems in your house are always in a merely temporary state of good repair."

"Sleeping in their clothes, eating pizza for breakfast, putting away their own laundry and not having a TV does not harm children."

And lastly, my favorite:

"Your kids won't care if you have a spotless house, brand new clothes or gourmet meals. But they will remember the 105 times you played Chutes and Ladders, all the books you read together, and the Ninja Turtle costume you made out of a cardboard box."

Of course, there are some people who believe that singles should not be allowed to adopt kids. If you're single and you want to adopt, it's critical that you understand their arguments (even though you probably adamantly oppose most or all of them). Here are a few objections you may come across—and some powerful counter-arguments:

♦ A child needs two parents so that one can fill in for the other when one is too tired, sick, and so on.

This is one of the strongest arguments against single adoptive parenting. Child-rearing is very difficult, and it can be especially tough when 100 percent of the work falls on one parent. For this reason, it's important for singles who want to adopt to identify family members, friends, or others who can pitch in on a regular as well as an emergency basis.

♦ A child needs to be raised by parents of both sexes.

Many people agree that it's important for girls to have adult males to relate to and for boys to have adult females to relate to. Singles argue that this person does not necessarily have to be a parent; it could be a close friend or family member of the opposite sex.

Familybuilding Tips

Adoption experts say that single males have a much more difficult time adopting than do single females. This is in part because several unspoken assumptions work against single males who want to adopt: that they can't be good parents or that they might even be pedophiles. Some experts advise men who feel that this may be an unstated problem to offer to take a psychological test such as the Minnesota Multiphasic Personality Inventory or to agree to an interview and evaluation by a psychologist of the agency's choice.

♦ If the single parent becomes ill or dies, the child will be orphaned.

When single men and women adopt, they are usually well aware that they need to plan for the unhappy contingency that they could become ill or very ill. Most agencies and attorneys want to know who (friends, family members, or others) can provide backup in the case of emergency. Singles who want to adopt should seriously consider this issue. (They should also periodically revisit it after they adopt. Former potential caregivers may move away or become ill or die themselves, necessitating a new plan.)

♦ The single person probably will have to work to support the child and, thus, cannot be an at-home parent.

The fact that most single adoptive parents must work is not a strong argument, because most parents in two-parent couples are employed. With a two-parent family, however, it is true that one parent can fill in for the other if one has to travel, becomes ill, and so forth. This kind of tag-team arrangement isn't easy for the single person, who must make special arrangements anytime the usual day-care arrangements fail.

◆ The stereotypical poverty-stricken, single biological parent is often confused, even by experts, with the single adoptive parent; however, single *adoptive* parents are overwhelmingly middle-class people who are employed and are ready and able to support their children.

Adoptinfo

In a 1991 study published in *Families in Society: The Journal of Contemporary Human Services*, researchers studied about 800 adopters, all who had adopted children with special needs, including 139 single adoptive parents.

They found that the average income of the single adoptive parent was about $21,300. At about that time, the income level for the average single parent in the United States was about $13,500. Thus, although many of the single adopters were not wealthy, neither were they poor.

Over half had at least some college education.

Some single adopters say that their pet peeve is being confused with single biological parents who are divorced. Divorced parents may face a number of obstacles single parents don't have to deal with: animosity from their former spouses, reduced incomes, and insecurity with their new status as single parent. On the other hand, divorced singles may also be able to rely on their former spouses when a crunch time comes.

Tips for Single Adopters

How do you apply for adoption if you're single? Here are a few suggestions:

◆ Join an adoptive parent group. Join a singles group if one is available in your area; if not, don't shy away from a couples group. You don't necessarily have to fit a "mold" to gain from a group.

◆ Investigate agencies and nonagency adoption arrangers in your area (see Chapters 6 and 7).

◆ Prepare for possible objections to you as a single adopter and arguments you can offer to counter them.

◆ Read *Adopting on Your Own: The Complete Guide to Adopting as a Single Parent*, by Lee Varon, a helpful resource for single adopters. (Farrar, Straus and Giroux, 2000.)

Gay and Lesbian Adopters

No one knows how many adopters are gay or lesbian, although some agencies openly welcome gay, lesbian, and bisexual applicants. It may well be that more gays and lesbians are seeking to adopt than in past years, as societal acceptance increases. But many people still don't reveal their sexual orientation to others, often because they fear that they'll be turned down by agencies (despite what they say) or because they want to retain their privacy.

Most state laws don't address whether gays may or may not adopt. Only one state—Florida—specifically bans homosexuals from adopting children. This law was challenged but was upheld by a federal court in 2004.

> ## Adoptinfo
>
> Gay and lesbian organizations, some adoption groups, and some adoption websites offer information on which agencies are amenable to applications from gays and lesbians and which are not. To learn more about a mailing list for gay, bisexual, and lesbian parents, go to www.cyberhiway.com/aparent/faq.html. Organizations for single adoptive parents may also be aware of friendly and unfriendly agencies or attorneys.

However, even if state law allows gays or lesbians to adopt children, many private adoption agencies and attorneys still turn away gay and lesbian applicants—often stating other reasons for their refusal. Some sectarian (religious) agencies oppose gays and lesbians adopting children outright. In addition, pregnant women in the United States who are considering adoption often choose an open adoption and select the adopting parents, and many prefer a married heterosexual couple. It's also true that some countries such as China specifically ban homosexual adoption, so agencies working with China are not allowed to knowingly place a child from that country with a gay or lesbian person.

As with single parent adopters, gay and lesbian adopters should understand—and be prepared to counter—the arguments made against their right to adopt. Here are some arguments made against gay and lesbian adoptions:

- ◆ They feel that only heterosexual couples should adopt.

    Many people continue to believe that a two-parent, mother-and-father family is the best. Gays and lesbians who are in committed relationships argue that they can provide a two-parent family. One way to show commitment could be to state (if this is true) that you have been involved in a relationship with the same person for two or more years and that you both intend for this relationship to continue. If you co-own a home or condominium or share other important financial arrangements, this could be seen as another indication of a commitment—just as such traits are seen as a sign of stability in a heterosexual couple.

Another important point to make is that adoption is not a right, like the right to vote. Instead, the primary goal of adoption is, or should be, to place the child with the best possible parents. Those who object to homosexuality believe that the best placement is with a two-parent, heterosexual couple.

◆ They see homosexuality as morally wrong.

This is a matter of personal opinion. It's not surprising that people who hold such beliefs would be opposed to the idea of gays and lesbians adopting children. Others, who view homosexuality as an acceptable personal choice, will likely be more receptive to the idea.

◆ They believe that gays and lesbians may abuse their children.

Studies indicate that gays and lesbians do not abuse their children more than heterosexual parents (in fact, some studies suggest that heterosexual biological fathers and stepfathers are more likely to be abusive than gay fathers).

◆ They believe that children will be embarrassed by having parents who are gays or lesbians.

It may well be true that children of gay or lesbian parents might have trouble explaining their situation to friends, although supporters of gay and lesbian adoption argue that this doesn't mean we should institutionalize stigma. Of course, the main issue and point of adoption is to consider the best interests of children, rather than to destigmatize gays and lesbians.

Adoptinfo

Those who argue against the embarrassment argument cite the 1984 case of *Palmore v. Sidoti*. In this case, a noncustodial biological father opposed having his child (who was white) live with his wife, who had married a black man. The U.S. Supreme Court ruled that although it might be difficult for the child to live in a mixed-race family, race alone couldn't be held as a constraint to child custody and that the courts couldn't sanction stigmatizing of race.

Some proponents of gay and lesbian adoption believe that the principle of not allowing racial stigma to prevail should also be extended to sexual orientation. Others argue that race and sexual orientation are two completely different issues. This particular argument is likely to continue.

◆ They believe that gay and lesbian parents will encourage their children to become gays and lesbians.

This suggestion is often made by people who object to homosexuality in general. However, all evidence runs counter to the notion that gay and lesbian parents somehow seek to transform their children into homosexuals. Also, most gays and lesbians point out that they were born and raised by heterosexual parents.

◆ Some foreign governments are opposed to gays and lesbians adopting internationally.

In that case, some gays and lesbians who want to adopt from those countries conceal their sexual orientation from the orphanage and foreign officials.

Some people take a halfway approach to the issue of homosexuals adopting. They believe that gays and lesbians should be able to adopt if they already have a relationship with the child. (For example, if they are related to the child or if they are a foster parent to the child.) In those cases, they believe it's preferable to reduce the losses the child has already suffered by keeping the child with someone familiar.

However, people who take the halfway approach are generally not in favor of placing a new child with a known gay or lesbian couple—for any or all of the reasons stated earlier.

Tips for Gay/Lesbian Adopters

Here are a few suggestions for gays and lesbians who seek to adopt:

◆ Read about adoption in general as well as the experience of homosexual adopters. Several of my previously published books may help with general information: *There ARE Babies to Adopt* and *The Encyclopedia of Adoption*, a reference book.

◆ Locate adoptive parent groups sympathetic to gays and lesbians. How? Well, one way is to ask them whether they have any objection to gays and lesbians adopting children. But if the idea of asking outright makes you nervous, you could first question whether they have any single members. If they do, then the next question could be whether or not gays and lesbians are welcome in the group.

◆ Understand your state laws. In most states, if there are two homosexual partners, only one is allowed to adopt; the other is usually required to give up her or his parental rights for the adoption to happen. However, increasing numbers of states are now recognizing *second parent adoptions*, in which a homosexual can become the legal adoptive parent of his or her partner's biological child.

- ◆ Locate agencies or attorneys that will accept you as a potential adopter. As with parent groups, you may want to first ask the agency or attorney whether they accept single applicants. If they don't, they probably wouldn't be accepting of gays or lesbians adopting; so the questions can end there. If they do accept singles, the only way to really know whether they will accept gays and lesbians is to ask. You could be somewhat oblique: ask "Have you ever had any gays and lesbians apply?" and see what kind of response you get.

Adopterms

Second parent adoption refers to the adoption of one person's biological child by his or her homosexual partner. Some people have compared it to stepparent adoption, in that one parent is a biological parent and the other seeks to create a legal relationship with the child. Usually, the person who wants to adopt has a parentlike relationship with the child already.

Parents with Disabilities

Moving on to another category of nontraditional adopters, let's talk about disabled people who wish to adopt children. What could a disabled person possibly offer an adopted child? First of all, the disabled person may be a very loving, kind, and accepting person, important traits in an adopter. It's also true that sometimes disabled people adopt children with similar disabilities.

One mom who has been in a wheelchair all her life adopted a child with a disability requiring a wheelchair. The mom can identify with the child's problems, and she knows how to cope with them, practically and psychologically. But she also knows the importance of discipline and won't put up with any nonsense—no "poor me" stuff works with her! She is probably a far better "fit" than the average nondisabled person.

A lot of people are surprised to learn that vibrant and perfect health is not always a requirement to adopt. Of course, most adoption arrangers want to place children with parents who will be able to raise them to adulthood, which pretty much excludes people who have terminal cancer or other life-threatening illnesses.

People who are able to master their disabilities, however, can apply to adopt. People with a variety of illnesses or impairments have succeeded at adoption. It isn't necessarily easy—nontraditional parents often have to try harder—but it is often possible.

In general, social workers will look at the severity of the disability as well as the type of child the disabled person wants to adopt. For example, a person who has difficulty moving around might find it very hard to parent an active toddler. Thus, the person should be prepared to discuss how he or she plans to keep up with a whirlwind of a child.

Mental Illness

Many people who have been treated for psychiatric illnesses (such as depression) are fearful that their medical histories might prevent them from adopting. When it comes to adoption, are psychological problems evaluated differently than physical ones?

What's important to most social workers is the nature of the illness and its current status. For example, most social workers will not have a problem with an applicant who was once depressed over a personal or professional setback but who has since recovered. Most social workers also don't object to applicants who take medication for depression. However, most social workers would hesitate to place a child with an applicant who has been suicidal or has suffered a recent severe depression.

A past psychosis presents the most serious problem. (A psychosis is a break with reality; often a person who becomes psychotic requires temporary hospitalization in a psychiatric facility.) Again, the nature of the illness, when it occurred, and the applicant's current status are most relevant.

Tips for Disabled Adopters

If you are disabled and want to adopt, here are some strategies to improve your chances:

- ◆ Understand that you may encounter some resistance from agencies and attorneys. Don't take it personally.

- ◆ Explore different avenues of adoption: agency or nonagency, U.S. or international, infant or older child.

- ◆ Don't be apologetic about your disability, but do be open about your limitations. Be prepared to discuss how you can accommodate them.

- ◆ Be patient with silly questions you may be asked.

- ◆ Be up front about whether you want to adopt a healthy child or a child with special needs. If you don't want to adopt a child with special needs, you don't have to.

Real Life Snapshots

Pat and Denise are both disabled—Denise had polio and Pat was born with spina bifida—and they successfully adopted a healthy biracial child several years ago.

In an article in *Accent on Living* magazine, Denise offered the following advice to disabled adoptive parents: "Be up-front about your disability and about the fact that you have the ability to be a parent. Address any issues before they worry about them, such as how you're going to handle child care. These are questions the social worker might not be inclined to ask but might make a lot of assumptions about your inability to do them."

Older Parents

As Baby Boomers age, the definition of how old is too old to adopt is changing. (To paraphrase an old joke, many Boomers think that middle age is about five years older than however old they are.)

Many men and women in their late 40s and beyond find that childbearing is not an option. Yet they still eagerly wish to be parents. Adoption is a good answer for some of them.

Adoptinfo

Older parents might actually have an advantage when they seek to adopt older children or children with disabilities. The reason? Many older adopters have grown children and are already experienced parents. Of course, children with special needs can be very challenging. But older parents may have the patience and the time to give the kids what they need: love, attention, and reasonable structure. It's also true that people in their late forties or even their fifties (and older!) are adopting babies and children from other countries because so many infants and children in orphanages urgently need families.

Here are some advantages that older parents might bring to an adoption:

- They might be more emotionally mature than younger parents.
- They might be more financially stable than younger parents.
- They might have more stable values than younger parents.
- They might have more time or patience for their children than younger parents.

Here are some disadvantages to older adopters:

♦ They might be less vigorous than younger adopters. Agencies and attorneys can investigate the health of the prospective adoptive parents to determine whether they seem to have enough energy and commitment to parent a child.

♦ They might have less patience and understanding than younger adopters. On the other hand, many younger people might be very impatient, while older adopters may be more willing to stop and listen.

♦ They might seem more like grandparents than parents. Yet in our society today, we see many people who have delayed childbearing and who have biological children while in their late 30s or even 40s. Nor is it important for every parent to look as if he or she stepped off a magazine cover: What's important is the love and commitment they give to a child.

Familybuilding Tips

Some foreign countries with overloaded orphanages have relaxed their age requirements so more children can be placed. In these countries, 50- or even 60-year-olds are able to adopt infants.

♦ They might become ill or die before the child is fully grown. These days, the average life expectancy for many people is well into the late 70s and beyond. What social workers can do is look at the health history of the prospective adopters' own parents and grandparents. At what age did they die? What did they die from? How was their general mental and physical health?

Many agencies, however, do set upper age limits (although those limits seem to be generally creeping up). In the past, the maximum age limit for adopting babies was around 40; today, many agencies will accept parents who are 45 years old and sometimes even older. Sometimes agencies average the age of a husband and wife to determine an age limit. If he's 50 and she's 40, their average age is 45, which may be fine. Some agencies have thrown out age limits altogether. (Although they would probably look askance if someone who was 80 years old wanted to adopt a baby!)

The Least You Need to Know

♦ Singles can adopt, but it might take a little more work. Single adopters must prove that they have a network of people who will take care of the child at times when they themselves cannot.

- ◆ Laws and policies on gays and lesbians adopting are evolving. Gays and lesbians who are interested in adopting should work with supportive agencies or attorneys.

- ◆ Disabled people who want to adopt kids should be ready to discuss how they'll handle their disability.

- ◆ Adoption is possible for people over age 45 or even 50.

Chapter 14

Getting Emotional

In This Chapter

◆ Telling your parents that you're going to adopt

◆ Explaining that you're adopting a new child if you already have kids

◆ Dealing with your adult siblings and other family members

You've applied to an adoption agency, and they've approved your application. Congratulations! You're awash with emotions: excitement, fears, and hopes for the future. Guess what—you're not alone. Your family and friends also care about what happens to you. Your adoption of a child will affect them in lots of ways. After you become a parent, everything will change: get-togethers, holiday plans, nights out, and how you spend your time with your new family.

Remember that however long it took you to reach the decision to adopt, you finally made it. By the time you tell your family and friends about it, you will have adjusted to the idea. However, they may well be at "start" in terms of their interest and knowledge about adoption. What they need from you is information, and what you need from them is support. You also may already have children in your family, and they'll have many questions and issues as well.

This chapter will talk about the attitudes of your family and friends toward adoption as you go through the process, before you even receive information on a particular child.

How Do Your Parents Feel?

If you have no children now and you plan to adopt, you can bet that your lifestyle will change. Your parents probably realize it. They know parenting isn't for sissies. Here are a few issues that might concern your parents and some thoughts that might be running through their minds:

♦ How will your relationships with them change?

After you adopt a child, you'll have to make some major shifts in your relationships with your parents and friends. You'll learn that parents must (usually) put their children ahead of other people outside the immediate family.

♦ Will you need and want their help with the adoption, or should they try to step back and wait until you ask?

Most people assume that a woman who has just given birth needs plenty of extra help because she is so exhausted from the childbirth. Yet, they don't often give this same consideration to parents who adopt a newborn infant.

Adoptive parents with a new baby can become extremely exhausted, too. Taking care of a new baby is hard work, whether it was born to you or adopted by you. Those 2 A.M. feedings and the 24-hour-a-day responsibility can get overwhelming. A little help if you can get it, especially at the beginning, can help you catch up on sleep and maintain a positive outlook.

Telling your parents that you would like their help when the baby comes might be a very good idea, even before a child is found for you to adopt. Another advantage of having your parents help you with child care is that they will become emotionally involved with the child. You probably will find yourself drawn closer to your parents, too. Don't expect all to be perfect, however! You may have a few disagreements about what's best for the child. But remember, *you* are the parent, and you may need to assert yourself in that role.

♦ Will you have a really long wait for your child? Will the adoption go through smoothly, or will there be problems ahead?

Your parents may be concerned that you'll have to wait some incredibly long period to adopt—and that will be difficult for you. Assure them that your plan is to adopt much sooner than that and you have developed a good strategy to reach that goal.

◆ Will the birthmother change her mind about the adoption?

Tell your parents that it's true that a minority of birthmothers change their mind about adoption, but in most states, when the birthparents sign their consent to an adoption, it is irrevocable, or they have only a brief period of time to change their minds.

If you are adopting a child from another country, explain to your parents that the orphanage (or other organization or individual) has custody of the child, and it would be almost impossible for the foreign birthmother to rescind her consent.

If you are adopting a foster child, explain that the state or county did a formal "termination of parental rights," and the birthparents are not allowed to interfere with that court order.

◆ How should they explain this to others in the family?

Familybuilding Tips

Some parents can be tremendously supportive in the preadoption phase by clipping articles, cheerleading you when you're down, and keeping their eyes and ears open for the latest information. Of course, this can be carried too far, and if your parents and friends are burdening you with adoption information, it's perfectly okay to tell them to lay off—you've got enough.

You may think that you receive far too many probing questions about adoption, but you probably don't realize that when people hear about the fact that you are planning to adopt, your parents often get interrogated, too.

Tell your parents what you want them to know about the adoption and be sure to emphasize that you want to create a family. You might want to add that you hope to be good parents like they were. Also tell them what information you want shared and what information is "off the record."

Sometimes when people don't have the nerve to ask you something, they have no qualms at all about calling up your mother and asking her the same thing. So your parents and other family members need to know what is *not* open for discussion with others. (If something is *really* off limits, maybe you shouldn't share it with your parents in the first place.)

◆ How will other children you already have be affected? And what will this child be like? What if he turns out to have problems? Or what if she just doesn't fit in with the family?

If they express such fears, or hint at them, you might tell them that children don't come with warranties, whether born to you or adopted. If they persist, you might gently mention a few people who are biological relatives and yet have had serious problems. Biology is no guarantee of a happy parental experience, and adoption doesn't foredoom one to an unhappy experience. Parenthood is a challenge, either way.

CAUTION **Adoption Alert** _____

You can bet that if you do tell family members you're planning to adopt, you and the adoption will be very hot topics of the day.

Resist the common prospective adopter tendency to tell all to anyone who asks anything. Put your brain in gear before your mouth starts moving. Why? Because the sad fact is that people tend to remember anything "bad" that you have to say; if it has something to do with the child, you probably don't want them repeating it later on when that child is a member of the family.

What if you're a single person and your mom thinks your plan to adopt a child is the craziest idea she's ever heard? To handle this emotionally, you might think about circumstances in the past that turned out okay, even though she disapproved of actions you took at that time.

You might also want to try to determine the underlying fear. Does your mom think she'll be constantly trapped into on-call babysitting? You can reassure her by telling her you've developed a child-care plan. Or she might think adopting will prevent you from ever marrying. Remind her that single people do get married.

Your Children Already in the Family

If you already have children, this new child (or children) you will adopt will become their sibling(s). They may have some powerful positive and negative feelings about this:

◆ They may fear that you'll favor the new child over them.

Whether you think it's an issue or not, it's a good idea to reassure the children already in your family—even your adult children who have already left home—that they still are very important to you and always will be. No one can replace them. You want to adopt another child (or children), but the new child will have a different relationship with you.

Also, be sure to tell them that love isn't like a pie that must be divided up into smaller pieces when there are more people. You can love the family that you have now, and you can love a child whom you adopt, without diminishing the love for the ones who "came first."

♦ They may worry that you'll spend less time with them.

Let's be realistic about one aspect that probably will change—your time. Especially if you are adopting an infant, your time will be more in demand than it was in the past. You'll need to be sure that after you do adopt and are over the initial adjustment stage, your other children—and your spouse—still receive loving attention.

Your family and children may especially worry if the child you plan to adopt is disabled. Won't this take too much time and energy out of you—and them? How long will it take to figure out exactly what the child needs and how to provide it? Will the disabled child become the center of attention *because* of the disability? As you can see, you need to think about many things here!

♦ They may worry that the household workload will increase.

Guess what? They're right! At least in the early days and until you get settled, you may find yourself calling on your children to help you with the new child. However, they should not be expected to sacrifice all their time and energy to the child whom *you* chose to adopt.

If you think you will really need extra help, you should consider your options even before you receive a referral for a child. Should you find a baby-sitting cooperative in your neighborhood or start one yourself? Should you check out day-care programs? (If you work, you definitely should decide ahead of time whether you will continue to work, how long you'll take off after you adopt your child, and other work-related issues.)

Be sure to keep in mind the possible reactions of the newly adopted child to whatever plans you make. A two-year-old adopted from another country, who speaks another language, may not adapt very well at first to a day-care center, to your children, or to you. She probably needs at least a few weeks with you before she can be placed in another new and strange environment. It's a mistake to hold off on thinking about these issues until after you adopt.

♦ Children already in the family may consciously or unconsciously wonder about their place in the family—for example, no longer being "the baby" or "the big kid." Again, reassure them of your love. When the child comes, make sure you still have "alone time" with them so they continue to feel special.

◆ They may wonder what their friends will think. (I talk about how to explain adoption to others in Part 4.) Others have strange ideas about adoption sometimes, based on TV shows, movies, or things they've heard. Yet most people don't believe in talking animals that they see on TV shows. Tell them that just as talking animals are mythical, the idea that all adopted children and adults are disturbed is also a myth. Just because you see it on TV doesn't make it real.

◆ If adopted themselves, your children might have new questions about their birthparents. If nonadopted, they may have questions about their births. Answer the "old" adopted child's questions honestly and openly and reassure him of your continuing love. Talk to nonadopted kids about their births and how important they are and always will be to you.

Real Life Snapshots

After my husband and I were approved to adopt, we began thinking about names for the baby that would come someday. (More information on naming is offered in Chapter 18.) We involved the two children already in our family, then ages six and seven.

We all pored over name books, looking at the meanings of different names, and also seeing if the name sounded right with our last name. We finally selected a boy name and a girl name, since we didn't know if our new baby would be male or female. Of course, my husband and I had veto power over some of the silly names the kids chose!

This task took many hours and also helped the children feel that they were important to the future adoption. And they were!

Of course, your children may exhibit many positive and excited feelings about the new child. They may be eager to hug the new baby or show the new older child the ropes. Children can be very affectionate and helpful—but don't expect that kind of behavior 100 percent of the time, or you will be disappointed. You'll also see jealousy, boredom, and other common reactions to a new person—and a rival—in the family. This is normal.

Your Adult Siblings and Other Family Members

Now that you've thought about your parents' reaction to adoption, as well as how your children (if you have any) may feel, it's time to consider how other family members will react to your plan to adopt. In most cases, they will greet the news in a positive and excited way.

As with your parents, if siblings or other family members express dismay about you adopting, you could remind them of past decisions you made that they were skeptical of but that worked out. Or better yet, remind them of decisions *they* made that everyone questioned but ultimately proved positive. Then tell them that this is a decision you are making and that you believe will work out for your family. If you're committed to adopting a child, be firm with your doubting family members. Let them know your decision is final and you hope and expect them to welcome your child into the family.

The Least You Need to Know

- ◆ Most adoptive parents' own parents worry about adoption, but most become very proud grandparents.

- ◆ Your relationships with others will change when you adopt. Make sure that you have a child-care plan in place before you adopt.

- ◆ Children already in your home need reassurance that you'll still pay attention to them after the adoption.

- ◆ When possible, involve family members in looking forward to the adoption with you.

Chapter

15

What You Should Know About a Child You Might Adopt

In This Chapter

- ◆ Inquiring about the health of the child
- ◆ Getting the birthfamily's medical background
- ◆ Discovering whether "good genes" matter
- ◆ Checking out prenatal care

How do you first learn about a child who may become *your* child? Sometimes the call with the information comes as the result of a pregnant woman who liked your adoption resumé and chose you as the potential parents to her child. Or maybe the social worker has gotten word of the child she thinks would be just right for your family, so she contacts you. The first inklings of a contact are made in many different ways. But how do you know whether to follow your head or heart? I recommend following both! This chapter will provide you with practical guidance on the "head" part.

On the "downside," many times when people adopt, they feel like they have little or no control over the process. They don't like this helpless feeling, so they try to find out as much information about a child and/or the birthmother as possible, to decide whether or not to adopt. This is a good thing.

They may be especially concerned about heredity. Medical and scientific advances have made us increasingly aware of how heredity affects our "predispositions" for various physical traits, health, even talents and personality traits.

This chapter covers genetic predispositions as well as environmental and medical factors that you should know about if you're thinking about adopting a child.

Vital Statistics

When the agency or attorney tells you about a child who's already been born, you should be sure to ask plenty of questions about the child's health and her environment.

Here's a sampling of questions you might ask about a child of any age:

- When was the child born? (If unknown, approximately when? Who determined this, and how did they come up with that date?)

- How much did the child weigh as an infant?

- What was the head circumference of the child as an infant? If not available, what is the child's head circumference now? The child's head size is relevant to a physician. A head size that is too small in relation to the child's age or body can mean a problem with brain development. A head size that is too large may mean hydrocephalus ("water on the brain"), and there may be problems with development.

- Does the child appear to be developmentally on track? How does she compare to her peers?

- Can the child hear and see?

- Is the child shy or outgoing? Noisy or quiet?

- Does the child have any siblings? If so, where are they?

- What illnesses has the child had and at what age? What treatments did she receive? Has she had any surgeries? Does she take any medications on a regular basis? If so, what are they and what are they for?

Adoptinfo

Growth charts for weight, length, and head circumference are available in most pediatricians' offices.

◆ What is the child's best feature? Biggest problem area?

◆ Has the child been immunized, and if so, can you obtain the immunization records when you adopt her? (The pattern of immunizations, particularly in children born in the United States, can be indicative of how often the child was seen for health care.)

If the child is older than age two, you might *also* consider asking the following questions as well:

◆ Where has the child lived since birth? In how many homes or with how many different caregivers?

◆ What major experiences have happened to the child—positive or negative?

◆ Has the child been physically or sexually abused? Has the child been neglected? Neglect can be as bad or even worse than abuse for children. (For example, not feeding a child is a form of neglect. Some children are underfed or even starved.)

◆ Has the child received any developmental interventions? (Such as speech therapy, physical therapy, or occupational therapy.) If so, from whom, and what were the results?

◆ Has the child received any counseling or mental health therapy? If so, from whom, for how long, and for what issues?

◆ Has the child been growing normally? Measurements, including weight, length/height, and head circumference (birth and current) are all helpful to assess a child's physical growth.

Deep Background

Aside from those basic questions, it's important to obtain as much medical background information about the birthparents (and their extended birthfamily) as you can. Unfortunately, much of the information you receive may be sketchy. If a child was abandoned, for example, there's no way to know the medical history of the birthfamily.

When the birthparents are available, however, the adoption arranger usually will provide them with a questionnaire they can respond to about their medical histories. The arranger should also ask for information from the birthparents' parents, if possible.

I strongly recommend that any health information provided on the birthparents and their parents be reviewed by a medical doctor before the adoption is finalized, so that the physician can give an evaluation on possible risks and problems. A listing of physicians with particular expertise in adoption and foster care is provided in Appendix F. You can find more names of physicians who are experts in adoption and foster care through the American Academy of Pediatrics at the following Web address: www.aap.org/sections/adoption/adopt-states/adoption-map.html.

Familybuilding Tips _____

Usually, the primary source of medical information an adoption arranger receives in a U.S. adoption will be from the birthmother (or pregnant woman) herself. She generally will provide all her current medical information. (If you're adopting your child from another country, the information usually will come through the orphanage director to your agency or attorney.)

But think about this. Were you in pretty good shape when you were 18 or 21? Probably you were healthier then than now! The point is that most birthmothers have not yet encountered serious health problems that they may suffer as they age, including those that may have a genetic basis, such as diabetes and arthritis. So what you really should know are the health conditions of the birthparents' *parents*, and if possible, other older family members.

Born in the USA

The medical information on a U.S.-born child is only as good as whatever information the birthparents supply to your adoption arranger. The amount of information available may vary due to state law. Some states may require very specific medical information from birthparents, while many others leave the amassing of information up to the arranger.

Adoption Alert _____

Information on birthparents is usually more difficult to obtain in international adoptions. In some cases, the agency may not even know who the birthmother is. You usually can forget about any information on the birthfather. It's still a good idea to ask for this information so that when it *can* be amassed, adoption arrangers will work to provide it to you.

Ask the adoption arranger for medical history information on both the birthparents and, whenever possible, their parents and other family members as well. Most birthparents are young and healthy when they place their child for adoption, but the health of *their* parents may provide possible clues to your child's future health. Is there a history of heart disease, cancer, rheumatoid arthritis, or any other serious diseases? If, for example, there is a history of cancer or heart disease, your child's doctor can keep an eye on potential problems.

Sometimes birthparents are not very well aware of the health of their own parents, so ask the adoption arranger if it's possible for him or her to obtain the medical history information directly from the birthgrandparents. If not, the birthparents can be asked to contact the birthgrandparents and request the information. Or a questionnaire can be provided for them to fill out, which may be less threatening than responding to questions from the birthparents or a social worker.

Adoptinfo

Here's an interesting innovation in adoption law: In 1996, Pennsylvania passed legislation to create an Adoption Medical History Registry.

According to the law, a Pennsylvania birthparent may fill out an Adoption Medical History Information form, which remains on file should the adopted child seek information as an adult. In addition, the form can be updated if the birthparent later develops health problems about which the adopted child should know. The information is voluntary and is disclosed only to adoptive parents or adopted adults over age 18. It is also completely anonymous.

Children in Foster Care

If you adopt a foster child in the United States, the medical information you receive will only be as good as the case records.

Since foster children may receive inadequate health care prior to their placement for adoption, children who have lived in foster homes need a thorough physical exam.

It's also a good idea before the adoption is complete to ask a medical expert to review whatever medical records you can obtain, to ensure that any known medical problems can be handled by your family and your doctor.

Children who have lived in foster care are at risk for developmental delays and mental health issues. Don't be afraid to request psychological evaluations of the child even if the health-care provider doesn't mention them. For information on how older foster children should be evaluated by a psychologist, read "Evaluating Older Pre-Adoptive Children," available online at: www.apa.org/journals/pro/pro295428.html.

Adoption Alert

For the latest information on the medical evaluation that doctors recommend for foster children, go to the policy statement search page of the American Academy of Pediatrics at http://aapolicy.aapublications.org. Then, under "title," use the search words "foster care." This search will help you find the most recent statement on the medical evaluation of children in foster care.

Health Issues Overseas

Obtaining background medical information can be an especially difficult problem in international adoptions, because the orphanage may know nothing about the child prior to his or her arrival. Also, sometimes children from other countries have illnesses that are not seen often in the United States. In addition, children who have lived in institutions for more than a few months can be severely impacted by the orphanage experience.

Children living in foster care (as opposed to an orphanage) in another country are also at risk for medical problems. For all children adopted internationally, there are increased risks of infectious diseases, exposures to toxins (such as lead) in the environment, and growth and developmental delays. The longer the child lives in an orphanage, the higher the probability that the child will have health or psychological problems later.

> **Adoption Alert**
>
> If you adopt a child from another country, all medical testing that was done prior to your child's adoption should be repeated by your pediatrician after your child is with your family.

If the agency doesn't provide you with enough information, ask the agency to ask their facilitator or the orphanage director for more. (See Chapter 11 for more information on international adoptions.)

Listen Up!

Unfortunately, some eager adopters seem deaf to the medical information that they're given. Social workers report that sometimes even when adopters are told of a child's possible health problems, they don't necessarily "hear" the information. They are too anxious to adopt to really consider the ramifications of what they're being told.

For this reason, some agencies list possible risks in writing and require adopters to sign these forms in front of a notary.

> **Adopterms**
>
> A genetic predisposition refers to a probability that a child will inherit some feature that occurred in the biological family, from something as simple as blue eyes to far more complicated issues such as alcoholism and mental illness.

Good Genes, Bad Genes

Most of us don't think about any of the "bad" genes that might run in our families. Yet, we all have positive and negative *genetic predispositions.* Some people inherit a predisposition for high blood pressure, for example. Many experts believe there are inherited predispositions for certain psychiatric problems as well.

When people have biological children, they can't selectively choose the good genes that they want and de-select the ones they don't. (Not yet, anyway!) It's pretty much a roll of the genetic dice. Yet adopters frequently want as much genetic information as they can obtain, because they want to control what they will and will not deal with in a child. Keep in mind that although a family history for a particular problem may exist, the birthparents may never actually develop the problem, and the adopted child may not develop it, either. However, if you would have difficulty dealing with a particular condition or illness, for whatever reason, be sure to make this clear to the adoption arranger.

Familybuilding Tips

All too often, adopted adults have inadequate medical or genetic background information. You can head off this problem by seeking this data for your child now. Not only will you be able to use the information, but you also can pass it on to your child when he or she grows up.

Baby on the Way: Prenatal Info

If the child you're planning to adopt isn't yet born, whatever information you can gain about the pregnant woman and about the child's prenatal condition is important. Researchers are discovering that prenatal conditions have an enormous impact on children's later mental and physical development.

Here are a few questions to ask about prenatal conditions that can affect a child:

♦ Is the pregnant woman receiving adequate prenatal care? This means care in the first or early second trimester of her pregnancy, when she should be examined at least monthly by an obstetrician or certified nurse midwife.

♦ Is the pregnant woman eating right? Is she taking prenatal vitamins?

Because unborn children receive all their nutrition from their birthmothers, the birthmothers' diet is crucial. Is the pregnant woman eating plenty of vegetables, fruits, whole grains, and dairy products? Is she eating a steady diet of junk food and nothing else?

♦ Is the birthmother abusing alcohol?

Physicians advise pregnant women to stop drinking alcohol altogether during the pregnancy; alcohol use can damage the developing fetus. At its most extreme, this damage can lead to Fetal Alcohol Syndrome (FAS), which causes severe neurological damage.

♦ Is the pregnant woman abusing drugs (legal or illegal)?

Abuse of illegal drugs (such as marijuana, heroin, and cocaine) during pregnancy can adversely affect the child's physical and mental development. The birthmother's gynecologist probably will check for drugs and hopefully will report any signs of drug use to the agency or attorney. However, this may not be possible because of patient confidentiality unless the birthmother signs a release. Ask the agency or attorney if they obtain such releases.

Also, remember that many legally prescribed medications can be dangerous to a developing fetus and so should not be taken by pregnant women. If the birthmother is getting adequate prenatal care, she will be aware of these restrictions.

♦ Does the pregnant woman smoke? Smoking while pregnant decreases oxygen delivery to the developing baby and may result in a baby having a lower birth weight at the time of delivery.

♦ Is the birthmother under severe stress? Is there any domestic violence, either physical or emotional?

What is the birthmother's general emotional and psychological state? Although it's inevitable that an unplanned pregnancy will cause some amount of stress, high levels of depression or anxiety will not be good for her or the developing fetus.

Real Life Snapshots

Before Carla and Bob adopted their baby, they asked the pregnant woman numerous questions about her medical history and those of her parents, the birthfather, and his parents. They collected as much data as they could (far more than the social worker had ever sought). When they were finally satisfied, they decided to adopt the child. He was born a very healthy boy.

Several years later, Carla and Bob had a biological child. Unfortunately, their second son was born prematurely and he suffered numerous complications for the first two years of his life. At that point, Carla wryly remembered her careful questioning of the birthmother and all her fears about adopting an unhealthy child. She'd had no idea she could have a very sick biological child herself. The moral of this story is that with kids, either adopted or biological, no matter how careful you are, you can't ensure there will be no health problems.

How to Say No

Why would you want to say "no" to an adoption arranger who's offering you a child? There are many reasons. Perhaps the child has a medical problem that is serious, and you don't have the resources or the schedule that would allow you to adequately provide all the care the child needs. Or you feel you just don't have enough information about the child.

If you feel that a referral for a particular child is *not* right for you, it's a good idea to explain to the arranger, as tactfully as possible, why you don't feel comfortable accepting this child. If the arranger pressures you to adopt the child anyway, I recommend that you consider finding another adoption arranger.

Most prospective parents are terrified to "turn down" a child, convinced the adoption arranger will never offer them another. The reality is that if the agency does indeed place the kind of child you seek, it will probably offer you another child. An agency would decide not to work with you only if you turned down, say, three or four healthy children for reasons that don't make sense to the arranger.

Real Life Snapshots

Todd and Vicky had applied to adopt through an attorney and were completely stunned when they were called a month later and told of a baby that was just born. Did they want to adopt her? They felt unready and scared, and they turned the child down. After that, they agonized that God would punish them by never ever giving them another chance to adopt.

Well, He didn't. Punish them, I mean. They adopted another child about six or seven months later. They felt, as most adoptive parents do, that the child they adopted was the child who was meant for them.

The Least You Need to Know

- ◆ If you are considering adopting a child who is already born, find out as much as possible about the child's birth size, growth, and current physical development.

- ◆ Try to obtain medical information on the child's biological grandparents, as well as the birthparents.

- ◆ If you are considering adopting a child who is not yet born, find out about the pregnant woman's health and prenatal care.

- ◆ Don't feel pressured to adopt a child you are not sure about.

Chapter 16

What You Should Know About Birthmothers and Pregnant Women Considering Adoption

In This Chapter

◆ How pregnant women choose adoption arrangers, and why you should care

◆ The pros and cons of meeting women considering adoption for their babies

◆ What to ask and *not* ask a birthmother

◆ Why some birthmothers change their minds about adoption

When you're concentrating on your own goal of adopting a child, it can be difficult—nearly impossible—to understand why a woman would contemplate placing a child for adoption. Yet it is important to understand not only why some women choose adoption, but how they choose the adoption arranger, whether an agency or attorney.

You also need to realize that birthmothers have fears and concerns about adopters—hey, they watch TV too! (Adopters are sometimes the bad guys on television, sadly.) This chapter takes a look at adoption from a birthmother's perspective and explains why you need to at least try to see the world through her eyes, if only briefly.

Choice of Adoption Arranger

First let's like talk about *why* birthparents choose agency adoption (and particular agencies), or independent (nonagency) adoption (and particular attorneys). If you know why the pregnant woman chose a particular agency, attorney, or third party, this can give you another piece of the puzzle to help you decide whether you want to adopt her child.

Here are some reasons why birthmothers choose agencies:

♦ They're young, and their parents chose the agency for them.

There are both pros and cons to young birthparents whose own parents bring them to the agency (from a prospective adopter's viewpoint). It's good that the parents know about the pregnancy and believe that adoption is the right path. However, if the young (under age 18) pregnant woman is not committed to the decision to place her child for adoption, she is more likely to change her mind.

♦ They called the agency, and the social worker seemed understanding and kind.

Younger birthmothers are probably more likely to turn to adoption agencies than attorneys, because they need more emotional hand-holding than do adult women. Thus, if they believe the agency social worker is understanding, they may decide to stay with the agency. Conversely, these women might be frightened of lawyers, or may feel that placing through an attorney is not quite acceptable or is in some way "cold."

♦ The adoption agency had an emotionally compelling ad in the Yellow Pages when the pregnant woman checked the phone book under "Adoption." She might be drawn to emotional appeals.

♦ Some birthmothers don't know about nonagency adoptions and think agencies are the only way to go.

> **Adoptinfo**
>
> This chapter concentrates on domestic adoption rather than international adoption. In other countries, birthmothers may abandon their child to an orphanage or place them in foster care. The adoption is usually not an open one involving meetings, although open adoptions are not unheard of. Read Chapter 11 for information on international adoption.

◆ The agency said they could choose the adopting parents from resumés of approved families, and this sounded good. The opportunity to choose the adoptive parents is a very attractive one to many pregnant women considering adoption.

◆ They might be suspicious that if they use a lawyer, their needs won't truly be represented.

◆ They heard about the agency from a friend or saw an ad and called the agency.

I think that most pregnant woman can find an agency that does meet their needs *if* they do some checking around. One problem is that sometimes they might call one agency, not like what they hear, and erroneously decide that all agencies are the same. Most birthmothers, however, will be satisfied with their first or second agency contact. Pregnant women who do a great deal of shopping around for an adoption arranger might be setting the adoption up for failure because they're finding something wrong with every contact, which might indicate that they are unsure about adoption.

Choosing an Attorney

As discussed in Chapter 6, in some states, lawyers can handle private adoptions from start to finish; in other states, the pregnant woman and prospective adoptive parents must find each other first and then come to the attorney to handle the legal work. In many cases, two attorneys must be hired; one for the birthmother and one for the adopters.

From a birthparent's perspective, there are pros and cons to arranging the adoption through a lawyer rather than an agency. Here are several reasons why pregnant women considering adoption might choose a nonagency adoption:

◆ They do not want to apply for welfare benefits.

Some adoption agencies require low-income birthmothers to apply for welfare programs (such as Temporary Aid to Needy Families [TANF], Food Stamps, Medicaid, and other state programs that might be available to low-income pregnant women) to help offset the cost of the pregnancy, although other agencies can and do pay for the birthmother's medical and living expenses through funds provided by the adoptive parents.

With an independent adoption, if state law allows it (and most states do), the adopting parents can pay the birthmother's medical bills. In many states, it is also legal for the adopting parents to pay for the birthmother's living expenses, such as rent, heat, electricity, and so forth. This may also be done by agencies as a "pass through" of expenses to the adoptive parents.

◆ They may want to live independently from their parents or other relatives during their pregnancy, and if they can receive living expenses from the adopters, this is an achievable goal.

◆ They want an open adoption or a confidential adoption.

If a pregnant woman doesn't like the idea of open adoptions but the agency she has dealt with promotes them, she may choose a nonagency adoption for more privacy. However, if the agency is into confidentiality and the birthmother wants more openness, she may turn to an independent adoption. (See Chapter 6 for more on open versus confidential adoptions.)

◆ They want a certain kind of family to adopt their child (for example, a family of a particular religion or racial background).

If an agency does not have the kind of family a birthmother wants, she might choose a private adoption to have more choices.

◆ They don't want counseling.

Some pregnant women turn away from agency adoptions because they *do not* want counseling by a social worker, therapist, or anyone else. In more and more independent adoptions, counseling is an option that the birthmother can take or leave.

◆ They don't know what adoption agencies are available in their area.

I've heard some birthmothers tell me that they aren't aware of local agencies that provide adoption services because the word "adoption" is not in their name. For example, Catholic Social Services and the Children's Home Society are two agencies that arrange adoptions. But because the word "adoption" isn't in their name, some pregnant women considering adoption might not think to contact them.

Meeting a Birthmother

Some agencies or attorneys (or other adoption arrangers) think it's a good idea for a woman to meet the people who want to adopt her child. Some arrangers recommend a meeting on a first-name basis, whereas others favor full disclosure of both first and last names.

Some adoption experts don't like the idea of meetings occurring before consent is signed because they worry that it could interfere with the pregnant woman's decision—making her feel pressured into the adoption. They prefer that meetings occur after the birthmother makes up her mind about adoption, independently of knowing the couple. (Others say that the birthmother needs to meet the couple to know whether adoption is the right choice for her.)

The argument that the pregnant woman might be less likely to change her mind if she meets the couple is actually used as a selling point by some open adoption advocates, who tell adopters that the birthmother will then know them and won't want to hurt them. Open adoption is also sometimes used as a marketing tool to convince pregnant women that placing a child for adoption won't be that painful, which I find troubling. Even when she knows the family that will be adopting her baby and likes them very much, the adoption of her child is still a loss for nearly all birthmothers.

The most important point to keep in mind for *you* is that most people are filled with trepidation about meeting a birthmother, and this is normal. It doesn't necessarily mean that a meeting would be wrong for you. However, if everything in you screams "No!" don't allow yourself to be pressured into a meeting.

If you think it's stressful to meet the woman who might give you her child—you're right. It's also stressful for *her*. It's also okay to not meet, if that is your choice. However, this might limit the number of agencies for you to apply to, since many agencies like the idea of a meeting.

CAUTION Adoption Alert _____

I've seen many people who are seeking to adopt become irrational, scared, and very unlike their normal selves when faced with the idea of meeting a real live birthmother. I call it "Rapture of the Adoption." It's similar to "rapture of the deep" in that the adopter has plunged to unknown depths far too fast to handle what's going on. This can also happen with *no* meeting; for example, if the arranger tells you about a child and says you have one day to decide.

If you reach this stage, you might feel out of control, silly, scared, overwhelmed, and excited. Keep your wits about you. Don't agree to adopt a child unless you have seriously considered the idea. Don't let Rapture of the Adoption overtake you.

Just as prospective adopters have concerns and/or fears about meeting birthmothers, pregnant women considering adoption are often frightened by the idea of meeting adoptive parents. It's always a good idea to consider the fears that a pregnant woman might have before meeting *you*, should you both choose to meet. Here are some examples:

- They (the adopters) will be smarter than me, and I might say something stupid.
- They'll think I'm too fat.
- They'll think I'm a slut.
- They'll think I'm a drug addict.
- I'll probably hate them, and they'll hate me, too.
- What if they're abusive?
- I'm scared.

When you want a child so intensely, it might be very hard for you to understand how someone could *not want* a child. It can be far too easy to assume that anyone who doesn't want to parent a child must be unkind or cold. Give her a chance! She might be the mother of the child you parent.

Questions to Ask

Whether you choose to meet with the birthmother yourself or decide to leave all birthmother interactions to the adoption arranger, you'll probably still want to obtain answers to some of the following questions.

- When is your baby due?
- When did you start thinking about adoption?
- Are you working with an agency or attorney? (If you've met her through your own advertising.)
- Are you feeling all right?
- How does the birthfather feel about the pregnancy? How does he feel about adoption?
- How do your parents feel about the pregnancy?
- How did you choose this agency/attorney/facilitator?
- Do you have a plan for your life, after the baby is born, either jobwise or educationally?
- What do you like to do in your spare time?

◆ Have you known anybody who placed a baby for adoption? Do you know any adopted people?

Questions to Avoid

Following are some questions you *should not* ask the pregnant woman in your first meeting, because they might make her very uncomfortable. (After you read these questions, you'll probably understand why. They are very intrusive and negative, and not good first-encounter questions.) This doesn't mean you should never ask these questions, either directly or through an intermediary. Just don't ask them in your first meeting.

◆ Are you sure you really want the baby adopted and you won't ever change your mind?

◆ Have you taken any illegal drugs during your pregnancy?

◆ Did the father refuse to marry you?

◆ Were you raped?

◆ How many times have you been pregnant?

◆ How many men might be the father?

◆ How many babies have you given up for adoption before now?

Interviewing Tips

If you decide to interview and screen birthmothers yourself, whether in person or by phone, follow these basic interviewing tips:

◆ Try to avoid holding preconceived notions about the birthmother as poverty-stricken, unintelligent, or anything else. Research indicates that she is more likely to be middle class and of normal intelligence. Listen to what she says with an open mind.

◆ If you have any questions that might be sensitive, don't ask them first. Instead, begin by making small talk. You need to build up a little trust. (Don't wait to ask them last, either. You might never get to them.) Some sensitive questions can be deferred altogether and left to the birthmother's attorney or social worker to ask.

◆ The way you word questions is important. Don't phrase questions in a way that implies what the answer is. (For example, "You're not working now, are you?" implies that the expected answer will be "no." Instead, ask "Are you currently employed?") Don't ask the question in a way that implies there is a "right" answer.

◆ After you ask a question, wait for the response. Don't answer for the birthmother or try to rush her.

◆ If the pregnant woman backs off from answering a particular question, ask other questions. Then consider rewording and revisiting the original question a little later, and you might get your answer. For example, if you asked, "Do you think prenatal care is important?" the birthmother might have shied away from the question because she hasn't been to a doctor yet. You could later ask, "Have you decided what doctor you plan to see?" By rephrasing the question and also asking it later, you are more likely to receive an answer. However, if the second try doesn't work, back off.

◆ At the end of the talk, ask the pregnant woman if there's anything important that you haven't discussed, then be silent and give her time to answer. Often people will say "No," and then they'll blurt out something they're worried about or that's important to them. It doesn't always happen, but it's worth asking the question.

◆ Understand that some birthmothers are not emotional or sharing kind of people, and they won't want to be your close friend. This doesn't mean they're not serious about adoption. Their primary concern is whether you would be good parents to the child and whether you seem to be good candidates; then they're satisfied.

Questions for *You*

Don't expect to be the only one asking questions when you speak with a pregnant woman considering adoption. In most cases, she'll have a few questions to ask you! Some of these questions might be appropriate, and some might not be. Here are a few questions you should be prepared to answer:

◆ How long have you been married (if you're married)?

◆ Can't you have children?

◆ Why do you want to adopt?

◆ What does your family think of adoption?

- ◆ Do you have any pets?

- ◆ How long have you been thinking about adopting?

- ◆ What religion are you?

- ◆ Will you work after the baby is born? If so, what kind of child-care arrangements do you favor?

- ◆ Who will take care of the baby if you're sick? (This question is more likely to be asked of a single person, and it's a valid one.)

There are also questions that you *should not* answer. Some of these might be answered later by your adoption arranger, and some are just no one's business. Even if you *want* to answer these questions, resist this impulse!

- ◆ What's your address? You may want to provide this information later, but *do not* provide it in your first encounter, which, by the way, should be in a public place like a restaurant or park. Not a fancy restaurant, either, because that might make her (or you) too nervous. Go for the mid-range.

- ◆ Who do you (and your spouse) work for? Don't get too specific, at least not during the first interview. It's okay to say, for example, that you're an engineer and your husband's a plumber. It's better to not say that you work for XYZ Electronics at 95 Maple Street. You don't want anyone involved in the adoption except the adoption arranger to contact you at work.

- ◆ How much money do you make? A birthmother who asks you this right away may be a scammer (see Chapter 9)—or a naïve person who doesn't know what to ask you. Either way, tell her that you make enough to support your family and to support a child.

CAUTION   **Adoption Alert** _____

If you have identified a birthmother and she asks you for money, refer her to your agency or attorney. Do the same if any other person she knows asks you, such as the birthfather, his parents, and so on.

Any exchange of money could be construed as "baby selling" by a third party, which might be a serious criminal offense, depending on state law. Note that I'm not talking about $20 for bus fare and a sandwich. I'm talking about significant amounts. (Although you should watch out for constant nickel-and-dime stuff.) Don't make this mistake.

◆ How much money will you give me? This is another sign of a possible problem or a naïve person. Tell the birthmother that you have to refer all financial aspects of the adoption to your social worker or attorney. If you are pressed very hard on the money issue, do not pursue this adoption. There will be other opportunities.

Real Life Snapshots
After advertising her desire to adopt, Alicia was contacted by a 15-year-old girl in another state, who wanted her to fly out to meet her. Alicia was ready to jump on the next plane out.
Ask yourself: If a 15-year-old girl who was a stranger from another state asked you to drop everything and fly there to meet her, would you? Without consulting with her parents, her attorney, or some other representative? I don't recommend it, especially knowing what I know about the high probability that this young teenager will change her mind. (Her age is a negative factor, because many younger adolescents change their mind about adoption.)
As stated elsewhere in this book, I think most adopters seeking a child from the United States should first look within their own state to adopt a child. They should retain the services of a competent and honest adoption agency or attorney. They should also strive to retain their own common sense.

"Dear Birthmother ..."

Another way for the birthmother to get to know you is to write a "dear birthmother" letter that explains why you want to adopt. (This is somewhat similar to the adoption resumé discussed in Chapter 12.) Often adoption agencies or attorneys show these letters to pregnant women considering adoption. It's a kind of sales pitch and can be a tough letter to write.

Basically, a "dear birthmother" letter is written by the potential adoptive couple or (usually) by the potential adoptive mom. The letter explains why the writer wants to become a parent and describes herself and her family. Often the letter includes positive and comforting words to the birthmother. Ask the agency or attorney who asked you to write such a letter to give you some sample letters that others have written. Although you shouldn't copy the sample letters, you can use them as a model to help you write your own letter.

Adoptinfo
The "dear birthmother" idea rose into prominence with the book *Dear Birthmother: Thank You for Our Baby* by Kathleen Silber and Phyllis Speedlin after its original publication in 1982.
This is a book that describes open adoption very positively and includes warm and realistic letters between adoptive parents and birthmothers.

"Dear birthmother" letters can get very emotional and can be very difficult to write. If you write one that makes you burst into tears, it's probably a good letter. Of course, you do *not* want the pregnant woman to think you're an emotional basket case. You want to convey the strength of your desire to adopt and at the same time show that you're emotionally stable and would be a good parent. Show it to your spouse, of course. But be sure to also show it to someone who is less emotionally involved (*not* your partner and *not* your parents). A trusted friend or someone you respect may be a good choice. Make sure they have a positive emotional reaction to the letter; if they don't, tear it up and start over again.

Birthmothers Who Change Their Minds

Probably the most intensely felt fear of adopters is that the birthmother will make an adoption plan—and then flip-flop and decide to raise the child herself.

Very few birthmothers change their minds about adoption after the baby is placed with a family. How do I know this? Because when I was researching a reference book several years ago (*The Adoption Option Complete Handbook*), I sent letters to hundreds of agencies and attorneys, and one of the questions I asked them was how many cases they had of an adoption falling through after placement.

Most had very few such cases. One agency said, "In 10 years, in 4 of 940 placements have children been returned to birthparents." Another said, "Of approximately 700 placements, there have been approximately 10 such cases."

Of the attorneys who responded to the question, I received such comments as "In over 1,000 adoptions, only 5 fall-throughs *after* the placement was made." And "One out of approximately 45 cases."

Of course, a birthmother may change her mind about adoption *before* placing the baby with you, such as right before or after the baby is born. This happens, and it's painful, but it's less agonizing than taking a baby home, getting attached to her, and then losing her.

Despite my research, you should ask each adoption arranger what their particular experience has been. Ask them what percent of birthmothers change their mind before the placement occurs and what percent change their mind afterward. This will help you gauge the risk that you face.

If Agency A says that 100 percent of their birthmothers go through with an adoption plan before placement, then you should probably be skeptical. Even the best arrangers have some birthmothers who change their minds. Conversely, if Agency B says only 10 percent proceed with the adoption, something is wrong—with their policy, procedures, or elsewhere. Too many women working with this agency are changing their minds. It's not your job to figure out what they're doing wrong. Move on.

Women who are in their second or third trimesters are less likely to change their minds about placing their baby for adoption because a woman still in her first trimester may be going through many emotional issues, may be under a lot of pressure from the birthfather and others, and the baby may not seem entirely "real" to her yet. Later, after she feels the baby kick and move around, she'll have a better sense of the reality of the situation. If she still is considering adoption then, that is a sign of potential commitment, although it's certainly no guarantee.

Familybuilding Tips

It's very important that a birthmother feel that the adoption decision is hers and that she was not forced into it by others—her parents, the birthfather, or anyone else. A study reported in a 1996 issue of *Clinical Social Work Journal* revealed that those birthmothers who felt pressured into adoption suffered significantly higher levels of grief than those who felt unpressured.

It's also true that a woman usually gives signals that she's ambivalent; for example, if she has no plan for her life after the birth, she is more likely to change her mind about the adoption. A good counselor should spot those clues.

Although it's impossible to accurately predict whether any particular woman will change her mind about placing her baby for adoption, researchers have studied birthmothers who changed their minds about adoption in the past and compiled the following list:

- The birthmother is under age 17.
- She has no immediate or future career/life plans.
- She lives in a big city.
- She was brought up by a single mom.
- She is nonreligious.
- She lives with the birthfather.
- Her mom disapproves of adoption.
- She lives with her parent(s).
- She is a high school dropout.
- Her mother or father has no education beyond high school.
- She (or her parents) are on welfare.
- She has friends who are single parenting and urging her to do the same.
- She has a very difficult delivery of her child.

You might think that some of these factors would lead the birthmother *toward* adoption rather than away from it. For example, a birthmother who is only age 15 is not in a good emotional or financial position to raise a child. But in most cases, she has not achieved the maturity to realize this. Also, she might be strongly influenced by her peers, and if her friends are parenting babies, she might choose parenting, too. (If she has friends who've placed their babies for adoption and are comfortable about that choice, that's a positive sign for you.)

Conversely, a 20-year-old woman is more mature and might decide that adoption is the best course for her child. She is less likely to be influenced by others.

> **Adoption Alert**
>
> Do not assume that if the birthmother you're talking to falls into one or two of these "likely to change her mind" categories, then all is lost. However, if she fits most of the high-risk categories, proceed with caution. Just because she doesn't have any of these characteristics, she can still change her mind. It's just less likely. Remember that nothing is 100 percent certain.

Education appears tied to the decision to place for adoption; the less educated the birthmother is, the more likely she will choose parenting over adoption. This may be because if a woman has no career goals (which is more likely with less-educated women), she may see parenting as a default choice. By "career goal," I don't mean the birthmother must be an aspiring brain surgeon. Wanting to be an X-ray technician or a hair stylist are career goals, too.

It's not clear why a woman would change her mind after a difficult delivery. Perhaps the birthmother has become worried about and attached to the child. Perhaps she fears she won't have more children in the future. Other factors are easier to understand. A woman who was raised by two parents is more likely to believe that her child should have two parents, but a woman raised by a single mom is more likely to think single parenting is okay. Also, if the pregnant woman is already on public assistance, she might not see a problem with single parenting; whereas, if the birthmother is very opposed to going on welfare, as many are, she might see adoption as a better choice.

A woman who is religious might believe that God has called her to place her baby for adoption, and she might also see adoption as a means to atone for having a baby when unmarried. (Some people think nonmarital childbearing is a sin.)

What to Do If It Happens to You

If she's going to change her mind, when does it happen and what should you do if she does?

During early pregnancy and even through the second trimester, the pregnancy may seem unreal to a pregnant woman, especially if she is in a crisis situation. (This is one reason why some adoption arrangers don't like to work with women in their first trimester. She has too many psychological issues to work through before she can decide for or against adoption.) Do not count heavily on adopting the baby of a woman who is only two months pregnant.

When birthmothers who have truly committed to adoption do change their minds, it's usually either close to the birth or just after childbirth. Sometimes the imminence of birth makes the birthmother realize that she wants to parent the child. In other cases, the birth itself has an impact. She may experience a change of heart after seeing the child. Or she may be affected by others, such as the birthfather or her relatives, who want the child to stay with the biological family. Very few women decide months after a child is born and with an adoptive family that they want the child back from the adoptive family—although it can happen.

Adoptinfo

In many states, when a birthparent consents to an adoption, the consent is either irrevocable or can be revoked only for a brief period. (Check the State Adoption Law Chart in Chapter 10 for more information.)

If an adoption falls through because a birthmother changes her mind about the adoption before the baby is placed with you, it hurts, and it hurts bad, even when you never saw the baby. It was already your baby, in your mind. I have heard from adopters whose adoption fell through that they would "never ever" think about adopting a child again. It was too painful, too scary, too hard. Clearly, they needed time to grieve. Do you know what happened later? After a few months, they decided to try again, and they ultimately did adopt a child.

How the Birthparents' Parents Feel

Often the birthmother's parents have a profound impact on her decision to place or not place her child for adoption. As a result, it's also a good idea to try to understand how they feel about the situation.

Although birthparents don't always tell their own parents about the impending adoption—or even about the pregnancy—when their parents do know, they are bound to have their own reactions, fears, and concerns. Here are some common issues among the birthparents' parents:

◆ Will the child be safe? Will he or she be loved?

No scientific studies have been done on what the primary concerns of a birth-parent's family are, but my take is that most are concerned about whether the child will be safe and loved.

The safety angle is a concern because many people are worried about child abuse. The agency (if you are using one) should tell birthparents to let their parents know that adopters are thoroughly screened by social workers in most cases.

They also might need reassurance that the child will be loved. Knowing that the adopters tried for five years to create a biological child and then considered adoption for another two or three years could help illustrate the couple's intense commitment to parenthood. Nonidentifying (or identifying, in the case of open adoption) information can also help the birthparents' family feel that the adoption is a good choice for the child.

◆ Will this be my only grandchild (if there are no others in the family)? Will my child have other children later on?

No one can know for sure whether the birthmother will have more children in the future. But many do. Had she chosen to parent her child as a single parent, the probability of marriage in her future would be diminished. Conversely, some studies have indicated that pregnant women who choose adoption for their babies are more likely to marry later on than single mothers who parent their babies.

The Least You Need to Know

◆ It's important to avoid stereotyping birthmothers.

◆ Birthmothers choose an agency or independent adoption for different reasons. It helps adopters to know why they make these choices.

◆ Birthmothers have questions about adopters.

◆ Birthmothers have different coping styles.

◆ Most birthmothers don't change their minds about adoption, but you should consider some risk patterns.

◆ If possible, convey reassurance to the birthparents' parents that you will provide a safe and loving family for the child.

Chapter 17

Playing the Waiting Game

In This Chapter

- ◆ Dealing with nosy family and friends
- ◆ Coping with your social worker
- ◆ Keeping a positive attitude
- ◆ Battling adoption jitters
- ◆ If you get turned down

You're pretty certain you'll be approved by the adoption arranger, or maybe you've already been approved, and you're waiting to hear about a baby or child. Now things should be easy, right? But you feel like you are slowly going crazy. Every day you wonder, will it be today that I hear something? Will it be tomorrow?

Waiting time is crazymaking for many adopters. They want the baby born *now*. They want the orphanage to release the child *now*. They want the foster-care system to send the child to his new home *now*. But they feel they have no control over when anything will happen. All they can do is wait.

Actually, there *are* things you can do. Like think about a name for your baby. Plan where her room will be. Pay some attention to *yourself*—remember, for the next 18 or so years, you'll be very busy attending to the needs of this other person!

This chapter shows you how to survive the "I got those waiting-for-my-new-child-to-come-home blues."

All in the Family

Your immediate family (your spouse and any children you already have) and your extended family (your parents, your spouse's parents, your siblings, and others with whom you're close) probably will drive you crazy during the wait to get approved to adopt and before your child's arrival.

This might not be very comforting, but people do it to pregnant women, too. Most pregnant women in their last trimester swear they are asked 20 times a day when they are due and why they haven't had the baby yet.

When people know that you're planning to adopt a child, they, too, will ask you repeatedly when the child will be coming. They're really not trying to drive you crazy—usually what they're doing is trying to show interest and that they care. You can tell them you're very excited and anxious but haven't heard anything, but as soon as you do, you'll tell the whole world. They'll probably hear your whoops of joy in Australia! This should stave off the questions for a while.

If you're faced with people telling you that you *can't* adopt, just tell them that the agency or attorney you're working with has approved you and does think you'll get your baby sometime. You can joke and say that it'll probably be sometime before you're eligible for Social Security. Later, when your baby does come, say that you're so fortunate, it worked out that you were able to adopt sooner than you expected.

If people ask you personal questions that you would rather not answer, you can be vague and say that you're not sure about that. If the questions are insulting from your perspective, such as how you possibly could want to raise someone else's problem, you could then say that you regard all children as blessings and will be thrilled when you can become a parent. Keep in mind that it is not necessary for you to share intimate details about your child or your life with others.

Curious Co-Workers

People outside your family—the people you work with and basically anybody who knows that you're adopting a child—can drive you bananas as well. They'll ask you how it's going and might also ask you probing questions that you'd rather not answer. You don't have to! Tell them what you want to tell them and then change the subject if that works for you. You can also say you are so pleased that they are really interested in your adopting a child. And you'll be happy to let them know if any news-breaking event occurs, and the stork suddenly drops off a child. Gentle and positive humor works well with most people.

Waiting Do's and Don'ts

The wait is the hardest of all for *you*, the future adopter. Sure, other people can aggravate you with interminable questions, but you have an awful lot of questions, hopes, and fears yourself. So how do you manage to get through these days, weeks, or even months of waiting?

Adoption obsession is very common for the person who has been approved and is waiting for a referral. It can be very debilitating and enervating.

You can do some things to distract yourself during this waiting period:

♦ Maintain a positive mental attitude, which is probably the most important advice I can offer. Sure, we all have doubts and fears. Try not to agonize over every problem that might happen.

♦ Keep a journal of your thoughts and how you feel about the adventure that lies ahead. You certainly don't have to be a professional writer to express your feelings and frustrations, your ups and downs. Many people find that the very act of writing down their thoughts frees them from considerable anxiety. It might also jog your unconscious into producing solutions to particular problems.

♦ Read books about parenting and adoption (but don't go overboard). You might also want to review children's books about adoption as well. (See Appendix G for specific resources.) Keep in mind that most authors have biases, whether they realize it or not. Some see adoption as an idyllic experience; others think adoption is a problematic institution that should be radically changed. The reality is probably somewhere in the middle.

Adopterms

Adoption obsession refers to constantly thinking about adopting a child. It usually occurs in first-time adoptive parents, although people adopting a second or third child might also experience it. A little obsession is beneficial, because it leads you to pursue different opportunities and to learn as much as possible. Just don't let it overtake your life!

◆ Meet and talk to parents, adoptive and nonadoptive. An effective adoptive parent group can be really helpful, because it allows you to see people with children they've adopted. You can learn the tactics they used to succeed, and the do's and don'ts of adoption.

◆ Take an exercise class or renew an old hobby. Staying involved with our interests makes us happy, and children derive benefit from happy parents. Hopefully you will maintain your hobbies and interests even after your child comes home. After all, don't you want to help your child develop her own interests? She may even share some of yours!

⚠ CAUTION **Adoption Alert** _____

Keep in mind that sometimes adoptive parent groups deteriorate into a kind of "gripe session" where members mostly come to complain about the woes of adoption or how tough it is to deal with their children's problems. Avoid those groups. (Fortunately, they are rare.)

⚠ CAUTION **Adoption Alert** _____

If you find yourself obsessing over adoption for more than a few months, ask yourself what the problem is. Is it fear that you won't succeed? Fear that you will have trouble parenting? Or something else? Make sure you want to adopt before you proceed.

Here are some things you should *not* do while you wait for an approval or to hear about your child:

◆ Worry about negative stories others tell you about adoption. Everyone will know a horror story, just as everyone seems to have a medical horror story they want to share with you when you are facing surgery.

◆ Make any other major life changes unless you have to. Adopting a child is big enough!

◆ Quit your job (if that's an option for you) unless you know for sure a child is coming or unless you're looking for a good reason to quit anyway. Believe it or not, some people quit their jobs after they're approved for adoption so they can devote their time to getting ready. That may be okay if you will be adopting within a month or two. What if the wait lasts as long as a year? You can find yourself with a lot of extra time on your hands.

Losing Your Nerve

People never get cold feet and decide that they really *do not* want to adopt, do they? Sure they do! As you get closer to the goal of adoption, you or your spouse may get panicky and fearful. Can you really be good parents? Can you deal with all the changes that will come with parenthood—or with parenting yet another child?

I like to compare the fear of adopting your first child to the fear many of us felt when we decided to get married. Getting the premarital jitters doesn't mean that you don't love your future spouse. What it means is that you're planning a major life change— and that can be frightening.

You don't need nerves of steel to adopt, but it's important to understand that there will be ups and downs in the process. If you know this is normal, it will make the experience much easier. Here are some ways to cope with the emotional highs and lows:

- Meet other people who have recently adopted. They can understand.

- Give yourself a set time to worry about problems that arise. When that time is over, order yourself to think about other things.

- Consider renewing a hobby you enjoyed in the past but have neglected.

- If you are spiritual or religious, try meditation or prayer.

- Remind yourself that there is a child at the end of this maze, and it's all worth it.

A little fear is normal. Of course, if you have very serious doubts and you are wondering if your motives are good ones, then you should think carefully before taking this major step—for your sake and for the child's sake.

Before you applied to adopt a child, you probably thought finding the agency or attorney was the hard part. Then you thought going through the home study was the *really* hard part. Then the toughest part was the waiting period after you filled out all the forms, had your home visit and answered all the social worker's questions, and waited for your home study to get approved. For many people, the last part of the waiting process is the hardest, once you are approved to adopt and you're waiting to adopt your child. You're in the final stretch before you succeed. Adoptive parents agree that although all this waiting for your child is hard, it's well worth it.

The Least You Need to Know

- If you feel your social worker is being unreasonable, discuss your concerns with her supervisor or the agency director.

- Keeping a journal, practicing your hobbies, and reading about adoption can help you get through the waiting period.

- Last-minute fears about adoption are nearly universal.

◆ If you are rejected by an agency, try to find out why. You might be able to re-apply later, or you can apply to another adoption arranger.

◆ The wait for your child after your approval to adopt is difficult, but well worth it.

Part 4

Raising Your Adopted Child

Too many people think that after the adoption is official, they can forget about it forever. Not true! Issues still can and will come up.

For example, your parents and friends will almost inevitably ask questions that you might not want to answer. So what do you do? One idea: Read this part first.

Your child will also have questions about adoption, and you need to be prepared to answer them—whether your child is 3, 13, or 33! This part includes a chapter on explaining adoption to children of all ages.

AS PAINFUL AS THIS IS, I THINK I NEED TO INFORM YOU THAT YOU CAN NOT BE MY BIOLOGICAL PARENTS.

Chapter **18**

Congratulations! We've Got a Child for You!

In This Chapter

- ◆ Clinching an adoption
- ◆ Preparing for your child
- ◆ Checking up on your newly-adopted child's health
- ◆ Finalizing your adoption

Sue and Tom knew that Cara was due any day now and that she had chosen them to parent her child. But when "The Call" came that Cara was in labor, they were stunned, nervous, excited, and scared.

Maureen had applied to adopt a foster child through the county social services agency. It had been six months since she'd been approved, and she wondered if she would *ever* receive a referral to a child. Then one day, the social worker called: They were thinking that Missy, an eight-year-old girl, might be a good fit with Maureen. Would she like to arrange a meeting? Maureen was so excited. She was maybe going to be a mom!

This chapter explains what to do when you finally find a child who is right for you, including how to handle the adjustment period just before and after your new child arrives in your home.

Sealing the Deal

Although there are no secret formulas or magic incantations you can say to be certain the adoption goes through once you've agreed to adopt a child, here are some tactics that may work for you:

◆ If you're religious, prayer may help. Not all adoptive parents are religious, and you don't have to be a member of an organized religion to adopt. But many adopters who are religious report that their faith helps them tremendously. If you aren't religious, try meditation.

◆ Show the social worker you're truly committed. Promptly fill out the forms you're given, arrange for your physical examination(s), and read any books she recommends.

◆ Compliment your adoption arranger. Not in a fake way—most people can tell when you're being nice only because you want something. But you can achieve the same goal more honestly by finding something that you genuinely like about your arranger, and complimenting her on it. Most people enjoy genuine admiration. And when your adoption arranger feels favorably toward you, she's more likely to go the extra mile for you.

Familybuilding Tips

One fascinating effect of finding something positive about another person is that, as you emphasize what you like about the person, you will probably find yourself liking him or her even more! Then the other person responds positively to you, and the relationship is further reinforced. This is a good tactic to use in adopting. (And in life.)

◆ Show your gratitude to your adoption arranger. If you are given a referral to a child, write a thank-you note expressing your joy, your hope, and your thanks for her help. Almost no one does this! I wonder why … I think it's very effective.

◆ Get into a PAM—*a positive adoption mind-set.* When you hear about a child you might be able to adopt, you must be realistic and understand that sometimes things don't work out. Still, be positive. Imagine yourself picking up your child. Think about how excited you'll feel. Imagine happy occasions with the child. Allow yourself to feel truly parental. I believe that a positive adoption mind-set can subconsciously enable you to work through many barriers that pop up. (Not all, but many.)

Adopterms

A **positive adoption mind-set** (PAM) is an attitude and feeling that you will succeed with this adoption and you will become a parent.

How is a PAM different from the adoption mind-set discussed in Chapter 2? The adoption mind-set refers to a goal-oriented state of mind in which you can develop a successful adoption plan. But when you reach the PAM stage, you have already found your child and are waiting for the adoption to go through.

Of course, one of the most important things you can do to help the adoption go smoothly is to take steps to prepare for the new family member who will soon enter your life.

Getting Ready for Your Child

Once it begins to sink in that you will actually be bringing a new person into your home and family, you'll start to think about just how much there is to do to prepare for him or her. In the following sections, I'll walk you through some of the physical and emotional preparations you'll need to make.

The Name Game

People preparing for adoption can spend countless hours choosing a name for their new child, particularly if they're adopting a baby or toddler. (If you don't know whether the child will be a boy or a girl, then choose names for both genders.) Here are a few issues to consider in naming a child—or changing names:

◆ The age of the child. If the child is two or over, her name is part of her identity, and many experts recommend that the name not be changed. (Some adopters give the child a new first name and they make the child's former first name her middle name, so it's not lost altogether. For example, if the child's birth name was Marie, they may change her name to Jenny Marie. They may also call her both names for a while, until she gets used to the "Jenny.") My view is that if the name of the child would cause embarrassment or taunting, perhaps it should be modified. Otherwise, don't take the child's name away unless there are compelling reasons to do so.

Sometimes when adoptive parents adopt an abused child, they want to wipe out all the pain of the past and give the child a "clean slate." To do so, they decide to change the child's first and middle names. They see it as a claiming tactic and as a loving act. The problem is that the child may come to the family with nothing but himself and his identity—a part of which is his name. If the child is old enough, consider allowing her to have a say in what her name will be.

◆ Naming the child after someone in the family. This is one way of showing a connection of the child to the family.

◆ To an older child you adopt, taking your last name is a very big deal. Danny, age 8, pleaded with his new family and even with his social worker to *hurry up* and finalize his adoption before September. Why? Because he wanted to go back to school as a "Smith." It was very important to him. The day that the judge congratulated persistent little "Mr. Smith" on the finalization of his adoption was a very happy day. (Danny's parents have the photos to prove it.) As was the day that he proudly registered for school as Daniel Smith.

> **Real Life Snapshots**
>
> Timmy, a very smart newly adopted child, told his new mom that he wanted to change *her* name. What did she say? She told him that by adopting him, she'd gained the best name possible: Mommy.

A Room of One's Own

Getting the child's room ready can involve a fresh paint job and new furniture or simply cleaning an existing room and supplying it with a few toys and decorations. In my family's case, we built an addition to our house so we could have an extra bedroom. At this point (before the child arrives), your child's room should be clean and safe and pleasant. And don't forget the childproofing, for infants and toddlers who'll be adopted. (Covering wall sockets, removing dangerous or breakable objects, and so forth.)

Have Health Insurance

Children sometimes get sick, so it's important to look into health insurance for your child *before* you bring him or her home. Federal laws now require most companies that offer health insurance to cover employees' adopted children right away, regardless of any "pre-existing conditions" they have. Be sure to enroll your child for your insurance within 30 days of placement in your home or, if you've adopted the child in another country, within 30 days from the day of the adoption. You don't have to wait until you finalize the adoption.

If your employer doesn't offer health insurance, consider the feasibility of purchasing
private or individual health insurance for
your family before you adopt, and be sure to
check into the provisions the company has
for new family members. Ask your doctor or
the business office in the local hospital for
information on private health coverage and
how you can find more information locally.

Adoption Alert

The Health Insurance
Portability and Accountability Act
of 1996 is a federal law that
states that "pre-existing" conditions
(health problems a child had
before entering your family) cannot
be excluded from insurance coverage that your employer offers.

Consider Child Care

Before the child comes home, you'll need to decide whether you or your partner will
stay home with the child and, if so, for how long. The federal Family and Medical
Leave Act requires employers of more than 50 people to allow workers to take off up
to 12 weeks of *unpaid* leave for the birth or adoption of a child. Of course, you don't
have to take the whole 12 weeks—a few weeks may be sufficient for you, depending
on your situation. If both partners work outside the home, each person may take up
to 12 separate weeks off, thus postponing the need for child care for 6 months. In
addition, some states and some companies allow for *paid* time off. Check with your
adoption agency and your employer's human resources department to see what's
available to you.)

When your child first arrives, try to budget at least a few weeks off to spend time
with him or her. Also remember that if you are adopting a child from another country, the cultural transition can be very shocking and upsetting for a while—you may
need to allow more time.

If both you and your partner will be returning to work, you will also need to arrange
a workable child-care plan.

Getting Your Newly Adopted Child a Checkup

Although you need not rush your baby or older child to the pediatrician on the day
you bring her home (unless she's ill), you should arrange for a physical checkup
within about two weeks. (Check with your pediatrician beforehand to find out what
she thinks is best.) Your doctor will want to review your child's immunization record
and, if they were performed overseas, might repeat the shots or check for immunity.
She'll also want to know whatever you know about the child's medical history and any
medical, developmental, or psychiatric problems that you're aware of. The doctor will

make sure the child's hearing and vision are evaluated as well as see if her growth seems on track, based on the information you have.

The pediatrician should also arrange for laboratory tests. If the child was adopted from another country, he or she should be checked for diseases and disorders common to that area, including anemia, hepatitis, sexually transmitted diseases, lead poisoning, and tuberculosis. Even if testing was already done overseas, it is important that it be repeated.

If the child has lived in an overseas orphanage or in substandard care in the United States, the doctor may order a stool check for intestinal parasites and a skin test for tuberculosis. Some children adopted from U.S. foster care may also be at risk for having contracted sexually transmitted diseases or bloodborne pathogens, and should be tested.

Repeat testing may be needed six months later, especially for hepatitis B and C, tuberculosis, and HIV. Your child's doctor can check with the American Academy of Pediatrics for the most updated recommendations.

Post-Placement Visits

If you adopted the child from another country, often the adoption was finalized in that country. However, if you're adopting a child in the United States or readopting a child from another country (more on readoption later in this chapter), the adoption process isn't over once you bring the child home. You can expect at least a few post-placement visits from your social worker before the adoption is finalized. (The time frame for finalization varies from state to state but it is often about six months after the placement of the child. See Chapter 10 for the laws in your state.)

The social worker will visit your home to make sure all is well and to answer any questions that you have. Based on these visits, the social worker will report to her agency and the courts on how things are going and, unless there is some serious problem, will recommend that the adoption be finalized.

An example of a serious problem is that your marriage is failing or your spouse has developed a substance-abuse problem, and there is clearly a detrimental impact to the child. The social worker's job is to make sure the child is safe and secure.

Finally! Finalization Day

Whether they admit it or not, most adopters breathe an inward sigh of relief when a judge says that the child is legally theirs. The adoption just doesn't seem "real" to most adopters until a judge decrees that it is.

The official process is called *finalization*, and it usually occurs in a courthouse (either in the courtroom or in the judge's chambers). It's a really good idea to have retained an experienced attorney to handle finalization to make sure it's done right. This is *not* the time to cut corners.

When you finalize your child's adoption in the United States, the finalization process varies, but you are given a date and time and place to appear.

The judge may ask several questions and review papers that have been drawn up. Many family court judges say that adoption finalizations are one of the few judicial proceedings they really enjoy—they enjoy playing a part in creating a family.

If you have other children, you may wish to bring them to the courthouse—assuming that you think they'll be well-behaved. (Most children are awed in the presence of a judge. But not all!) This is a momentous day for them, too, and it's good if you can make them a part of their sibling's formal entry into the family. Many families also plan a formal or informal celebration after the courtroom finalization.

Subsequent to the adoption finalization, you will receive an *adoption decree*, which officially states that you are the parents of the child. You will also later receive an amended birth certificate, which lists your names as the parent(s). These are very important papers. Be sure to keep them in a safe place!

Adopterms ___

A **finalization** of an adoption refers to the legal process wherein a child is declared to be the lawful child of the adopters, who now have all the rights and obligations of any parent.

An **adoption decree** is a statement in a legal document that grants the adopters full parental rights. It is usually given to the adoptive parents after the finalization. The document itself may also be referred to as the decree.

Adoption Redux: Readoption

In the case of intercountry adoptions, some countries issue a final adoption decree to the adoptive parents while they are in the country. But the parents may seek a *readoption*, an additional adoption in their home state beyond the one that occurred in the child's country. A readoption allows them to obtain an adoption decree and birth certificate from their state. Your adoption agency can provide information on readopting.

Adopterms ___

A **readoption** is a process in which international adopters adopt their children a second time, in front of a U.S. judge. (The first time was in the country of the child's birth.)

Why readopt? For several reasons. For one, a foreign document may be challenged by some people such as school authorities. The family who readopts may believe that a U.S.-issued birth certificate is a lot more credible to the average bureaucrat—and they're probably right. Another reason: Some states require readoption, not recognizing adoption in other countries as valid.

Readoption also ensures that a child has the full rights of inheritance from adoptive parents in the event of the death of one or both of them without a will. If only one parent travels to another country to adopt the child, then readoption is the only way the other parent can become a legal parent. In one case, an adoptive father who traveled alone to Russia was diagnosed with late-term cancer shortly after he returned. The family had to rush through the readoption before the father died so that the child would have a legal parent in the United States.

A readoption also may protect families from possible legal changes overseas that might retroactively affect adoptions finalized in the foreign country.

Familybuilding Tips

Some families celebrate two special days for their adopted children: their birthday and "Adoption Day."

Should you celebrate both? My feeling is that the child's birthday is most important and should never be subordinated to the day she arrived in your family. However, go ahead and celebrate both days, if you like.

Keep in mind that as children grow older, they might not want a big celebration on Adoption Day anymore. In addition, if you have biological children, they may be jealous that the adopted child gets two special days and they only get one. Some families with both biological and adopted children celebrate birthdays and also celebrate a "Family Day" rather than an "Adoption Day." Celebrations of Family Day should be tailored toward your own family's style and your children's ages.

Readoption procedures are not uniform from state to state (or even from county to county within a state). Some areas make it a lot tougher than others. It's a good idea to find out ahead of time (before you adopt) what the procedure is in your area so that you can have everything ready to go by the time you bring the child home. Ask your agency for information on readoption and check with your adoptive parent group for assistance.

Bringing Your Child Home

The day you finally bring your child home you'll probably experience a mixture of euphoria, tiredness, confusion, and a host of other emotions. You may have waited for this day for years. Even if it's only been months, those were very intense months indeed!

Don't forget to document the big day! Have someone take photographs or videotape the event. As your child grows up, she'll want to look back on that very special day when she officially joined her family.

The Least You Need to Know

- ◆ While you wait for the adoption to be finalized, prepare for the child's arrival: Arrange a room, choose a name, and investigate health insurance and day-care options.

- ◆ Set up an appointment with a pediatrician to have your newly adopted child get a checkup within the first two weeks of arriving in your family.

- ◆ Make sure you save your child's birth certificate and adoption decree in a safe place.

- ◆ If you finalize an international adoption, you may wish to readopt the child in the United States.

Here's Johnny! Introducing Your New Child to Others

In This Chapter

- Establishing your own adoption rituals
- Telling people about your adopted child
- Using "positive adoption language" and why it matters
- Explaining transracial adoption

Some people throw a big party and invite all their friends and relatives when they bring home their newly adopted child. Others wait a few days, a few weeks, or even a few months and then gradually introduce the child to new people. Others hold special ceremonies or rituals with other adoptive parents or even, in the case of an open adoption, with the birthparents. They may also tie in their adoption celebration with religious rituals such as christenings, naming ceremonies, and the like. Still others celebrate the day they finalize the adoption.

What's the best and most successful way to introduce your child to his or her new family? Does an adopted child need any more introduction than a birth child? This chapter covers these and other issues that come up when you adopt a child of any age.

Adoption Rituals

Although it may be instant love for you and your child, don't expect an immediate positive response from other family members, including your siblings, your parents, and your other children (if you have them). Your family will need time to get to know the child. If you're adopting an older child, don't expect him or her to take to your family immediately, either. After all, imagine yourself as a 6-year-old child being confronted with a new family and a horde of new people. It might be pretty scary.

Adopterms

An **adoption ritual** is a ceremony that acknowledges that a child has been (or will be) adopted into the family. Some people choose to incorporate mention of adoption into a traditional religious ceremony; others prefer to create special religious or nonreligious rituals that celebrate adoption.

Sometimes you can ease the introduction of your adopted child to the family with a special *adoption ritual*. This can be an established religious or secular ceremony or a unique event that you design yourself.

Parents celebrate adoption rituals for a variety of reasons. They may feel they need something beyond the usual christening or bris religious ritual, one that acknowledges the uniqueness of adoption. In addition, if the child is older, he or she might benefit from a ceremony that indicates that this family is his or her "forever family." Rituals can help solidify these concepts in the minds of children as well as adults.

Real Life Snapshots

Debra Smith, former director of the National Adoption Information Clearinghouse, and her husband, Gary, chose a formal Jewish ceremony to celebrate the entry of their son and daughter into their family.

First Justin, age 4, had a ceremonial *bris* (religious circumcision), and Talia, 2, had a naming ceremony. Both children were immersed in a ritual bath.

Then the Smiths and their children were honored by being allowed to bless the Torah. The rabbi offered a special blessing to the children and then gave them their Hebrew names. Said Smith, "We said that the children will learn from their Jewish family members, and they will also bring special talents and abilities to us from their birthfamilies."

Of course, not everyone wants to hold a special ritual associated with adoption. Although they don't deny the importance of the adoption, they don't feel compelled to create a special ritual to celebrate it. Instead, they rely on the same rituals used by parents whose children were born to them, such as christenings, family parties, and so forth.

If you participate in a religious ceremony in front of members of your church, synagogue, or mosque, you'll need to decide whether to mention that the child was adopted. Because adoption is a positive family-building option that you should be proud to be a part of, I encourage you to consider making the fact public.

> **Adoptinfo**
>
> In *Designing Rituals of Adoption for the Religious and Secular Community* (Resources for Adoptive Parents, 1995), Mary Martin Mason describes adoption rituals that could be used by Christians, Jews, and those who prefer a nonsectarian ceremony.

> **Real Life Snapshots**
>
> Since 1961, the Adoptive Parents Committee (APC) in New York City has celebrated its own annual candle-lighting ritual for new adopters.
>
> At the beginning of the nonsectarian APC ceremony, a poem is read. Then the candle-lighting begins. Families proudly display their children as they bring them to the stage.
>
> Part of the ceremony includes the lighting of the "Wish Candle" by a couple who has been trying to adopt. They represent all the other potential adoptive parents, and will, hopefully, light a candle for their own adopted child a year later.

Some rituals include the birthparents as well as the adoptive parents. For example, a birthmother I knew who wanted an open adoption arranged a ceremony with the couple who adopted her child in which she formally handed the child to the couple and then read a statement she had written. Afterward, the couple read promises that they were making to the birthmother and to the child. Everyone who attended the ceremony said there was a lot of beaming—and also some sniffling.

Some people choose to hold their adoption rituals shortly after the child is placed in their family; others delay until the adoption has been finalized, when they feel the adoption is truly official. How *you* feel may be entirely different, so when you hold your adoption ritual (if you choose to have one) is up to you.

Adoption Q & A

After you've adopted your child and introduced him or her to your family, friends, and acquaintances, be prepared for an onslaught of questions—some of them quite rude. For instance, don't be surprised if someone asks you whether the child's birth-mother used drugs or was an alcohol abuser, or how much the child *cost*. Of course, if the child had been born to you, no one would dare ask you those questions. You are under no obligation to answer them.

Here are some of the most common questions people ask new adoptive parents—in the way that they ask them—so get ready to cringe:

♦ Are you sure you'll be allowed to keep her?

 Many people have heard of those few—and very unusual—headliner media cases in which adopted children were sent back to their birthparents. So when they ask whether you'll be able to "keep" the child, in most cases, the sentiment behind the question is really a sincere caring and concern for you.

 If you want to explain your state law—for example, that consent is irrevocable after so many days—go ahead. If you're not comfortable with this, you can just say that everything is fine.

♦ She's so cute! How could her real mother give her away?

 When people wonder aloud how the birthmother could ever "give up" such an adorable child, explain that birthmothers usually make the adoption decision before the child is born. Physical beauty (or the lack thereof) is usually not a fac-tor; other reasons are the driving force. Whether you share those reasons with others—and I strongly advise caution before you blurt them out—is up to you.

♦ Are you sure the mother didn't have any diseases or use drugs?

 This line of questioning is intrusive and unfair. When a woman gives birth to a child, her relatives wouldn't think of asking her whether anything is wrong with her health. So why assume that just because a child was adopted, the birthmother was unhealthy? To answer, you can just say that the child is healthy, and you feel very blessed.

Real Life Snapshots

Sometimes you may feel like you *want* people to know your child was adopted, espe-cially if you are worried you might get blamed for a child's problem. For example, Tracey adopted a baby with fetal alcohol syndrome (FAS). Often she finds herself ex-plaining that the baby was adopted because she doesn't want people assuming that it was she who was an alcoholic and caused the baby's medical problems.

Adoptive parents like Tracey may need to work on how they feel about their child's ill-ness and to decide whether it is really that important to tell everyone that they weren't responsible for making their children sick.

◆ How much did you pay for him?

This is one of the most annoying questions that new adoptive parents report. It makes your child sound like a commodity, not a human being.

It's illegal to buy or sell children. What you paid were adoption fees, and whether or not you tell people how much they were is up to you. Remember, however, that there are heavy expenses associated with having a biological child as well.

My advice is to limit the number of people to whom you divulge the amount of adoption fees that you paid. Some people may attach a mental price tag to the child forever, and you don't want them viewing your child in this way for the rest of his or her life.

If, however, people inquire about fees because they sincerely want to adopt, you can give them a "ballpark figure," or you can refer them to your agency, attorney, or the local adoptive parent group.

◆ She'll probably be really good in math and science! (To the mother of a newly adopted Chinese infant)

When we think of racist assumptions, most of us think of negative ones. However, there are some "positive" ones as well, such as assuming children of a certain race will naturally be smart. In my opinion, the best thing to say is, "Some children are good at math and science, and some aren't as good, so we'll just have to wait and see."

Real Life Snapshots

"My mother-in-law will never forget that I told her Sharon's birthmother had a drug problem," sighs Julia. "Every time Sharon gets a cold or even misbehaves a little bit, my mother-in-law has to bring it up. She says, 'Do you think this has something to do with that cocaine?' I really regret telling her!"

It would have been better if Julia hadn't told her mother-in-law about the birthmother's drug use. But it's too late for that. Instead, Julia needs to face the problem head-on, before Sharon gets older and starts wondering herself. (Sharon is 3.)

Julia should tell her mother-in-law very clearly that Sharon is a healthy child and that there is no indication that her birthmother's drug use has hurt her at all. She should also say that the subject is closed, permanently. If her mother-in-law attempts to bring it up again, Julia should respond only with silence. Her mother-in-law will eventually get the picture.

Think Before You Speak

One common mistake new adoptive parents make is to tell everyone every minute detail about the baby. I know one woman who is very sorry she mentioned that her baby was born with traces of cocaine in her bloodstream—people still remember this fact about the child years later.

> **Adopterms**
>
> **Entitlement** is the feeling of being worthy and ready to take on all the responsibilities and obligations of parenthood. Everyone assumes that biological parents are entitled to parent their children. But adoptive parents feel like they must "prove their worthiness." Feelings of entitlement don't always come the first few days or weeks after the adoption. But as the parents take on caregiving tasks, this feeling usually does develop.

It's really not necessary to share private information about the child with everyone, including your parents. "My mother-in-law will never forget that I said my baby's mother wasn't sure which of two guys was the father," says Sue, an adoptive mom. "I don't want that to reflect on my daughter. I wish I had just kept my mouth shut."

Yet many adoptive parents think that they have to answer even the most insensitive questions. Perhaps this is because they don't yet feel a full sense of *entitlement* to their child; perhaps also because they've already had to share so much of their personal life with the social worker or attorney. *Remember:* You do not have to answer any questions that others ask you about your child's background and medical history. The Adoption Police won't show up to arrest you if you don't.

Positive Adoption Language

In Chapter 4, I mentioned the importance of avoiding adoption "slanguage" when speaking of birthparents. Now that you're an adoptive parent yourself, you may be especially sensitive to negative phrases and words.

Here's a sampling of words and phrases that may have a negative connotation, along with more positive substitutes:

Adoption Language

Negative Adoption Language	Positive Adoption Language
Real mother, natural mother	Birthmother, biological mother, genetic mother
Real father, natural father, "sperm donor"	Birthfather, biological father, genetic father

Negative Adoption Language	Positive Adoption Language
Give away, give up, put up for adoption	Place for adoption, chose for adoption, made an adoption plan
She kept her baby	She chose to parent her baby
Fake mother, foster mother**	Adoptive mother, mother
A child of their own, their real child	Their biological child
Foreign adoption	International adoption, intercountry adoption
Mixed race child, mulatto	Biracial child, multiracial child

** *"Foster mother" is an appropriate and positive term when used correctly: to describe a woman who is providing temporary care to a child. When it is used to describe an adoptive mother, it is inaccurate and is also often seen as a disparagement.*

As an adoptive parent, you may hate the suggestion that a mother is only *real* if she gives birth. Especially when you're the one who gets up every night to feed, change, and watch over your child! Those nights will seem pretty *real* to you and to your child. And they are.

Does this mean that the birthparents are then *unreal?* One birthmother says that people ask her whether she feels like she's not the real parent of her child who was adopted. She answers that she doesn't feel like an "un-mother." But she understands and accepts that her daughter was parented by a Mom and Dad who both love her very much. To her, they are all real.

It can be tremendously frustrating when you learn positive adoption language and you hear even your close family and friends using those old, bad words. Try not to get too angry! They don't have adopted children, so they might not understand. After they get to know your child, you may be surprised to find your family being outraged by negative comments others make about adoption and adopted kids, and smile to yourself as you hear them correcting others who say things like "real mother," and so forth.

 Familybuilding Tips

Want to teach people to use positive adoption language without lecturing them? Try *modeling*. If you're speaking with someone who keeps using the phrase "real" or "natural" mother, for example, respond by using the word "birthmother" whenever you can. After a while, you'll usually find the other person using the term, too! They're modeling your use of language, and often they don't even notice it.

Special Situations: Transracial Adoption

How will your family members react if you decide to adopt a child who looks very different from them and from you? They may be shocked and upset, or they may be accepting and positive. Or, more likely, they will be shocked and upset at first, and accepting and positive later.

Luckily, time seems to be a positive factor when it comes to transracial adoptions. As your extended family members become used to your child and get to know him or her as a person, they will likely become more accepting and loving. However, there might always be some family members who cannot or will not accept your child. If

> **Adoptinfo**
>
> One book that offers many practical and helpful suggestions to people who adopt transracially is *Inside Transracial Adoption* (Perspectives Press, 2000), by adoptive parents Gail Steinberg and Beth Hall.

you feel that your child is being treated negatively by certain relatives, you may have to adjust or curtail your visits. Before you take such a drastic step, however, confront the issue head on with the offending relatives, just don't do it in front of the child. Maybe there is something about the adoption or the child that they don't understand or that confuses them, and you can clear it up. Give it a try—communication is often a problem between extended family members, and it's best to resolve it when you can.

Some strangers or acquaintances will always ask rude or inappropriate questions about your transracially adopted child. You may be especially annoyed when strangers ask you intrusive questions like where you "got" your Chinese child from, making it sound like you either tripped over her and thus found her, or maybe you illegally purchased her.

First, try to keep in mind that most people are not trying to annoy you or violate your privacy. You could answer such questions by saying that the child was adopted from China, but if they persist, wanting to know what agency she was adopted from and other details, you could ask why they want to know. The answer might be that they are interested in exploring adoption themselves, or they know someone who is. In that case, you might want to provide information or recommend a parent group. If it's just nosy busybody stuff, you could say—if you are religious—that the child was sent from God, as all children are.

As your child grows older (older than two or three), she'll start listening to what you tell people about her. Maybe you don't want to be so forthcoming about her adoption anymore. So what should you say?

Here are a few choices:

- Tell the questioner that you can't talk right now.

- Give them the name and phone number of your parent group.

- If it's someone you know and you want to discuss the adoption with them, ask them to call you later.

- Tell them that *you* will call them later. If the person is a total stranger and wants to offer his or her phone number—and you're willing to do so—then you could call later or have a parent group representative call instead.

Real Life Snapshots

When Mona was asked where she "got" her baby from, she said, "Texas." But the person said, "No, I mean, what country, since I know from TV that there are no white babies in America, and you can only adopt mixed race crack-addicted ones."

Mona, a quick thinker, quipped, "Well, he's actually Swedish and came from a small town, called Nordstrom's" the name of a popular department store in Texas. The other person foolishly believed her.

- Tell them that you're really in a rush and just don't have time to talk about anything right now.

- Sometimes people will say that you are "wonderful" for adopting this "poor little orphan." Turn that statement around by saying that you are very blessed to be the parent of your child.

Keep your sanity intact by remembering that the most important thing is to educate yourself, listen to the advice of others, choose what works for you, and follow your own gut-level instincts. Do what is right for your child and for your family.

The Least You Need to Know

- Decide for yourself the best way to introduce your new child to your family.

- Give your family a chance to get used to your adopted child—and vice versa.

- Adoption rituals or ceremonies can be meaningful and helpful.

- Keep negative information about a child or birthfamily to yourself unless it's necessary to tell others.

Chapter 20

Using the "A" Word

In This Chapter

- ◆ Deciding when to explain adoption to your child
- ◆ Explaining adoption to young children, school children, and teenagers
- ◆ Answering sensitive adoption questions
- ◆ Explaining special situations

Lois was going through some old papers in the attic when she noticed a document that said something about adoption and starting reading it. To her shock, she realized the document referred to *her*. Thirty-five years ago, she'd been adopted—a fact she'd never known. Lois felt bewildered, betrayed, and shaken to the core.

This chapter is about talking to your child about being adopted. So why begin with a story about an adopted adult? To make an important point: There are still people out there who think the best thing to do is to pretend that an adopted child was born to you. Don't be one of them. Adopted children almost always find out about their adoptions. When they find out as adults (or worse, as adolescents), they may be shattered.

Your child will have questions about adoption as he grows up. I think the biggest mistake adoptive parents make in explaining adoption is either talking about it too much or not talking about it at all, as if it's a bad thing. This chapter will show you how to strike a balance.

Explaining Adoption: Like Explaining Sex?

Many people have compared explaining adoption to explaining the facts of life. How can talking about adoption possibly compare to talking about sex? Here are a few ways:

◆ You can't talk about adoption just once—as the child gets older, he'll have newer and tougher questions.

◆ The child's level of understanding of adoption becomes more sophisticated as the child grows up.

◆ Talking about adoption can be hard for adoptive parents, especially the first time. Talking about sex can be tough, too.

Why is it so hard for many adoptive parents to discuss adoption with their kids? Here are some reasons:

◆ It brings up memories of the pain of their infertility.

◆ They worry that it will make the child feel unwanted.

◆ They may not have much information to share.

◆ The adopters may feel like second-class parents.

◆ They may prefer to avoid the negative emotions an adoption discussion would bring up.

◆ They're afraid they can't explain adoption so the child can understand it, so they delay and often worry about it.

> **Adoptinfo**
>
> The discomfort some adoptive parents have when discussing adoption reminds me of a quotation I read in *Dialogues About Adoption: Conversations Between Parents and Their Children* by Linda Bothun (Swan Publications, 1994). When Carin presented her daughter Ashley, age 8, with yet another adoption book, Ashley said, "I don't need that book. *You* need that book."

Your child needs to hear about adoption from you. The following sections will give you advice on what to say and when to say it.

What to Tell—and When

Many experts agree that 3 or 4 is the youngest age at which a child can begin to have any concept of being born to a different mother. This is the earliest time to begin discussing adoption in little detail but very positive terms. As your child grows, you can tailor the information you give to fit the child, both individually and developmentally.

Adoptinfo
Some people advise new parents to tell their infants, "You're my beautiful adopted baby." Others disagree because infants don't understand adoption. Also, this constant repetition can make some parents fixate on the "adopted" part rather than the "beautiful baby" part.
As psychiatrist Denis Donovan, author of *Healing the Hurt Child*, says, "Babies have no need to 'know' about adoption. They need love, care, nurturance, safety, and challenge."

In the following sections, I break down childhood into three age groups and give you ideas for explaining adoption to children in each of these categories. Keep in mind that these stages are *not* cast in granite. For example, an explanation described here for "early childhood" might still work for a 7- or 8-year-old. Or it might be too simplistic for a more mature 5-year-old. When discussing adoption, consider your child's emotional and intellectual maturity.

Early Childhood: Ages 3–5

A simple story about adoption can suffice for the child who is 3 or 4. Most children like to hear their "adoption story." When my son was little, he loved his story. He wanted to be told again and again how Mommy and Daddy ran around the house when they heard he was born and how they called everyone. And how when they saw him, Mommy was so excited she jumped up and down like a little girl. And how she told Daddy to drive extra, extra careful on the way home with him.

Your child's story won't be the same—it'll be unique. Here are a few details to include:

◆ How you felt when you first learned about your child

◆ How you felt as you waited for the child to enter your family

◆ Your reactions when you learned the child would be coming

- What it was like when you first saw your child, in person

- What were the reactions of others in your family—your spouse, other family members, the child's siblings, and so on

- What the first few days with the child were like

The good news about explaining adoption to preschoolers is they like to hear about it and generally react very positively. In *The Psychology of Adoption*, psychologist David Brodzinsky explains: "They generally are told about being adopted in the context of a warm, loving, and protective environment. Thus the emotional climate surrounding the telling process is one which fosters acceptance and positive self-regard."

Familybuilding Tips

Children, especially younger ones, can be amazingly resilient. One minute, 5-year-old Tamara is upset that she didn't grow in Mommy's tummy. Then, while Mommy is agonizing over whether she said the "right thing," Tamara is running out the door to play with her neighbor. However, sometimes issues and concerns *do* bother children. If you sense your child is upset, some careful probing can often reveal what's going on.

Of course, very young children can't really understand adoption yet! This doesn't mean that when they *do* understand adoption, they'll feel badly about it. It just means that you should not assume your 3-year-old child has accepted adoption for life just because he is happy hearing the adoption story now. There will be other questions as your child grows up.

In fact, while you might feel that you should talk about adoption to your 3- or 4-year-old, your child doesn't really need to hear about it much. As the authors of *Talking with Young Children About Adoption* (Yale University Press, 1993) say, "Adopters and adoptees are often out of phase with each other regarding worries, concerns, and pain around adoption. For parents these worries and concerns surface before adoption and are often strongest during the child's toddlerhood, when the issue of beginning to talk with their children about adoption is often negotiated with some trepidation and sadness." But your young child might not even understand or care.

You can also supplement the personal adoption story with one or two books about adoption. I strongly recommend *Tell Me Again About the Night I Was Born* by Jamie Lee Curtis, a charming and beautiful book.

Adoptinfo
In *Parenting Your Adopted Child: A Positive Approach to Building a Strong Family* (McGraw-Hill, 2004) by Andrew Adesman, M.D., Dr. Adesman emphasizes that no matter how old your child is, or what the reason for the adoption, one best explanation is that the birthparents were unable to be parents. This covers all situations and takes the burden off the child, who may fear that he or she in some way wasn't good enough and that's why the birthparent chose adoption.

Information Overload

Some parents go overboard when they explain adoption to their young children. They buy five or six (or more!) books about adoption. They talk about adoption constantly. They press the child to ask questions. In their over-eagerness to discuss the subject, these adoptive parents can make their children tense and distressed.

Real Life Snapshots
Be careful that you don't overburden your preschool child with too much adoption talk. Adoptive mom Lindsey found this out the hard way. She'd discussed adoption frequently with her 5-year-old son, Jason, because she wanted him to accept being adopted. But his behavior began to deteriorate, and she could not figure out why.
One day he began sobbing over nothing. He said he was afraid she was going to have him adopted. Apparently, he thought all the talk about adoption was preparation for his leaving!
A child psychiatrist told Lindsey the constant references to adoption were making him feel alienated from his parents. The doctor said it was okay to talk about adoption if the subject came up—but that Lindsey should stop focusing on it. After Lindsey laid off, Jason's behavior improved.

Here are a few points to keep in mind:

 ◆ Select one or two adoption story books. Read them to your child. If she likes them, read them again. If she doesn't like them, put them away.

 ◆ Don't obsess if your child doesn't seem to accept her adoption. Give the kid a break: She's 4 years old.

 ◆ If your child asks a question when you don't feel ready to answer—such as why her mother didn't want to raise her—try not to clutch up. Take a deep breath and answer. If you really don't feel up to it, tell her you'll talk about it after dinner, tomorrow, or some other definite time. Make sure that you talk to her then.

♦ Take your child to adoptive parent group parties where other adopted children attend. At one party, an amazed 8-year-old told me that almost *all* of the children at the party were adopted! She had thought she and her brother were the only ones.

"Why Did Mommy Give Me Away?"

Kids often do *not* use positive adoption language and instead use what they hear on TV, in day care, or other places. So don't jump down your child's throat if she uses words like "gave me away," "real mother," and so forth. *You* use the appropriate terminology, and after a while your child will model on you.

The whys of the adoption choice by birthparents is probably the toughest question your child will ask you. I can't tell you how many adoptive parents answer, "Because she loved you." I think this answer is too simplistic for a young child. Think about it. You love your child, too. Does this mean that you might have her adopted? Does love equal leaving someone? That's the way your child may perceive it.

The point is, the birthmother may have loved the child plenty, but that is not the sole or even primary reason why she chose adoption. So what are some valid explanations that your child can understand—ones that don't put the birthparents down? Here are a few that might work for you:

♦ "Your birthmother wanted you to have both a mommy and a daddy and not just one parent. She couldn't provide two parents." (Of course, this explanation works only for two-parent families, and not for single adoptive parents.)

An older child may ask *why* wasn't a daddy around? But for most small children, it won't occur to them. If it *does* occur to the child, you could state that neither the birthmother nor the birthfather were ready to be parents, and they wanted someone who was ready and very excited and happy to be the parents—you!

It is a good idea (if it is true, as far as you know) to mention that the adoption decision was made before the child was born, so that the child will know there was nothing wrong with *him*. Instead, it was the birthparents who just weren't ready or able to be parents.

♦ "Your birthmother didn't feel ready to be a parent, but she wanted you to have good parents who were ready."

♦ "Your birthmother had problems that she couldn't fix, and she knew you needed parents who were ready to be parents."

For young children, I would not provide elaborate explanations on what the "problems" were. If the birthmother was young, that's understandable to kids. But I'd try to avoid stressing the point if she was a drug addict, alcoholic, and so on. Instead, it's enough to say she knew she couldn't be a good mom so she decided that finding someone else who could be a good parent was a good idea. And that lucky person was you!

♦ "Your birthmother was poor and also not ready to be a parent, and she knew that she couldn't provide what you needed. She knew that you would be well cared for with us."

I would not make a huge deal about the poverty thing (although it is true in most cases of intercountry adoption) because some bright children might wonder why you didn't give the mother money so she *could* be a parent. Another (and possibly more compelling) reason for the birthmother choosing adoption was the cultural stigma against unwed motherhood. This is particularly likely in other countries. However, I would avoid this explanation because it's too difficult for most young children to understand. You could say that you never had a chance to meet her and the decision was made before then.

Your "Chosen Child"?

Chosen child or *special child* are two phrases some parents like to use when discussing adoption with their young children. It's understandable: All parents think their children are very special! But if you use these expressions constantly with your adopted child, she may grow up believing that because she was chosen or special, she needs to be extra good or do really well in school. You don't want your child to feel she must always have to prove her worthiness. So don't make a big deal about her being a chosen child. Being adopted is a good thing, and it's good enough.

School-Age Children: 6–12

As children grow, they start to ask even tougher questions about adoption. For example, if the birthmother was poor, why didn't someone give her money so she could be a parent? Or, if she wasn't ready to be a parent, why didn't someone teach her what she needed to know? Why did she think a child had to have two parents? Your child might know lots of kids who have just their mom or dad. In fact, maybe you're a single parent yourself. If so, why couldn't the birthmother be a single parent?

The thing is, although school-age children often have the intelligence to ask these tough questions, they also usually still see the world in simplistic terms. People are either good or bad. You're either starving, or you're not hungry. If there's a problem, somebody should figure out how to fix it and solve it.

You probably can't explain the difficult social problems that lead some birthparents to choose adoption. You can, however, admit the obvious: The world can be an unfair place sometimes. The birthmother couldn't solve her problems, and the people she knew didn't know how to help her solve them, either.

Here's a tough thing to admit: You don't know how to solve all of the problems in the world, either. What you do know is that you wanted to adopt a child and when you learned about your child, you knew you wanted to be his parent.

Here's another aspect that's tough for adoptive parents to accept: Although the pre-school child may (and usually does) blithely accept whatever cheery explanation of adoption you offer, the older child is more skeptical and might feel sad for his birth-mother. He will have his feelings hurt if classmates and friends ask him why his "real mother gave him up." He might not want anyone to know he was adopted.

How can you make the pain go away? You can't make it all go away, any more than you can protect your child from many of the other slings and arrows involved in growing up. However, it really helps when you accept and acknowledge your child's feelings. If your child says he's sad about his birthmother not being able to be a parent, admit that it *is* sad. All the emotions associated with truly understanding adoption are not positive ones. And that's okay.

What if your child is teased about being adopted? Sometimes it's because the teasers are feeling inadequate themselves. In *Talking with Young Children About Adoption*, the authors cited the teasing of Teddy, who was told by other children that he didn't have to listen to his mother when she said to put his seat belt on because she wasn't his real mother. Said Teddy, "What do you think she is, a cartoon character?" The author later discussed the incident with her child, who said, "Gary is jealous. He doesn't have a father, and I do, so he's attacking my adoption."

Of course, not all children react so matter-of-factly. Here are some important points to convey to your child:

- Kids tease other kids about a lot of things: wearing glasses, being thin, being chubby, not doing well at math, or not being good at baseball. Sometimes, if they can't think of anything else, they'll choose adoption.

- Convey to your child that *you* are a real parent, and you will always love him and be his real parent. He's real, and you're real. You're not a "cartoon character," and neither is he.

- You might tell your child that he can tell his friends they can see you and touch you and hear you. This means you exist. This might sound silly, but I think it makes an important point.

- Do understand that sometimes teasing hurts. If you were teased because you're a "mere" adoptive parent and told you weren't "real," you'd be mad, too! In fact, adoptive parents sometimes are treated as if they were inauthentic parents by others, who don't understand adoption. The reality is that we can try to protect our children, but sometimes the teasing happens anyway. If they're prepared for it, however, they'll have a little more psychological armor. So that's your job.

Teenagers and Adult Children: 13–18 and Up

It's important that children know they were adopted before they reach adolescence; it's too turbulent a time to suddenly surprise them with the news. Even if your teenage child already knows, however, he may still have questions.

In fact, although you might be fully comfortable with the adoption by the time your child is a teenager, your child may be more curious about it than ever. As the authors of *Talking with Young Children About Adoption* say, "By their children's adolescence [adoptive parents] have often reached a deep love of comfort and satisfaction about adoption and truly feel that it was "no big deal." Yet the adolescent may question everything about adoption and need to acknowledge and work through a host of positive and negative feelings about it."

Why talk to teenagers or adult children about adoption? There are several reasons:

- They might have unresolved questions or issues and be afraid to ask you.

- They might want to search for birthparents but not hurt your feelings.

> **CAUTION**
>
> **Adoption Alert**
>
> Some adopted adults decide to seek out their birthparents when they grow up. Realize that the decision to search should be up to the adopted person, and not you. Don't press your grownup child to search. If she or he wants to search, try to be supportive and understanding. It's almost never a renunciation of you and your love.

- They might have forgotten the information you've given them before.

- They might have misunderstood information.

- Some information, such as medical or genetic background, will be helpful to them if they have biological children.

Bringing up the subject of adoption with an older child might be awkward. Try saying something like, "Joyce, I know you know you were adopted, but I'm wondering if you have any questions you want to talk about. A lot of people do. But of course, not everyone does." Then listen. Maybe your child won't want to talk about it right away. (Or ever!) Or maybe she needs time to frame her questions—rather than blurt them out as children do.

It might also be a good idea to review what you've told her in the past and update it to the adult version.

Sensitive Situations

In many cases, parents can tell their children that birthparents made a positive choice to place them for adoption. But sometimes the situation was not so upbeat or easy to explain. Here are a few situations that make telling problematic for some adopters:

- You have an open adoption, and the child already knows the birthparents.

- The child was the result of a rape, or the child of a birthparent with severe problems, such as drug addiction or mental illness.

- The birthparent's parental rights were involuntarily terminated by the state (usually in a foster child situation) because the parents were abusive or neglectful, or because they abandoned the child.

Open Adoption

Many people think that if an adoption is open (and especially to the extent that the child actually knows and has met with his birthparent), then there is no need to explain anything. After all, the child knows who you are and knows who the birthmother is, right? It's all known.

Wrong. Even in an open adoption, children need explanations about why they were adopted and what adoption is. Here are some issues that might come up:

♦ Why the child doesn't live with his birthmother. As I said before, most pre-school children readily accept whatever you say, so at that point you can explain that his birthmother was not ready to be a parent.

As your child grows older, he might wonder *why* she wasn't ready and how come he doesn't get to see her all the time. Then, you might want to explain more about the birthmother's circumstances. You'll also want to emphasize the permanency of adoption.

♦ If the birthmother is raising other children, why didn't she parent your child? This is a tough one. Remind your child that the birthmother wasn't ready to be a parent at that point in time. It was *not* the child's fault, nor did she think he was "bad." She just couldn't handle a child, any child.

If the birthmother already had children when she placed your child for adoption, she must have felt unready to parent more than one child. If she had children *after* your child was placed, she was older then, and might have felt more capable of parenting.

♦ If the child becomes angry with you, he might threaten to go live with the birthparents. You need to explain, as calmly as possible, that *you* are his legal parent. He may not choose to live with anyone else until he grows up. At one level, he won't like this. At another level, it'll make him feel safe. Children really don't want to call all the shots, even when they think they do.

Unfit Birthparents

Are there some things children should not be told? My opinion is that it's a bad idea to tell small children that they are the product of rape or that their birthmother was psychotic. This is tough information for anyone at any age to grasp and to accept.

So when do you tell them, if ever? I'm going against the grain here, but I think the child should be an adult (or nearly an adult) before hearing such painful and sensitive truths. Certainly she should know well before she is old enough to search for her birthparents—finding out the circumstances of her birth then would be extremely traumatic.

If the problem was something like alcoholism or drug addiction, it's probably a good idea to tell your child as a young adult or perhaps as early as age 10 or 11. Remember, children are very judgmental at that age. Try *not* to chime in if your child condemns her birthmother for her "bad" behavior, but explain that some people have addiction problems.

Be sure you know what your child is learning about substance abuse in school. If he is told that alcoholism is hereditary, and he knows a birthparent had a substance-abuse problem, he might feel doomed to becoming an alcoholic or a drug addict. You need to reassure him that studies show that substance abuse *can* sometimes be hereditary but certainly that no one is condemned to such a fate. You can tell your child that some people think such problems are mostly due to the family environment, and no one really knows for sure what's true. Tell him it's important for all kids to avoid drugs and alcohol, no matter what their family background, because they're too risky for kids.

Real Life Snapshots

Jennie says her daughter's birthmother was a crack addict who was also HIV-positive. How did she explain that to her adopted daughter?

Jennie told her daughter that her birthmother was very sick. When the birthmother learned that there was a special medicine (AZT) she could take during pregnancy to keep her baby from getting sick too, she took it. She took the awful-tasting medicine, and she got into a special program to help her baby be as safe as possible. But she knew that she was too sick to be a good parent. So she chose adoption.

This is a good explanation, because it's true. It doesn't romanticize the birthmother, but it doesn't demonize her either. It makes her sound like a real person—which she was.

Foster Children

If you've adopted a foster child, usually the birthparent's rights were involuntarily terminated because of abuse, neglect, or abandonment.

When you've adopted a child who was abused or badly neglected by a birthparent, it can be extremely hard to work up any positive feelings or sympathy for the birthparents. In fact, you might be very angry about what they've done to your child. It's not easy to forgive someone who has hurt your child so badly.

But if you don't try to find it in your heart to somehow accept what has happened, you could end up hurting your child. Many children think that what their parents did was their fault. They also sometimes think that if their birthparents were "bad," then they might grow up to be bad, too. So avoid saying unkind words about the birthparents to your child.

This doesn't mean you can say only sweet things about the birthparents. Try instead to convince yourself (and your child) that the birthparents simply could not be good parents. Maybe nobody ever taught them how. Maybe they couldn't overcome their problems, or they didn't realize they had problems. Don't excuse their problems or depict them as victims. While you don't want to condemn them, neither do you want the child to think their behavior was okay or unavoidable.

With the child in foster care, the birthparents were given a chance to solve their problems, but they did not. For whatever reason, they weren't capable of being good parents. So the child was placed with someone who was ready and capable: you.

The Least You Need to Know

- It's important to tell your child he was adopted, preferably before he starts school.

- Younger children will be happy with a simple story about their adoption. Older children and teenagers may be given more details.

- Don't tell the child that her birthmother chose adoption only "because she loved you." Explain that the birthmother was not ready to be a parent.

- Don't say negative things about the birthparents to your child.

Chapter 21

As They Grow

In This Chapter

- ◆ Dealing with differences between adopted children and their parents
- ◆ Common fears of adopted children
- ◆ Bad behavior: disciplining the adopted child
- ◆ Coping with serious problems

Carol was worried that something was seriously wrong with Maria, the child she'd adopted from Russia at the age of three. Three months after the adoption, Maria was nearly obsessive about food. Sometimes she over-ate to the point of gorging. She also hid food in her closet. Was Carol a bad mother?

As discussed in earlier chapters, most adopted children grow up to be healthy adults. But some adopted children, like some biological children, will need medical or psychological treatment.

This chapter discusses common physical, emotional, and behavioral issues that may occur after the adoption.

Your Kid Doesn't Look Like You—Deal with It!

Some adopters have difficulty accepting a child who looks very different from what they envisioned. (However, most adopters don't have a problem with the fact that their kids probably won't look much like them. The people who have the problem are usually outside the family.) Instead, it's often behavior problems that are the toughest part of parenting, whether your child enters your family by birth or adoption.

Adoptinfo

Back in 1976, Michigan researchers looked at a large sample of adoptive and non-adoptive families to see whether there were any physical similarities between parents and children. They found significant similarities between the biological parents and their children, which was no surprise. But although the significance was less, the researchers *also* found significant similarities in the stature and weight of the adopters and their children.

How we view ourselves and each other affects how we act and even how happy we are with each other. In 1980, researcher Lois Raynor studied adopted adults and their adoptive parents and reported her findings in *The Adopted Child Comes of Age*. She found that the more they saw themselves as similar to each other, the happier they were. For example,

- Of adopted adults who said they were "very much like" their adoptive parents, 97 percent said their adoption experience was satisfactory.

- Of adopted adults who said they were "unlike" their adoptive parents, 52 percent said their adoption experience was satisfactory.

- Of those adoptive parents who thought their adopted children were "like" them in appearance, interests, intelligence, or personality, 97 percent were happy with the adoption experience.

- Of those adoptive parents who thought their adopted children were "unlike" them in appearance, interests, intelligence, or personality, 62 percent were happy with the adoption experience.

The important thing to note in Raynor's study is that it did not matter whether the adopted child and adoptive parent actually seemed similar to outsiders! Adoptive parents and their children who saw similarities between each other were happier with each other, regardless of whether anyone else saw those similarities. One suspects that if a similar study were done on biological children and their parents, the happier ones would also be those who perceived similarities in each other.

Eventually adopted children *do* notice physical differences between themselves and their parents, whether it's their and your skin color, ethnic appearance, or some other characteristic. Your child may say that she wishes her skin was the same color as yours or that she had curly hair like yours, instead of straight hair. She will also realize (by the age of five or six) that other people notice that she doesn't look much like you.

It's best to not deny that there are differences or try to avoid the topic. Tell your child that not all biological children resemble their parents—some look very different. But do acknowledge the physical differences between you. And do realize that it is positive that your child wishes she could look like you. You might share with her that you wish she had been born from you and your spouse, but that it wasn't possible.

Remember, too, that sometimes adopted children *do* resemble their adoptive parents. Just because someone is not genetically "yours" doesn't mean she will have nothing in common with you.

Familybuilding Tips

Many adoption experts urge adopters to acknowledge and accept the differences between themselves and their children. I think this is good advice for any parent, because it helps to see your children as individuals. However, some parents go overboard and tend to concentrate on those differences. Try to do both: Acknowledge the differences and celebrate the samenesses. Achieve a balance.

Different Strokes for Different Folks

Other potential differences beyond physical appearance also exist. For example, you may have trouble understanding why your child isn't more athletic/bookish/outgoing/musical, like you are. If you love to party, you may have trouble understanding a child who is shy.

As an adoptive parent, it's understandable if you wonder about the potential effect of heredity and environment on your adopted child. In fact, one rather humorous tendency among some adoptive parents is to unconsciously blame any health or behavioral problems the child may have on heredity, while taking credit for positive achievements of the child.

Of course, this isn't even close to being true. Most people are a product of both their heredity and their environment, and it's usually impossible to sort out which is the driving force.

Real Life Snapshots

Sandy's son, Todd, is not performing very well in school, but she's doing her best to give him the help he needs. She doesn't know why he's having so much trouble. But sometimes she secretly wonders whether it's because his birthparents were poor students, too. Or maybe it's because he was adopted?

Change the scenario. Sandy's son, Todd, just graduated *summa cum laude* from Harvard Medical School. He's brilliant and has a great future ahead of him. Sandy knows in her heart that the wonderful environment she and her husband Jim have provided have made this special graduation day—and Todd's stellar future—a possibility.

What's important to keep in mind here is to avoid laying *too much* blame on heredity because often you can take many actions to correct problems a child has. The best thing to do is to encourage various interests in your child and see what works. Maybe your daughter will love ballet just like you did; maybe she'll prefer field hockey. Maybe your son wants to be a benchwarmer at the football game like you were; maybe he longs to be the star quarterback. What you should do is tailor your parenting and lifestyle to meet the needs of your child.

Common Fears of Adopted Children

All children have fears, no matter how good a parent you are. Adopted kids have the normal fears of the dark and monsters under the bed. But sometimes adoptive children may have special fears (especially if they were adopted after age two). Here are some of those fears:

- Fear of separation/fear of losing parents
- Fear of being kidnapped by birthparents

- Fear of what other people will think about them being adopted

- Fear of repeating the mistakes of the birthparents (suicide, drug or alcohol abuse, early pregnancy)

- Fear that biological siblings or birthmother are suffering or have died

Adoptinfo

Studies suggest that adopted children who most frequently need help are those who are adopted after age three.

If your child exhibits any of these fears, it's a good idea to be supportive and listen, and let her know that you will always be there when you're needed. If the fears start to dominate your child's life, consider seeking therapy for her.

Problem Child

Do adopted kids ever have emotional or psychological problems? Sure they do. Sometimes they hit a temporary rocky road; other times they may need professional help. Probably the biggest time when kids experience trouble is during adolescence, generally a difficult time for most children. In this section, I'll look at some of the most common problems some adopted children face.

"You're Not My Real Mom"

"I hate you! You're not my real mom! My real mom would never be as mean as you are!" If you hear these words from your child, it can be a shattering experience. You may wonder about your competence and whether your child loves you at all.

The good news is that in most cases, your child doesn't mean what she said. She's had an emotional outburst because she's mad that you didn't buy her the CD she wanted. Or you wouldn't let her do what she thinks everybody else is allowed to do. Or you are punishing her for a wrongdoing.

Adoptinfo

An adoption issue is a problem that preoccupies and distresses an adopted child and is related to adoption. For example, fear that a birthparent might kidnap the child is an adoption issue.

So what *is not* an adoption issue? Any problem not related to the adoption. For example, a child who is temperamentally shy or a child who hates his teacher isn't experiencing an adoption issue. Remember, many problems adopted kids experience have nothing to do with being adopted.

You should handle outbursts like this exactly as any biological parent would. Evaluate whether you were right or wrong. Are you being fair? Is the punishment appropriate for the crime? If you feel you've done everything right, hold your ground. If you cave in every time the "real parent" charge comes up, your child will use it repeatedly to control you, and that's not good for either of you.

So what you can say, in response to the "you're not my real mom" outburst, is that you *are* her real mom, in the first sentence. And then say that you have decided it's important for her to do what you've said. Say you love her and you feel sad that she's angry, but you'll talk about it later when you're both calmer. (You might also add that parents who raise biological children don't let their kids do whatever they want, either.) Then take a deep breath, shed a few tears in private, and move on. (Your child might cry, too. She might be surprised at her own outburst.)

Discipline Disasters

Sometimes adopters are so thrilled they've finally adopted a child that when the child misbehaves later on—as children invariably do—they let the behavior go because they are unwilling to discipline their child. But if any parent, adoptive or nonadoptive, lets a child rule the household, that parent is in for big trouble. To obtain many more parenting tips for kids from infancy through adolescence, read *Parenting Your Adopted Child* (McGraw-Hill, 2004) by Andrew Adesman, a noted pediatrician in New York. (For the record, I helped him write the book.)

Familybuilding Tips

The authors of *The Adoptive Family in Treatment* discuss a problem sometimes inadvertently caused by adopters who overly coddle their child—the creation of a little prince or princess who rules the household.

Parents need to realize that they, not the child, are in charge. Don't let your child run wild and take charge of your family. Even though you wanted this child for so long and you love her intensely, you do her no favors by constantly giving in to her demands. The cold, cruel world won't do that.

Other adopters don't feel a sense of entitlement to be a full and complete parent to the child. They imagine the birthmother thinking of them as bad parents for losing their tempers and yelling. The truth is that if the child *had* remained with the birthmother, she would probably punish him for his misbehavior, too. Because you are parenting the child and she's not, it's your job.

Echo Response

Sometimes a child adopted at an older age can display what therapist Claudia Jewett calls an *echo response*. This refers to hypervigilant behavior based on fears the child has developed from past experiences. For example, Jewett counseled a child who would never get into blue cars (although other color cars were okay). Through questioning the child, Jewett learned that the state social services cars had always been blue. The child associated blue cars with being taken away and put in yet another foster home. Understanding and desensitization can work to solve these kinds of problems.

Food Fights

If "food is love," then an early-life shortage of food can be interpreted very strongly and negatively by some children. Actually, food problems are fairly common among kids who are adopted after infancy, particularly older kids from other countries. Here are a few food issues:

♦ Extreme pickiness about foods. Kids who've lived in an orphanage, group home, or other place where they didn't always get enough to eat—or got extremely bland food—need to get used to the many new foods you serve.

♦ Gorging on food. Food gorging can really upset parents, especially when a child gorges to the point of vomiting. This is not a sign of bulimia; usually, the adopted child who gorges wants to be sure that he or she will have enough food to eat, unlike the past. Food gorging is especially common if the child was malnourished. The problem is nearly always temporary.

Adoptinfo

If your child is exhibiting problematic symptoms that are not causing imminent harm to himself or others, don't rush your child off to the nearest psychologist or psychiatrist. (This is especially true if you just adopted your child from another country. It takes time to get used to a new family/culture/lifestyle/climate!) Instead, start with your pediatrician. Ask the doctor to give your child a complete physical examination. If all is well with your child physically, your doctor sometimes may advise you to seek the help of a mental health professional.

♦ Hoarding and hiding food. This is a common problem for children who never knew where their next meal was coming from. They need time to learn that food is plentiful in their new home. Remember Maria from the beginning of this chapter? After her parents discovered her hoarding food, they told her she could have her own kitchen shelf stocked with foods she liked. For a while, Maria repeatedly checked the cabinet to make sure that the food was there. After a while, she stopped looking—and hoarding.

Serious Trouble

This section is about more serious behavioral and psychological problems that some adopted children sometimes have, problems that are difficult for them and for their parents. They may stem from earlier abuse or from a lengthy stay in foster care or an orphanage. Or they may just be caused by problems that life throws at them, and they need some help. (Even kids have problems, although adults often forget this.)

Troubled adopted children (like troubled nonadopted children) will often display observable signs that they need help. The following list shows a few possible indicators.

If your child exhibits just one or two of the problems described in this section (with the exception of the last four items on the list), your child may have a temporary problem. But if three or more of these problems show up, or any of the last four, your child needs professional help.

- ◆ Sudden loss of appetite or extremely increased appetite

- ◆ Change in sleep habits (needing too little sleep or sleeping all the time)

- ◆ Serious drop in grades

- ◆ Frequent lying or evasion

- ◆ Deteriorating personal hygiene

- ◆ Obsession with fears and worries

- ◆ Loss of interest in hobbies or friends

- ◆ Lack of friends

- ◆ Association with undesirable friends

> **CAUTION**
>
> **Adoption Alert**
>
> Keep in mind that after placement and for at least several months, older adopted children will nearly always act out. This is normal. If they're bad, will you still want them? They want to know, so they have to test you. As you discipline the bad behavior, make sure you always show that you still love the child.

- ◆ Persistent "orphanage behavior," such as rocking or head-banging that occurs beyond the toddler years

- ◆ Slow physical or mental development

- ◆ Physical violence or attacks

- ◆ Antisocial behavior such as stealing, starting fires, or harming animals

- ◆ Self-injurious behavior (cutting or harming oneself)

- ◆ Substance abuse

Adoptinfo

Some research indicates that adopted children are more likely to see therapists than nonadopted kids. Does this mean adopted kids are more troubled than nonadopted kids?

Not necessarily. For one thing, many studies include abused children and children who were adopted after years in foster care, whose problems most likely stemmed from their early life experiences. Also, some biased therapists may be more likely to find problems in adopted kids than in nonadopted kids. Finally, adoptive parents are more likely to take their children to therapists when they see signs of a possible problem.

Remember, the majority of adolescents who were adopted as infants or children adopted under age three do very well, based on study after study.

For example, preliminary results from the Sibling and Interaction Behavior Study (SIBS), released in 2002 and reported in *Adoptive Families* magazine, are very favorable. The SIBS study is a large study based at the University of Minnesota of nearly a thousand kids, about half of whom were adopted as infants or toddlers and the rest born to the family. Most of the children are adolescents now. The study has shown that the adopted children have the same warm relationship with each other that nonadopted siblings have. (It's not all happiness and light all the time, of course! It never is, with sibs.) The study has also shown that, so far, the adopted kids don't have any more emotional problems than the nonadopted kids. This is good news for parents who are worried that adoption may inevitably mean neurosis. It doesn't.

Getting Help

What if your child needs a therapist? It's important to find a sympathetic, knowledgeable therapist to help you and your child. Some therapists are biased against adoption in general; they attribute all problems to the adoption itself. Others think adoption is completely irrelevant and look for some other cause, without realizing that some children are genuinely confused and troubled by their adoptive status.

Psychiatrist Steven Nickman has bluntly stated that sometimes mental health professionals can make already-existing problems worse for adopted children. Nickman cites several problems that therapists may display when treating adopted children:

◆ Not understanding the difference between adopting a child from foster care or from an orphanage and adopting a newborn infant. That's a big difference!

◆ Not understanding the difference between confidential adoption and open adoption.

◆ Not recognizing or acknowledging the bond that exists between the parents and the adopted child; not perceiving similarities between the parents and adopted child.

Adoptinfo

A 1993 issue of the *Journal of Child Psychology and Psychiatry* studied adopted and non-adopted children referred for therapy. Researchers found that adoptive families had more supportive resources than nonadoptive families.

◆ Providing inappropriate therapy. The therapist might insist on working exclusively with the child and shutting the family out, or might ignore the child's previous history.

So how do you find a qualified therapist? Don't be afraid to ask your pediatrician or other physicians for recommendations. You can also contact a local teaching hospital and request a referral. Your network of friends and family might also be able to help.

Adoption Experts

A therapist who identifies herself as an adoption expert is more likely to see adoption as problematic. But a therapist who knows nothing about adoption may not understand the conflicts that can occur in an adopted child. Try to choose someone who is experienced in childhood or adolescent problems and who is neither fixated on adoption as inevitably *the* problem or someone who blithely ignores it.

Whatever type of expert you choose, ask the therapist the following questions as a screening tool:

◆ How many adopted children have you treated? If you feel it's important that the therapist have experience in treating adopted kids, then if she has only treated one or two adopted children, she wouldn't work for you.

◆ Of the adopted children you've treated, in how many cases was the main problem related to adoption? If the therapist says 95–100 percent of the adopted children she treated had problems directly related to adoption, seek another therapist. Adopted kids may have life problems and distresses that are related to adoption *and* **not** related to adoption. If the therapist sees an adoption monster behind every adoptee, she'll miss important information needed to help a child.

◆ Do you think adopted children are often very disturbed because they were adopted? If the therapist says that some children are distressed about adoption, that's okay. If she says all adopted children or the overwhelming majority of them are distressed, this reveals a bias related to the example given in the preceding bullet item.

◆ Do you think adopted children are rarely disturbed about being adopted? If the therapist thinks adoption never bothers kids, then she could miss something important, as well. In fact, it's unlikely you'll receive this answer from a therapist. If you do, I'd seek out someone else.

◆ Do you have any connection to adoption—are you an adoptive parent, adopted person, or birthparent? Or do you perform adoption evaluations? It's usually okay if the therapist has a connection to adoption—but it's best to *know* what her bias might be. For example, if she is a birthmother who thinks adoption causes scars in everyone involved, she obviously would be the wrong therapist for your child. Conversely, if she's an adoptive parent who believes in some sort of Adoption Nirvana, just say no to her as your child's therapist!

When a Problem Is Too Hard

Some adopters decide they cannot handle severe physical, emotional, or psychiatric problems that show up in their adopted child. What happens when a child's behaviors fall too far short of the parents' expectations?

Researchers at the University of Southern Maine identified several stages of an impending adoption failure:

1. In the first stage, *diminishing pleasures*, the joys of parenthood were far overwhelmed by the hardships.

2. Next, the parents want the child to change his behavior, but he can't or won't change. The parents may begin complaining how difficult this child is. It's a good idea for the parent to gain feedback and support from an adoptive parent group at this point.

3. At the *turning point* stage, an event causes the parents to feel they can no longer parent the child. The child may exhibit frightening or cruel behavior, or he may run away repeatedly. The parents start to imagine what life would be like if the child were no longer part of the family.

4. The *deadline* stage is just what it sounds like: The parents give the child an ultimatum. If the child doesn't do what the parents ask, they take steps to take the child away from the family.

Sometimes the adopters ask the agency or attorney to take the child back and place him with another family. In other cases they request that the state social services department take over the child's case (however, if they do so, they usually lose control over what happens to the child). These situations are referred to as *disrupted adoptions*. They are extremely rare for children placed in infancy. If an intercountry adoption disrupts, then the adoptive parents must find another placement. This can be very difficult. In the extremely unlikely event it happens to you, contact an experienced adoption agency for help.

Keep in mind that disrupted adoptions are rare. Some factors that may lead to disruption are prior severe abuse, multiple homes, and foster homes—although children who fit this profile can do well and should not be ruled out as adoptive candidates.

Adoption researcher Victor Groze estimates that only about 2 percent of all adoptions fail. Of course, the best plan is to work on resolving the problem well before it reaches the latter stages and before the parents and the child give up on working together.

Adopterms

A **disrupted adoption** generally refers to an adoption that fails before finalization, although many people also use the term for any failed adoption. (Some people use the term *dissolution* for adoptions that fail after finalization.) How adoption disruptions are handled depends on state laws.

Bottom line: Although the large majority of adopted children turn out just fine, sometimes they will experience serious medical or psychiatric problems. If that happens, then, of course, you will need to seek treatment for the child. First, get the child a physical examination to rule out a readily treatable problem. Then, if the problem may be behavioral or psychiatric, seek out a competent therapist. Finally, take into account your own needs as a human being. Don't blame yourself and don't obsess on the problem. You're one of the good guys!

The Least You Need to Know

♦ You and your child probably won't look alike or act alike—but you can still accept differences and find common interests.

♦ Most adopted kids are fine. If temporary emotional problems surface, cope with them without making a big deal out of them. But do get your child help if she needs it.

♦ Don't spoil your child. Remember that you're the parent and you are the one in control.

♦ Hoarding food and overeating sometimes occur with newly adopted orphans. These problems usually go away.

♦ If your child shows signs of a serious behavioral or psychiatric disorder, contact a therapist.

22

If Birthparents Remain in Contact

In This Chapter

- ◆ How to deal with a "middleman"
- ◆ How to handle parenting conflicts with the birthparents
- ◆ What to do if birthparents drop out of contact
- ◆ What to do as your life situation changes

Annie had been telling everyone she knew that she wanted to adopt. One day her friend Charlotte called. She knew a young woman who was pregnant and wanted her baby adopted. She was a good person in a bad situation—her boyfriend had walked out on her when he found out she was pregnant. She was due in about three weeks. Would Annie like to meet her?

Tom and Lola have an open adoption relationship with Sheila. But lately she has been calling a lot and dropping by rather frequently. They feel like something is up, and they don't feel comfortable with Sheila. They wonder what to do.

Open adoptions (described in Chapter 6) don't work equally well for everyone. If you have chosen an open adoption or are considering one, this chapter will show you key issues to consider so you can create a beneficial relationship with the birthparents of your child.

Dealing with a "Middleman"

As explained in Chapter 6, most open adoptions are facilitated by a "middleman"— usually an agency worker or attorney. The middleman may help initiate the adoption (by introducing you to the birthparents and helping you develop a successful relationship) or may get involved after you've found suitable birthparents (to legally finalize the adoption).

If you have a semi-open adoption (one in which occasional meetings with the birthparents are arranged through the middleman), the middleman will facilitate your contacts with the birthparents.

Using a middleman throughout one's relationship with a birthmother has its advantages as well as its disadvantages, as the following list makes clear:

Pros	Cons
Allows you to avoid direct contact with birthparents	Inhibits direct contact with the birthparents
Retains your privacy	Slows communication
The middleman can present requests or messages to and from the birthmother	Messages or requests might get distorted as they are passed on
The middleman provides counseling to you and the birthparents	You might not want counseling

Real Life Snapshots

Sometimes contact between birthparents, adoptive parents, and the adopted child can startle others. When birthmother Sue was planning her wedding, she asked adoptive parents Hal and Jenna whether their daughter Bonnie could be the flower girl. They thought it was a charming idea and agreed. There was a lot of talk among family members about whether or not this was appropriate—but it worked for them. Bonnie was thrilled to have an important part in the wedding.

Making Direct Contact

Maybe you prefer the direct approach. You want to be able to call or write the birthmother directly, and you want her to be able to contact you directly as well.

If direct contact is a concept that works for you and the birthparents, fine! But if you decide to manage the open adoption on your own, with no third-party intervention or assistance, realize that you might make mistakes and end up hurting the other party's feelings or getting hurt yourself. Frequently, these are the kinds of mistakes that, had you been working with an intermediary, he or she would have pointed out to you before a serious problem arose.

Some proponents of open adoption compare the negotiations, confusions, and tensions that take place to those that occur in any extended family. However, a closer and clearer comparison is probably the case of divorcing parents when one parent will not share custody. In that case, as with open adoptions, all the parties who are involved need to work out the emotional and practical issues of a noncustodial parent who will have some contact with the child.

The success of this relationship depends on the maturity of the adults involved and their clear understanding of their roles. Children will take their cues of what is expected of them from the adults in their lives.

In addition, birthmothers need to work on resolving the problems that led them to place their child for adoption, grieve the loss of their child, and make sense of their new roles. Adoptive parents need to feel secure as parents and bond with their child.

> **Familybuilding Tips**
>
> If you do have an open-adoption experience, you are far more likely to have contact with the birthmother than the birthfather. Birthfathers seem far more reticent about maintaining contact, although some do create a relationship with adopters and adopted children.

If Problems Occur

Although your relationship with the birthparents may start out great, sometimes problems develop later on. Keep in mind that relationships with family members (including one's own parents) are sometimes strained, so it shouldn't be surprising if problems occasionally surface with an open adoption.

Even very strong proponents of open adoption emphasize that relationships between adoptive parents and birthparents can change, sometimes quite a bit,

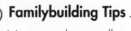

Familybuilding Tips

No matter how well you get along with the birthparents before the adoption, it's a good idea to put your expectations and plans in writing. These contracts are discussed in Chapter 18.

after the adoption. Being aware of the emotional and psychological experiences of others can help prepare adoptive parents for the situations that come up in their relationship with their child's birthmother. It's also important to realize that neither party can fix the problems of the other. If there is serious conflict, it is critical that you seek a third party to help everyone address the issues.

Birthparents Drop Out of Sight

When adopters agree to an open adoption, they are often very enthusiastic about it. Which is why it's hard for new adopters to understand why birthparents sometimes pull away or even drop out of communication for an extended period of weeks or months. Was it something that you said? Probably not.

One of the most difficult adjustment periods appears to be the first year after the adoption. The birthmother might want to step back for a while and *not* see the child or the adoptive parents. She might find contact painful, and yet she doesn't want the adopters, whom she likes, to feel responsible for her pain, so she doesn't explain her actions.

Even if the birthmother remains in close contact for the first year or two, it's not unusual for her to start calling and writing less (or even drop out of sight altogether) after that time. This is normal. Birthparents pull away because they are "getting on with their lives." They can see that you are doing a good job as parents and the child is safe and happy. Although they still care about the child, they are moving into other areas of their own lives.

Adoption Alert

Holidays may cause conflicts in the first few years of an open adoption. Will you allow the birthparents to see the kids on special days like birthdays, Christmas, Hanukkah, and so forth?

You can liken this issue to the learning curve of a newly married couple over the first year together. What most newlyweds learn to do is negotiate and compromise.

Similarly, you can negotiate issues like holiday and birthday visits with the birthparents. Make sure everyone accepts the solution and understands what their responsibilities are.

Needy or Demanding Birthparents

Sometimes birthparents (especially young and immature birthparents) become op-pressively demanding of adoptive parents, insisting on a lot more contact with the baby and with the adoptive parents than is comfortable for the adopters. Sometimes the adopters may feel like the young birthmother wishes she was adopted, too. And maybe she does wish that in some ways. But the needs of the child must be placed first. It's not the job of the adopters to parent the birthparent.

If this is going to happen, it's usually within the first few months or year of place-ment, when everyone involved is struggling to define their roles. Although you should be flexible and willing to negotiate changes, it's essential that you always do what is best for your child.

As new adopters, you may be tired from caring for the child, or you may just want to be left alone for a while. You probably don't want the birthmother dropping in when-ever she feels like it or constantly calling you. She may need to learn—by you telling her tactfully—that you have a life and a right to privacy.

The birthparent then may panic, and mistakenly assume that you are reneging on your agreement. Birthparents and adopters can become quite upset with each other at this point. The problem is that the relationships are still so new, and they need to be worked on.

Here are a few issues you and the birthparents should agree on before the baby is placed with you:

- ◆ Whether or not the birthmother will be allowed to spend time with the child alone. Don't agree if you think that it would be unsafe to allow it (for example, if the birthmother has a drug or alcohol problem).

- ◆ What the child should call the birthmother.

- ◆ What to do with birth relatives, primarily birthgrandparents. Will they, too, be involved with the open adoption, or will your child's relationship be mostly with the biological parents?

Whatever the issue, make it clear that *you* are the parent with the ultimate and final say over the childrearing and that this is not a co-parenting arrangement.

I like what the authors of *The Open Adoption Experience* say about boundaries: "… open adoptions do not require that you live without rules or by someone else's set of rules … An adoptive family can and should have appropriate boundaries about its relationship with the birthfamily. The difference between open adoption and confidential adoption is not that there are no longer boundaries but that there are boundaries where there used to be walls."

Real Life Snapshots

Adopters Corinne and Ted felt that open adoption was the right choice for them and Ava, the birthmother. But a month after baby Leda was born, things started to unravel. Ted and Corinne were exhausted new parents. On a few occasions, Ava called them, and they forgot to return her calls.

On her end, Ava was anxious. Corinne and Ted had seemed so nice! But now they didn't seem that friendly. Maybe she had been deceived, just so they could get her baby. Maybe she should see an attorney.

Ava eventually did get through to Corinne and Ted and told them that she was angry. They got peeved as well. After more disagreements, Corinne and Ted decided to hire an adoption mediator, and Ava agreed to participate in mediation.

The mediator explained what the strains of new parenthood were like to Ava and also helped her work through her own anxiety and fears about adoption. She helped Ted and Corinne understand Ava's fears. Finally, the mediator sat them all down and worked out a plan they could live with. Of course, mediation cost Ted and Corinne money. But they felt it was worth every penny.

Your Life Changes

As we move on through life, our situations change—sometimes for the better and sometimes not. For example, you may get divorced (although studies indicate that adoptive parents have a lower divorce rate than nonadoptive parents). Or you may find yourself facing health or financial problems.

When you're in difficult straits, you may find yourself cutting back on contact with the birthparents. Maybe it's because you're just too tired or upset to talk to them. Or maybe it's because you're afraid they will be disappointed in you. Most birthparents do realize that life situations change. And even if they don't realize it, they will need to accept it.

The Birthparent's Life Changes

You may have stayed about the same, but perhaps the birthparent's life has improved or worsened. If the birthmother had a problem with drugs or alcohol, she may have recovered and really turned her life around. You may need to re-evaluate her as she is now, rather than as she was when you first met her.

However, the birthmother may have developed some problems that weren't there before, as far as you know. Remember that you can always renegotiate how much time you allow her to spend with your child.

More Than One Child

Things can get tricky when you adopt more than one child from different birthmothers. No matter how hard you try, the open-adoption arrangement with one birthmother cannot be exactly equal to the arrangement with the birthmother for the other child. One birthmother may be very responsive to the child, while the other birthmom sends a card once a year and that's about it. Parents may feel upset for the child who has been "shortchanged" in the open adoption.

No matter how hard we want to equalize the situation for our children, it's impossible for their lives to be on an exactly even footing. Children need to learn that life will not provide equal opportunities for all. The open adoption experience will be different, even when both birthmothers are very enthusiastic participants.

Real Life Snapshots

Rachel is a birthmother who sends cards and gifts to her son and calls him once in a while. But she knows that his brother, not her biological son but also an adopted child, doesn't have an open adoption with his birthmother. Rachel says she thinks that it must make him sad that his birthmother never contacts him, and she feels kind of like a "surrogate birthmother" to him. She always remembers her son's brother on his birthday and at holiday time.

The Least You Need to Know

- ◆ Open adoptions take work, but proponents believe they are worth every effort.

- ◆ Adoptive parents and birthparents sometimes disagree. This is normal.

- ◆ It's a good idea to get your open adoption agreement in writing so everyone understands the terms and conditions up front.

- ◆ The first year of an open adoption involves adjustments for all.

Part 5

If Your Adult Child Searches

There's constant disagreement among people who care about these things as to how many or what percent of adopted adults search for their birth-parents; it's enough to know that some of them do. If your child grows up and wants to search, your family will need to face plenty of issues. This part covers why and how adopted adults search.

The bottom line is that whether or not they decide to search for birth-parents, nearly all adopted children still need the love of their parents who adopted them. Read this part to enlighten yourself on a much-talked-about (and little-understood) topic.

Chapter 23

Why Do They Search?

In This Chapter

- ◆ Which adopted adults are most likely to search for birthparents
- ◆ What adopted individuals hope to find by searching
- ◆ Common search myths and realities
- ◆ Dealing with your own feelings about the search

Some adopted adults are drawn to—even obsessed by—the desire to seek out their birthparents. But many adopted people say it's no big deal and never search.

Why do some adopted adults search while others have no interest? Does searching for biological parents mean that an adoptee doesn't love the adoptive parents? This chapter explores the major reasons why some adopted adults seek their birthparents.

Who Searches?

To *search*, in adoption terminology, means to seek out a biological relative. Most searchers try to locate their birthmothers, sometimes followed by a search for the birthfathers. Some searchers try to find birth siblings as well.

CAUTION

Adoption Alert _____

What if your minor child (under age 18) tells you that she doesn't want to wait until she's 18 to search? Should you get involved in the search for her birthparents?

My view is that unless you have some compelling reason to start now, the search should be delayed until your child is an adult. Children under age 18 are unprepared for the emotional turmoil an adoption reunion can sometimes generate. (In fact, sometimes people who *are* 18 are still unready.)

Here are the primary traits of most searchers:

♦ Most are female.

♦ Most are in their childbearing years (whether male or female). Having their own child can propel them into thinking intensely about what their own birth must have been like and wonder what their biological mother was like. They may also worry about possible inherited diseases.

♦ Many are well educated. A well-educated person would consider it possible to find a birthparent; a less-educated person might not know how to begin a search.

♦ Many are only children in the adoptive family. If the adopted person is an only child, he may wonder whether he has any siblings out in the world. If he grew up with siblings, whether biological or not, the desire for sisters and brothers may have been fulfilled. (Certainly he would not idealize siblings, having lived with them!)

♦ Many have very little information on what their birthmother looks like, what her medical history is, and what kind of personality she has. This can spur adopted adults into searching. (Lack of medical history is especially frustrating to some adopted people.)

♦ Some report learning late (in adolescence or adulthood) about their adoption or learning about it in a traumatic way. This might also spur an adopted person into searching, but not always.

♦ Some people are more curious by nature than others, and they need to know everything they can about virtually every subject. Information about their biological family members is no exception.

Why Do They Search?

Over the next few pages I'll talk about some of the main reasons adopted adults give when asked why they decide to search for birthparents.

Adoptinfo

Researchers Katherine Kowal and Karen Maitland Schilling found several major reasons why adopted people search. The most prevalent (24 percent) was birth, pregnancy, or the adoption of a child. One subject stated, "As I rocked my newborn son in my arms, I wondered who had rocked me."

Other reasons included encouragement by another person, medical problems in themselves or their children, and a change in the relationship with the adoptive parents. Another precipitant was a "life-cycle marker"—the timing of a particular birthday or the time in general seemed right to the adopted person.

Curiosity About Their Roots

Probably one of the easiest motives to understand is sheer curiosity. Maybe the adopted person doesn't resemble her adoptive parents or anyone in the family—and wonders whether she looks like anyone in her biological family. She may feel very different because she is of a different ethnic background.

She may wonder about similarities beyond physical ones. Does her birthmother share any of her interests? Is she athletic or musical? Does she hate to get up early, too? What's her pet peeve? What's her favorite holiday?

Personality traits may also be inherited. Is the birthmother an introspective, shy type or a bouncy, gregarious person? Is she the first one to try something new, or does she like to stick with the tried and true? These are a few more issues the adopted adult may wonder about—and probably has wondered about for years.

Medical History

Many adopted adults want medical background information for themselves, as well as for any children they have (or may have). They may wonder whether their birth families have any history of heart disease, cancer, or other illnesses that have a genetic link.

> ### Adoptinfo
>
> Researchers Kowal and Schilling studied the information adopted individuals said they were looking for when they searched. Their findings: 75 percent of the adopted adults studied wanted medical history; 71 percent wanted information on the personalities of their biological parents; 68 percent wanted a physical description of their biological parents; 66 percent wanted the names of their birthparents.
>
> More than 50 percent also sought the following information: ethnic background; their own early medical history; the hobbies of their birthparents; the reasons why their adoption occurred; the marital status of their birthparents; the educational level of birthparents; and the birthparents' occupations. (Interestingly, whenever possible, this type of information is provided to most adoptive parents now, so they can give it to their children.)

For some adopted adults, the desire for medical information is really a subterfuge. It's the socially acceptable reason they offer for searching. However, the real reason they search is for one of the other reasons listed here.

Why Adoption?

Many adopted adults report that they want to know *why* they were adopted. No matter how carefully told and truthful the adoption story was, some adopted people feel that they need to hear it from the person they were born to: Why did she choose adoption?

Many older adopted adults learn that the decision was not a choice but more of a societal mandate. Women in the 1950s through the 1970s (and earlier) were considered to be bad if they parented a child as unwed mothers. So adoption was considered the right thing to do. Of course, for many women it *was* the right thing to do, while others had doubts and regrets.

Search for Siblings

Some adopted adults I've talked to say they really want to meet their siblings—if they have any. Especially if they are only children, they wonder whether there are any brothers or sisters out there. Their sibs are often a lot closer to them in age than their birthparents, so they may share more things in common than they do with the birthparent.

> **Familybuilding Tips** _____
>
> I could find no studies on the relationships of adopted adults with their biological siblings. Anecdotally, however, it does appear that biological siblings are generally accepting of the adopted adult.
>
> Sometimes, however, siblings who were parented by the birthmother are in a lower socioeconomic strata than the adoptee. In that case, they may be jealous of the advantages that the adopted person has obtained—an affluent life, a college education, a good job, and so forth.

Adoptive Parents Are Gone

Adopted adults who have never done anything about searching may find themselves interested when an adoptive parent dies. This close link is gone, and they might want to see whether they can find the woman who created them and perhaps forge a relationship with her. In other cases, the adopted person may have been interested in searching for a long time but was afraid the adoptive parents would be upset or offended. (Sometimes they are right about this.) So the adopted person didn't search until the adoptive parents died.

Finally, some adopted adults seek out their birthmother simply to thank her for having chosen adoption. They may worry that she feels guilty about it.

Unrealistic Expectations

Other, more negative motivations apparently lead a few adopted adults to search.

Some adopted adults believe that their personal problems stem primarily (or solely) from adoption. This viewpoint is more often heard from adopted adults who are estranged from their adoptive families, but it may still occur even if the adopted person and adoptive parents are on good terms. Here's how blaming adoption for everything can work: The person has a problem, maybe a lot of problems. She thinks her problems all relate to adoption in some way. (If she hadn't been adopted, she would have gone to a different school, had a different job, married a different person, and so on.)

Based on this reasoning, the only corrective action the adopted person can think of is to seek out her birthmother and create a strong relationship with her. The problem with this answer is that no birthmother, no matter how loving and caring, can erase all life's problems. The adopted person is bound to be disappointed—unless she adjusts her thinking to conform more to reality. An adopted adult who feels unwhole will not resolve an identity crisis through meeting a birthparent, even if this may seem true at the euphoric first few meetings.

Real Life Snapshots

In their article on the search process in a 1986 issue of *Social Casework: The Journal of Contemporary Social Work,* researchers Patricia Auth and Shirley Zaret described a patient, K, who "blamed all the shortcomings in her life on that fact that she had been deprived of ever knowing her birth mother."

K's parents supported her in the search process, and she also received counseling. Fortunately, by the time K did meet her birthmother, she no longer expected her birthmother to be a fairy godmother with a magic wand and was able to see her as a real person, with good and bad points.

Many adopted adults don't receive good counseling, however, and it can be very distressing when they meet a flesh-and–blood person instead of a perfect mother.

In fact, both the birthparent and the reunion that the adopted person hopes for may be nothing like reality. The following table lists some unrealistic search fantasies and the more common realities.

What Are You Afraid Of?

Many adoptive parents have powerful negative feelings about the idea of an adoption search. Should they feel guilty? I don't think so. I think they should feel human. But frankly, they don't have much to worry about.

Search Expectations versus Search Realities

Expectation	Reality
Birthparent will be beautiful, glamorous, famous, or rich.	Birthparent may be none of those things.
First meeting will be euphoric. It will be like a fairy tale come true.	First meeting may be positive or negative. (The birthparent may even refuse the meeting.)
Birthparent will welcome adopted person with open arms and unconditional love.	Birthparent may accept or deny parenthood. The birthparent may reject the adopted person.

Expectation	Reality
Adoptee will control the first meeting.	Birthparent may surprise the adopted person by bringing the extended family to the first meeting.
Adopted person can control the relationship.	Birthparent may want more or less contact than the adopted person wants.
Birthmother will identify the birthfather.	Birthmother may refuse to identify.
Adopted person will have new extended family.	Birthmother may be unwilling to tell the extended family about the adopted person.
Birthparent will be a lot like the adopted person.	Birthparent may be very different from them.
Adoptive parents will understand the need to search.	Adoptive parents may not accept/understand.
Birth siblings will accept adopted adults with open arms into their lives.	Birth siblings may be jealous of the adopted person.
Adopted person's life problems will end.	Life problems usually continue.
Adopted person and birthmother will have a smooth relationship.	Relationship may be rocky.
Birthparent will want same kind of relationship adopted person wants, whether intense, at arm's length, and so on.	Birthparent's needs may be very different from adopted person's needs.

Whether they admit it or not, adoptive parents whose children search often feel jealousy and even anger toward the birthparent. The adoptive parents may feel that they've done all the hard work of parenting—and now this interloper, the birthparent, will take over. This rarely happens—but the fear is there.

One adoptive mom I know found the search painful and scary, even though she struggled to be supportive of her child's need to search. Other adoptive parents are more philosophical and accepting. There are adoptive parents who actively launch the search to locate the birthparents themselves, in an attempt to gain information the child can have when she is grown up.

> **Adoptinfo**
>
> As many as half of all searchers don't tell their adoptive parents about the search until it's over or they're well into it. Most are afraid of hurting their adoptive parents.

Remember, it isn't inevitable that your child will search—most don't. Questions about birthparents' medical history may only mean that your child wants information rather than contact. Don't assume your child wants to search—many adopted adults express a feeling that they are expected to search and are concerned that something is wrong with them because they don't want to. It's okay to *not* search. However, don't blind yourself to the possibility that your child may want to search.

> ### Familybuilding Tips
>
> It's hard to find information about how adoptive parents feel when children search. Many parents remain silent—whether they feel happy, sad, or ambivalent. It may not be politically correct for the adopters to admit to being upset, but that's a normal human reaction.

Adoptive parents might experience a host of emotions when they learn that their adult child has searched—or plans to search—including fear of being abandoned, concern for the adopted child's emotional well-being, feelings of rejection, or even a hopeful and supportive attitude. Their child's search might also bring up long-forgotten memories of infertility issues and the reasons for adopting.

Fear of Abandonment

Some adoptive parents worry that if the adopted person likes the birthparents better, then he may devote all his spare time to them and forget he was ever adopted.

Does this make any sense? Of course not. No adopted person, whether they had a great, mediocre, or even terrible relationship with his adoptive parents, can forget that he was adopted and that he was parented by the adopters. You might forget where you parked your car. You might forget what day it is. You don't forget who raised you.

Still, it may be true that when the adopted adult first locates a birthparent, the birthparent will receive the lion's share of attention. Usually, though, after the excitement fades, the adopted person's relationships with both the birthparents and the adoptive parents becomes more balanced.

You'll Like Them Better Than You Like Us

Adopters often fear that their children will like the birthparents better than they like the adoptive parents. Why? One reason is that the adopted person has no history of bad times with the birthparents. They didn't yell at Susie for smoking in the shed. They didn't tell Jimmy that if he wanted a car, he'd have to save his own money for it.

Real Life Snapshots

When Alicia met her birthmother, Barbara, adoptive mom Ellen had reservations. "I worried if my relationship with Alicia would change. Would she want to do more things with Barbara than with me?" Ellen feared that Barbara would be more attractive and appealing, that she would lose time with Alicia, that Alicia would be rejected by Barbara, and that Alicia would be disappointed in Barbara.

In reality, the reunion was a happy one. She advises adoptive parents in this situation "to feel confident in their relationship with their child. When the newness of the relationship with the birthmother wears off, they remember who loved them and raised them. Nothing can replace the relationship of a mother and child."

She also says adoptive parents should be helpful, supportive, and willing to listen. Ellen says the best part of a search is, "The child is closer to you now than before, and you don't have to worry about birthparents anymore, now that you know them."

First, realize that most birthparents are normal people who probably would have parented the child in the same ways you did. They would have punished Susie for smoking, too.

Remember the flip side. The birthparents didn't see Susie play the lead fairy in the school play. They didn't sew her dress and create her gorgeous wings, which she treasured. Nor did they see Jimmy win a science fair prize. Or help him catch his first bass. You did.

Finally, some adoptive parents fear that the genetic similarities of the birthparents will prove irresistible to the adoptee.

It's very common for adopted adults and birthparents to explore mutual likes and dislikes when they first meet. If the relationship progresses, however, your child will begin to realize that although she and her birthmother share traits, they are also unlike in some ways as well.

It's notable that most adopted adults take great pains to insist that they love their parents and that their search was not initiated because they didn't think the adopters were "good enough." They weren't looking for better parents. They just wanted to know the people who were responsible for their creation.

CAUTION

Adoption Alert

Many adoptive parents are scared and apprehensive about an adopted adult's search. But some actually press their child to search. I don't think this is a good idea.

If your child wants to search, then be supportive. But don't pressure her and try to take over this important aspect of your child's life. Let your child decide whether and when to search for a birthparent.

> **CAUTION**
>
> **Adoption Alert** _____
>
> Some studies indicate that adopted adults who search are more likely to see adoptive parents as different from them than adopted adults who choose not to search. This doesn't mean that searchers don't love their parents; in most cases, they do love them. But they may not feel like they are similar to them. Hence, they search in the hopes that the birthparent is similar to how they perceive themselves. Of course, it doesn't always work out; sometimes adopted adults and their birthparents are very different people.

Adopted Adults Who Don't Search

There is great disagreement about how many people actually search for their birthparents, but it does appear to be a minority of all adopted adults. So what about the ones who don't search? Many report that they don't like to tell people they were adopted because the first thing many people say to them is, "So have you found your mother yet?" If they say that they don't want to, they get puzzled looks.

In other cases, adopted adults find the identifying information they need—and then decide not to contact their birthparents. They may delay for months or even years, for a variety of reasons: fear, ambivalence, confusion, or an insufficient desire to continue.

My suggestion to all adopted adults is this: If you want to search and contact your birthparents, go ahead. If not, don't. Follow your own heart and do what's right for you and not what your friends, spouse, adoptive parents, or anyone else says.

The Least You Need to Know

- ◆ Adopted adults have different reasons for searching. Many want to understand where they come from or find out why they were placed for adoption.

- ◆ Some adopted people think finding their birthparents will solve their problems. They need to understand that this is not the case.

- ◆ Adoptive parents should realize that just because a child searches, it doesn't mean that he or she does not love them.

- ◆ Not all adopted adults search. Each adopted person must decide what is right for himself or herself.

Chapter 24

How Do They Search?

In This Chapter

- ◆ Finding a birthparent
- ◆ Using state registries
- ◆ Using search groups and private investigators
- ◆ Searching on the Internet

Finding a birthmother or birthfather is usually a lot more complicated than paging through a phone book. Why? Many adopted adults have no idea what their birthmother's first or last name was when they were adopted or what it is now. (The birthmother may have married or divorced since the adoption.) Furthermore, in most states, the adopted adult's original birth certificate is sealed (confidential), and the new birth certificate lists the adoptive parents' names as the parents. So just finding out the name of their birthmother is the first hurdle for many adopted adults who wish to search. (This is one advantage cited by proponents of open adoption: They already know the names of their birthparents.)

Getting Involved

If your adopted child decides to search, you may want to get involved. In fact, the authors of *The Adoptive Family in Treatment* say that therapists should encourage families to become involved when a search occurs. "The impact of the search, whatever the outcome, will be felt throughout the family, and the support of the family system makes the search process itself far more bearable for the searcher," they say. I recommend, however, that the adopted adult should be the person who takes the lead in deciding if and when to search and also in choosing whether or not a reunion occurs with a birthparent. Not you.

Don't pressure your child of any age to meet a birthparent because your friends tell you it's a great idea or you saw it on television or for any other reason. Let your adult child initiate this task, if he or she wishes. Do, however, let your child know you are ready and willing to help, if any help is needed or wanted. Some adopted adults have held off from searching, fearing that they would offend their parents if they searched. Let your child know you're open to the idea (if you are).

If you do decide to take an interest or get involved in your child's search, I've included this chapter to give you a brief overview of searching tactics and techniques. Entire books are devoted to searching; I will only touch on some basics here.

It's important to keep in mind that searching for birthparents was not considered acceptable in the past and was actively discouraged. It has only been in the past 15 to 20 years or so that birthmothers have been told at the time of adoption that the adopted adult might search for them someday. It's also true that most professionals (and most laws) are careful to ensure contact is made only when the birthmother consents to contact. Some adopted adults and adoptee groups, however, believe that it is their right to search for birthparents and to contact them, whether the birthparents want contact or not.

The Right to Search?

Should adopted adults be able to find their birthparents if they so choose? The entire issue of an adoptee's right to know versus a birthparent's right to privacy is a heated one.

Some adoption rights groups, such as the former Adoptees Liberty Movement Association (ALMA) in New York, have asserted that the adoptee has the right to know who her birthmother is—although of course she cannot force her birthmother into an ongoing relationship.

Others believe that birthparents should not have to respond to the inquiries of children they've placed for adoption if they don't wish to. They may be embarrassed about the adoption or angry about the circumstances surrounding it, or they may feel they have closed the door on the past.

The existence of birth siblings raises even more complicated issues. Does an adopted adult have the right to contact siblings by birth when her birthmother opposes this contact? Or do siblings have the right to search for an adopted biological sister when their mother is against the idea? Such tough calls are hotly debated and are beyond the scope of this book. Instead, I touch on the bare bones issues of searching in this chapter.

Stating Your Case: State Registries

More than half the states in the United States have some sort of registry that adopters may be able to use to find information about their birthparents (and vice versa), even without information on their birthparents' names. These registries generally are managed by the state social services department (usually located in the state capital or in the state vital statistics branch). I'll explain the different kinds of registries over the following pages. (States continue to change their laws on matters related to adoption, including search, so don't assume that this information is cast in granite for all time. It isn't.)

Mutual Consent

If both an adopted adult (over 18 or, in some states, over 21) and a birthparent register in a state with a mutual consent registry (also known as a voluntary consent registry), identifying information will be provided to both.

The following states offer mutual consent registries (some states with registries may be missing from this list):

Arkansas	Michigan
Colorado	Missouri
Connecticut	Nevada
Florida	Ohio
Georgia	Oregon
Hawaii	Rhode Island
Illinois	Texas
Louisiana	Vermont
Maine	West Virginia

> **Adoptinfo**
>
> Keep in mind that not everyone is aware of the state registries and not everyone chooses to use them; consequently, searchers shouldn't depend solely on the state registry but may also wish to register with private organizations, such as the International Soundex Reunion Registry (ISSR), described later in this chapter.

Search and Consent/Confidential Intermediary

Some states provide a *search and consent system*, otherwise known as a *confidential intermediary* system. In this system, the adopted adult can request identifying information on the birthparents. The confidential intermediary locates the birthparents and asks for their permission to release identifying information. If they consent, the adopted adult is given their names. Some detractors have called this system "search and confront" because sometimes birthparents may be pressured into a rushed meeting by harried or inexperienced workers.

States that offer confidential intermediary systems, include the following:

Arizona	Montana
Colorado	North Dakota
Illinois	Oregon
Indiana	Vermont
Michigan	Wisconsin
Minnesota	Wyoming
Mississippi	

> **Adopterms**
>
> A **search and consent** or **confidential intermediary system** is a system whereby one person, usually the adoptee, requests that a search be made for the birthparent. The birthparent is identified, contacted, and asked whether she or he wants contact with the adoptee. If the birthparent agrees, then the identifying information is provided to the adopted adult.

Note that some states offer *both* a mutual consent registry and a confidential intermediary system.

Open Records

Open records refers to a system wherein the adopted adult can request his original birth certificate with the names of both biological parents, and it will be provided. Obviously the search process is much easier when the names of the birthparents are known. At present, Alabama, Alaska, Kansas, New Hampshire, and Oregon have open records systems. (The New Hampshire law passed in 2004.) Tennessee also allows some individuals to open their records, but it is a more complex system than in the other states.

> **Adopterms**
>
> **Open records** refers to a system in which the adopted adult can request his original birth certificate, and it will be provided. No court orders are needed.

Many adoption groups are eager to institute open records laws, so that adopted adults in any state can gain access to their original birth certificates for the asking. This information won't help adopted adults who are seeking medical or social information but who do not wish to make contact with the birthparent in order to gain this information. Instead, the original birth certificate provides only the identifying information on birthparents.

Petitioning the Court

Many states do not have mutual consent registries, confidential intermediary systems, or open records; in those states, if an adopted adult wants to open his birth records, he must obtain a court order to do it. To obtain a court order, the adoptee must convince a judge that it's a good idea for the records to be opened.

An adopted adult who chooses to go before a judge should be prepared to state why he needs to see his records. If there is a medical necessity (for example, the adopted person needs a bone marrow transplant), most judges would agree to open the records but generally will try to discreetly obtain the information from birthparents and their consent before releasing information to the adoptee. Sheer curiosity, on the other hand, is often not convincing enough to a judge.

Documentation—such as a letter from a physician, psychologist, or counselor stating that the adoptee needs the information to deal with issues he's struggling with—might help. It's also a good idea for the adoptee to prepare counter-arguments for every reason why a judge would say "no."

Judges hold varying opinions on whether or not adoptees should have access to their birth records. Adopted adults who want to approach a judge should consult an attorney in their state of birth about the best way to do so.

> ### Adoptinfo
>
> *Searching for a Past: The Adopted Adult's Unique Process of Finding Identity*, by Jayne Schooler (Pinon, Colorado Springs, CO, 1995), emphasizes both the practical and emotional aspects of searching for birthparents.
>
> There are also general "people-finding" books, such as *The Complete Idiot's Guide to Private Investigating*, by Steven Kerry Brown.

I'm All Grown Up! Contacting the Agency

Another way that some adopted adults find birthparents is by asking the adoption agency that originally arranged the placement. The agency may have a policy to release information if the birthparent agrees.

Adopted adults who are interested should speak with the agency director or social worker. If the contact says no, he or she may still be a source of good information about alternative search methods.

The theory is that if the agency has a policy to provide identifying information, things will work out well. However, the implementation isn't always effective.

Real Life Snapshots

In one case, Pennsylvania adopted adult Carol Sandusky sued the Cumberland County Children Services because a social worker gave her personal information to a biological sister—even though Sandusky had told the social worker that she did not want that information released.

Sandusky also learned more than she wanted to know about the circumstances surrounding her birth. The biological sister offered Sandusky graphic descriptions of how Sandusky had been abused by her biological parents before she was adopted.

Sandusky ultimately lost her lawsuit because a judge ruled the statute of limitations on the allegations had run out; however, she publicly stated her anger at the violation of her privacy.

Hiring Magnum, P.I.?

It's possible to hire someone else to do the legwork and find the information. Private investigators, search consultants, and search organizations are all available to perform searches—for a fee.

Numerous *search groups* are available nationwide—probably a group is near you. Many online groups are also available. However, be very skeptical of anyone who contacts you (or your adopted adult child) out of the blue, offering to find a birth-parent instantly for a substantial fee.

Adopterms

A **search group** is an organization that assists adoptees and birthparents with the search process. They may provide information, or they may actively involve themselves in the process. Hundreds of search groups exist nationwide.

No one should be hired without a thorough interview first. Here are some questions to ask:

◆ How many adoption searches have you performed?

Go with someone who knows what he or she is doing. If the person has performed only 5 or 10 searches in 10 years, stay away! On the other hand, if the person says she's performed 10,000 searches (or some other ridiculous number), be wary. Use common sense.

◆ About how long does it take to find the information?

The longer the person drags out your case, the more the bill might be. Find out the typical time frame.

◆ Do you have to break any laws to get it?

Although it's rare, search consultants have been arrested for illegal searches of government databases. An adopted adult should not be connected with anyone performing criminal acts. So if the searcher hesitates when you ask how she plans to obtain the information, go elsewhere.

◆ What are your fees? What is the upper limit of your fees?

You don't want an open-ended search that might ultimately cost you thousands of dollars. Find out up front what the fees are and what you will get for your money. Get it in writing, too.

◆ Do you have contracts for adoption searches? Can I see one?

Ask to see a sample contract the investigator or agency uses. Read it over carefully and see whether it seems reasonable to you. If possible, show it to your attorney before you sign it.

Before you engage the services of a private investigator or search consultant, ask for references from other customers. Also, check with the Better Business Bureau. Your local search groups may also have an opinion of the person's work.

Other Search Methods

Besides tapping into state registries, petitioning the court, or hiring a PI, adopted adults can begin their search in a number of other ways. Here are a few of the most common:

◆ Register with the International Soundex Reunion Registry (ISSR) in Carson City, Nevada. This valuable resource has helped thousands of people locate each other. Both the adopted adult and the birthparent must be registered in order for a match to take place. For information, contact: International Soundex Reunion Registry, P.O. Box 2312, Carson City, NV 89702-2312. Their phone number is 775-882-7755, and their website is www.plumsite.com/issr.

◆ Consider the use of Internet resources.

Many online registries are available. Many adopted adults use the Internet to personally advertise their desire to find their birthparents. The Internet also houses many public records and databases, which makes it a convenient search tool.

◆ Advertise in newspaper classifieds. A typical ad will announce that an adopted adult with such-and-such a birth date is searching for a birthmother. Some adopted adults advertise in the area of their birth or where they think the birthparent might reside.

◆ Try a personal investigation.

The adopted adult could try to reconstruct what is known about her birth: For example, what hospital was she born in? Who were the attending physicians? Individuals at the hospital may be willing to provide information. The problem with this is that medical records and documents are held as confidential in virtually all cases, and, thus, doctors and nurses would be violating state confidentiality laws if they provided such information. People have sued medical staff for releasing just such information.

Adopted adults may be able to tap into public databases and computerized phone records for more information.

Real Life Snapshots

In 1997, a wire release reported that Colorado adoptee Carolyn Donahower found her birthfather very rapidly in the privacy of her own home by using her computer.

Donahower knew her birthfather's name and also suspected that he might be living in Kansas. She used a CD-ROM program of business and residential phone listings, and found a match. She left a few phone messages. "The next morning, my birthfather called me, and we spoke for the first time in 30 years."

Bottom line: In many cases, adopted adults can locate their birthparents if they are still living. But whether their birthparents will agree to see them and whether a meeting will occur is a whole other story.

It's also important to consider the impact of the search on the person "found." Contact may completely disrupt a person's life and cause them great distress. However, many searches result in happy and successful relationships, and the individuals involved are very pleased about the reunion. Keep in mind that your adult child's life will be changed, *and* other lives will also be changed if and when he or she chooses to search.

The Least You Need to Know

♦ The adopted adult's right to search is hotly debated; thus, finding birthparent information can be difficult for many adoptees.

♦ Some states help with mutual consent registries or confidential intermediaries.

♦ Some adoption agencies help searchers; others don't.

♦ The Internet is a useful resource for many searchers, but searchers need to exercise caution.

♦ Be careful when choosing a private investigator or search agency.

Appendix A

Selected Adoption Agencies

Although this state-by-state list of adoption agencies is by no means exhaustive—hundreds of other agencies are out there—it should help you get started on your search for an agency that's right for you.

However, just because an agency is included in this book doesn't guarantee its quality. I cannot promise you that you will be happy with any of the agencies listed here (although I hope that you will be). Agency directors and boards of directors change; be sure to screen an adoption agency thoroughly before contracting for its services. Read Chapters 6 and 9 carefully and use your common sense when choosing an adoption agency. Finally, some agencies have websites, and others do not. Having a beautiful website is *not* a guarantee of a good agency, nor does the low quality of a website indicate the agency *isn't* good.

Alabama

Children of the World, Inc.
110 South Sector Street
Fairhope, AL 36532
251-990-3550
www.childrenoftheworld.com

Lifeline Children's Services, Inc.
2908 Pump House Rd.
Birmingham, AL 35243
205-967-0811
www.lifelineadoption.org

Villa Hope
4 Office Park Circle, Ste. 218
Birmingham, AL 35223
205-870-7359
www.villahope.org

Alaska

Alaska International Adoption Agency, Ltd.
308 G St., Ste. 225
Anchorage, AK 99501
907-677-2888
www.akadoptions.com

Catholic Social Services
225 Cordova Street
Anchorage, AK 99501
907-277-2554
www.cssalaska.org

Arizona

Christian Family Care Agency
1102 South Pantano Rd.
Tucson, AZ 85710
520-296-8255

Dillon Southwest
3014 North Hayden Rd., Ste. 101
Scottsdale, AZ 85251
480-945-2221
www.dillonsouthwest.org

Hand in Hand International Adoptions
931 East Southern Ave., Ste. 103
Mesa, AZ 85204
480-892-5550
www.hihiadopt.org

Arkansas

Children's Homes, Inc.
5515 Old Wolcott Rd.
Paragould, AR 721450
870-231-4031
www.childrenshomes.org

California

Across the World Adoptions
399 Taylor Blvd., Ste. 102
Pleasant Hill, CA 94523-2200
925-356-6260
www.adopting.com/atwa

Adopt A Special Kid (AASK)
7700 Edgewater Dr., Ste. 320
Oakland, CA 94621
510-553-1748
www.adoptaspecialkid.org

Adopt International
1000 Brannon St., Ste. 301
San Francisco, CA 94103
415-934-0300
www.adopt-intl.org

Adoption Options, Inc.
4025 Camino del Rio South,
Ste. 300
San Diego, CA 92108
619-542-7772
www.adoption-options.org

Adoptions Unlimited
4091 Riverside Dr., Ste. 115
Chino, CA 91710
909-902-1412
www.adopting.com/aul

Bay Area Adoption Services
465 Fairchild Dr., Ste. 215
Mountain View, CA 94043
650-964-3800
www.baas.org

Heartsent Adoptions
15 Altarinda Rd., Ste. 100
Orinda, CA 94563
925-254-8883
www.heartsent.org

Life Adoption Services
440 West Main St.
Tustin, CA 92780
714-838-5433
www.lifeadoption.com

Vista Del Mar
3200 Motor Ave.
Los Angeles, CA 90034-3740
310-836-1223
www.vistadelmar.org

Colorado

Chinese Children Adoption
International
6920 South Holly Circle
Englewood, CO 80112
303-850-9998
www.chinesechildren.org

Friends of Children of Various
Nations, Inc.
1562 Pearl St.
Denver, CO 80203
303-837-9438
www.fcvn.net

Hope's Promise
309 Jerry St. #202
Castle Rock, CO 80104-2442
303-660-0277
www.hopespromise.com

LDS Family Services
3263 Fraser St., Ste. 3
Aurora, CO 80011
303-371-1000

Connecticut

Lutheran Social Services of
New England
2139 Silas Deane Hwy., Ste. 201
Rocky Hill, CT 06067-2336
860-257-0340

Thursday's Child
227 Tunxis Ave.
Bloomfield, CT 06002
860-242-5941
www.tcadoption.org

Wide Horizons for Children
776 Farmington Ave.
West Hartford, CT 06119
860-570-1740

Delaware

Adoption House, Inc.
3411 Silverside Road, Ste. 101
Webster Bldg.
Wilmington, DE 19807
302-477-0944
www.adoptionhouse.org

Catholic Charities
2601 West Fourth St., Ste. 9
Wilmington, DE 19947
302-856-9578

Children's Choice, Inc.
25 South Old Baltimore Pike
Lafayette Bldg., Ste. 101
Newark, DE 19702
302-731-9512

District of Columbia

Adoption Center of WA
1726 M St. NW, Ste. 1101
Washington, DC 20036
202-452-8278
www.adoptioncenter.com

Adoption Services Information
Agency/ASIA
7720 Alaska Ave. NW
Washington, DC 20012
202-726-7193
www.asia-adopt.org

Adoptions Together, Inc.
419 Seventh St. NW, Ste. 201
Washington, DC 20004
202-628-7420
www.adoptionstogether.org

Florida

A Bond of Love Adoption
1800 Siesta Drive
Sarasota, FL 34239-4501
941-957-0064

Adoption By Choice
4102 West Linebaugh Ave. #200
Tampa, FL 33624-5239
813-960-2229
www.abcadopt.com

All About Adoptions, Inc.
503 East New Haven Ave.
Melbourne, FL 32901
407-723-0088
www.allabout adoptions.org

Children's Home Society
P.O. Box 5616
Jacksonville, FL 32247-5616
904-348-5616

Heart of Adoptions, Inc.
418 West Platt St., Ste. A
Tampa, FL 33606
813-258-6505
www.floridaadoptionagency.com

Shepherd Care Ministries
5935 Taft St.
Hollywood, FL 33021
954-981-2060

Universal Aid for Children, Inc.
Cypress Village East
167 SW 6th St.
Pompano Beach, FL 33060
954-785-0033
www.uacadoption.org

Georgia

Georgia AGAPE, Inc.
3094 Mercer University Dr., #200
Atlanta, GA 30341
404-452-9995
www.georgiaagape.org

Hope for Children, Inc.
24 Perimeter Center East, Ste.
2400
Atlanta, GA 30346
770-391-1511
www.hopeforchildren.org

New Beginnings Adoption and
Counseling Agency
1316 Wynnton Court, Ste. A
Columbus, GA 31906
706-571-3346
www.ebcadoption.org

Open Door Adoption Agency
P.O. Box 4
Thomasville, GA 31799
229-228-6339
www.opendooradoption.org

Hawaii

Adopt International
820 Mililani St., Ste. 401
Honolulu, HI 96813
808-523-1400
www.adopt-intl.org

Hawaii International Child
1168 Waimanu St., Ste. B
Honolulu, HI 96814
808-589-2367
www.adopt.h-i-c.org

Idaho

LDS Social Services
10740 Fairview, Ste. 100
Boise, ID 83713
208-376-0191

New Hope Child and Family Agency
700 West Riverview Dr.
Idaho Falls, ID 83401
208-523-6930

Illinois

Adoption-Link, Inc.
1145 South Westgate, Ste. 104
Oak Park, IL 60301
708-524-1433

Catholic Charities
651 West Lake St.
Chicago, IL 60661
312-655-7086

Children's Home & Aid Society
910 2nd Ave.
Rockford, IL 61104
815-962-1043

The Cradle
2049 Ridge Ave.
Evanston, IL 60201-2794
847-475-5800
www.cradle.org

New Life Social Services
6316 North Lincoln Ave.
Chicago, IL 60659
773-478-4773
www.nlss.org

St. Mary's Services
717 West Kirchoff Rd.
Arlington Hts., IL 60005
847-870-8181

Sunnyridge Family Center
2 South 426 Orchard Rd.
Wheaton, IL 60187
630-668-5117
www.sunnyridge.org

Indiana

Americans for African Adoptions
8910 Timberwood Dr.
Indianapolis, IN 46234-1952
317-271-4567
www.africanadoptions.org

Bethany Christian Services
5650 Caito Dr.
Indianapolis, IN 46226
317-568-1000
www.bethany.org/indiana

Catholic Charities
315 East Washington Blvd.
Ft. Wayne, IN 46802

Childplace
2420 Highway 62
Jeffersonville, IN 47130
812-282-8248
www.childplace.org

Coleman Adoption Service
615 North Alabama St., #419
Indianapolis, IN 46204-1434
317-638-0965

Iowa

Bethany Christian Services
8525 Douglas, Ste. 34
Des Moines, IA 50322
515-270-0824

Gift of Love International
Adoptions, Inc.
7405 University Blvd., Ste. 8
Des Moines, IA 50325
515-255-3388
www.giftoflove.org

Kansas

Adoption Centre of Kansas, Inc.
1831 Woodrow Ave.
Wichita, KS 67203
316-265-5289
www.adoptioncentre.com

Lutheran Social Service of Kansas
2942 SW Wanamaker Dr.
Building B, Ste. 1C
Topeka, KS 67214
785-272-7883

Special Additions, Inc.
19055 Metcalf Ave.
Stilwell, KS 66085
913-681-9604
http://specialad.org

Kentucky

Adoptions of Kentucky, Inc.
One Riverfront Plaza, Ste. 1708
Louisville, KY 40202
502-585-3005

A Helping Hand Adoption Agency
501 Darby Creek Rd., Ste. 17
Lexington, KY 40509
Toll-free: 1-800-525-0871 or
859-263-9964
www.worldadoptions.org

Bluegrass Christian Adoption
Services
1517 Nicholsville Rd., Ste. 405
Lexington, KY 40503
859-276-2222

Louisiana

Children's Bureau of New Orleans
210 Baronne St., Ste. 722
New Orleans, LA 70112
504-525-2366

St. Elizabeth Foundation
8054 Summa Ave., Ste. A
Baton Rouge, LA 70809
225-769-8888

Volunteers of America
360 Jordan St.
Shreveport, LA 71101
318-221-2669
www.voanorthla.com

Maine

Maine Adoption Placement Service
(MAPS)
58 Pleasant St.
Houlton, ME 04730-0772
207-532-9358
www.mapsadopt.org

St. Andre Home
283 Elm St.
Biddeford, ME 04005
207-282-3351
www.saintandrehome.com

Maryland

Adoption Service Information
Agency (ASIA)
8555 16th St., Ste. 600
Silver Spring, MD 20910
301-587-7068
www.asia-adopt.org

Adoptions Together, Inc.
5750 Executive Drive, Ste. 107
Baltimore, MD 21228
410-869-0620
www.adoptionstogether.org

The Barker Foundation
7945 MacArthur Blvd., Ste. 206
Cabin John, MD 20818
301-229-8300
www.barkerfoundation.org

Cradle of Hope Adoption Center
8630 Fenton St., #310
Silver Spring, MD 20910-3803
301-587-4400
www.cradlehope.org

Creative Adoptions, Inc.
10750 Hickory Ridge Rd., #108
Columbia, MD 21044
301-596-1521
www.creativeadoptions.org

International Children's Alliance
8807 Colesville Rd., Third Floor
Silver Spring, MD 20910
301-495-9710
www.adoptica.org

World Child International
9300 Columbia Blvd.
Silver Spring, MD 20910
301-588-3000
www.worldchild.org

Massachusetts

Bethany Christian Services
1538 Turnpike St.
North Andover, MA 01845
978-794-9800

Brightside for Families and Children
2113 Riverdale St.
West Springfield, MA 01089
413-827-4315
www.brightsideadoption.org

Wide Horizons for Children
38 Edge Hill Road
Waltham, MA 02451
781-894-5330
www.whfc.org

Michigan

Adoption Associates
1338 Baldwin St.
Jenison, MI 49428-8937
616-667-0677
www.adoptassoc.com

Adoptions of the Heart
4295 Summerwind Ave.
Grand Rapids, MI 49525
616-365-3166

Americans for International Aid
and Adoption (AIAA)
2151 Livernois, Suite 200
Troy, MI 48083
248-362-1207
www.aiaaadopt.org

Bethany International Services
901 Eastern Ave. NE
Grand Rapids, MI 49503

Family Adoption Consultants
P.O. Box 50489
Kalamazoo, MI 49005
269-343-3316
www.facadopt.org

Hands Across the Water
2890 Carpenter Rd., Ste. 600
Ann Arbor, MI 48108
734-477-0135
www.hatw.org

Minnesota

Bethany Christian Service
3025 Harbor Lane #316
Plymouth, MN 55447
763-553-0344

Children's Home Society of Minnesota
1605 Eustis St.
St. Paul, MN 55108
651-646-7771
www.chsm.com

Crossroads Adoption Service
4620 West 77th, Ste. 105
Minneapolis, MN 55435
952-831-5707
www.crossroadsadoption.com

HOPE Adoption & Family
5850 Omaha Ave. N
Oak Park, MN 55082
651-439-2446

Lutheran Social Services
2414 Park Ave.
Minneapolis, MN 55404-3713
612-879-5230

Mississippi

Acorn Adoptions, Inc.
113 South Beach Blvd., Ste. D
Bay St. Louis, MS 39520
1-888-221-1370
www.acornadoption.org

Bethany Christian Services
2618 Southerland St.
Jackson, MS 39216
601-366-4282

New Beginnings of Tupelo
P.O. Box 7055
Tupelo, MS 38802
662-842-6752

Missouri

Children's Hope International/
China's Children
9229 Lackland Rd.
St. Louis, MO 63114
314-890-0086
www.childrenshopeint.org

Christian Family Services
7955 Big Bend Blvd.
Webster, MO 63119
314-968-2216

Creative Families, Inc.
9378 Olive Blvd., Ste. 320
St. Louis, MO 63132
314-567-0707

Lutheran Family & Child Services
8631 Delmar Blvd.
University City, MO 63124
314-534-1515

Small World Adoption Foundation
15480 Clayton Rd., Ste. 300
Ballwin, MO 63011
636-207-9229
www.swaf.com

Special Additions, Inc.
701 Berkshire Dr.
Belton, MO 64012
816-421-3737

Montana

A New Arrival
804 Bayers Lane
Silver Star, MT 59751
406-287-2114

Catholic Charities of Montana
25 South Ewing
Helena, MT 59624
406-442-4130

Nebraska

Adoption Links Worldwide
5017 Leavenworth
Omaha, NE 68106
402-556-2367
http://alww.org

Holt International Children's
Services
10685 Bedford Ave., Ste. 300
Omaha, NE 68134
402-934-5031

Nebraska Children's Home
Society
3549 Fontenelle Blvd.
Omaha, NE 68104
402-451-0787

Nevada

Catholic Charities of Southern
Nevada
808 South Main St.
Las Vegas, NV 89101
702-385-2662

LDS Social Services
513 South Ninth St.
Las Vegas, NV 89101
702-385-1072

New Hampshire

Bethany Christian Services
P.O. Box 320
Candia, NH 03034
603-483-2886

LDS Social Services
547 Amherst St., Ste. 404
Nashua, NH 03063
603-889-0148

Wide Horizons for Children
11 Powers St.
Milford, NH 03055
603-672-3000

New Jersey

Adoptions From the Heart
451 Woodland Ave.
Cherry Hill, NJ 08002
856-665-5655

Children of the World
685 Bloomfield Ave., Ste. 201
Verona, NJ 07044
973-239-0100

Children's Home Society of
New Jersey
635 South Clinton Ave.
Trenton, NJ 08611
609-695-6274

Golden Cradle
1050 North Kings Hwy., #201
Cherry Hill, NJ 08034-1909
856-667-2229
www.goldencradle.org

Lutheran Social Ministries
6 Terri Lane, Ste. 300
Burlington, NJ 08016
609-386-7171

Seedlings, Inc.
375 Route 10 East
Whippany, NJ 07981
973-884-7488

New Mexico

Chaparral Adoption Agency
1503 University Blvd. NE
Albuquerque, NM 87102
505-243-2586

Christian Placement Service
1356 New Mexico 236
Portales, NM 88130-9411
505-356-4232

LaFamilia Placement Services
707 Broadway NE, Ste. 103
Albuquerque, NM 87102
505-766-9361
www.la-familia-inc.org

Rainbow House International
19676 Highway 314
Belen, NM 87002
505-861-1234
www.rhi.org

New York

Catholic Family Center
25 Franklin St.
Rochester, NY 14604
716-262-7134

Children of the World
27 Hillvale Rd.
Syosset, NY 11791-6916
516-935-1235

Community Maternity Services
27 North Main Ave.
Albany, NY 10022
518-482-8836

New Beginnings Family and
Children's Services, Inc.
141 Willis Ave.
Mineola, NY 11501
516-747-2204
http://new-beginnings.org

New Life Adoption Agency
430 E. Genessee St., Ste. 210
Syracuse, NY 13210
315-422-7300

Parsons Child and Family Center
60 Academy Rd.
Albany, NY 12208-3103
518-426-2600
www.parsonscenter.org

Spence-Chapin
6 East 94th St.
New York, NY 10128
212-369-0300
www.spence-chapin.org

VIDA
354 Allen St.
Hudson, NY 12534
518-828-4527

North Carolina

Carolina Adoption Services
301 North Elm St., Ste. 500
Greensboro, NC 27401
336-275-0582

Catholic Social Services
627 West 2nd St.
Winston-Salem, NC 27106
336-727-0705

Christian Adoption Services, Inc.
624 Matthews-Mint Rd., #134
Matthews, NC 28105
704-847-0038
www.christianadopt.org

Gladney Center for Adoption
217 Commerce St.
Greenville, NC 27858
252-355-6267

New Life Christian Adoptions
500 Benson Rd., Ste. 202
Garner, NC 27529
919-779-1004

North Dakota

Adoption Option
1201 25th St. South
Fargo, ND 58103
701-235-6433

Catholic Family Service
1809 South Broadway, Ste. W
Minot, ND 58703
701-852-2854

Ohio

Adoption by Gentle Care
389 Library Park South
Columbus, OH 43215
614-469-0007
www.adoptionsbygentlecare.com

American International Adoption Agency
7045 County Line Rd.
Williamsfield, OH 44093
330-876-5656

Bellefaire Jewish Children's Bureau
22001 Fairmount Blvd.
Cleveland, OH 44118
216-932-2800

Building Blocks Adoption Services
P.O. Box 1028
Medina, OH 44258
330-725-5521 or
toll-free: 866-321-ADOPT
www.buildingblocksadoption.com

New Hope Adoptions
101 West Sandusky St., Ste. 311
Findlay, OH 45840
419-423-0760

Oklahoma

Cradle of Lawton, Inc.
902 NW Kingswood Rd.
Lawton, OK 73505
580-536-2478

Deaconess Home Pregnancy and
Adoption Services
5300 North Meridian, Ste. 9
Oklahoma City, OK 73112
405-949-4200
www.deaconess.okc.org/dpas

LDS Social Services
4500 South Garnett, Ste. 425
Tulsa, OK 74146-5201
918-665-3090

Small Miracles International, Inc.
1148 South Douglas Blvd.
Midwest City, OK 73130
405-732-7295
www.smint.org

Oregon

ASIA of Oregon
5935 Willow Lane
Lake Oswego, OR 97035
503-697-6863

Cascade International Children
133 SW Second
Troutdale, OR 97060
503-665-1589

Holt International Children's Services
P.O. Box 2880
Eugene, OR 97402
541-687-2202
www.holtinternational.org

Journeys of the Heart
P.O. Box 39
Hillsboro, OR 97123
503-681-3075
www.journeysoftheheart.net

New Hope Child and Family
Agency
4370 East Halsey St., Ste. 215
Portland, OR 97213
503-282-6726

Orphans Overseas
14986 NW Cornell
Portland, OR 97229
503-297-2006
www.orphansoverseas.org

PLAN Loving Adoptions Now, Inc.
P.O. Box 667
McMinnville, OR 97128
503-472-8452
www.planlovingadoptions.org

Pennsylvania

Adopt-A-Child
Maxon Towers, Ste. L-111
6315 Forbes Ave.
Pittsburgh, PA 15217
412-421-1911
www.adopt-a-child.org

Adoption Horizons
899 Petersburg Rd.
Carlisle, PA 17013
717-249-8850

Adoption Unlimited
2148 Embassy Drive
Lancaster, PA 17603
717-431-2021
www.adoptionunlimited.org

Adoptions from the Heart
30-31 Hampstead Circle
Wynnewood, PA 19096
610-642-7200
www.adoptionsfromtheheart.org

Bethany Christian Services
694 Lincoln Ave.
Pittsburgh, PA 15202
412-734-2662

Common Sense Adoption Service
5021 East Trindle Rd.
Mechanicsburg, PA 17050
717-766-6449

International Assistance Group
531 Fifth St.
Oakmont, PA 15139
412-828-5800
www.iagadoptions.org

Pearl S. Buck International
Welcome House Adoption
Program
520 Dublin Rd.
Perkasie, PA 18944
1-800-220-BUCK
www.pearlsbuck.org

St. Joseph's Center
2010 Adams Ave.
Scranton, PA 18509
570-342-8379
www.stjosephscenter.org

Tressler Lutheran Services
836 South George St.
York, PA 17403
717-845-9113

Rhode Island

Catholic Social Services
311 Hooper St.
Tiverton, RI 02878
401-624-9270

Gift of Life Adoptions
1053 Park Ave.
Cranston, RI 02910
401-943-6484

Wide Horizons for Children
245 Waterman St., Ste. 504
Providence, RI 02906
401-421-4752

South Carolina

Bethany Christian Services
1411 Barnwell St.
Columbia, SC 29201
803-779-0541

Carolina Hope Adoption Agency
819 East North St.
Greenville, SC 29601
864-268-0570
www.carolinahopeadoption.org

Christian World Adoption
111 Ashley Ave.
Charleston, SC 29401
1-888-972-3678
www.cwa.org

Tennessee

Bethany Christian Services
400 South Germantown Rd.
Chattanooga, TN 37411-3842
423-622-7360

Catholic Charities of TN
30 White Bridge Rd.
Nashville, TN 37205-1401
615-352-3087

Heaven Sent Children
307 North Walnut St.
Murfreesboro, TN 37130
615-898-0803
http://heavensentchildren.com

Holston United Methodist Home
404 Holston Dr.
Greeneville, TN 37744
1-800-628-2986

Porter-Leath Children's Center
868 North Manassas St.
Memphis, TN 38107-2516
901-577-2500

Small World Ministries
401 Bonnaspring Dr.
Hermitage, TN 37076-1147
615-883-4372

Texas

Adoption Alliance
7303 Blanco Rd.
San Antonio, TX 78216
210-349-3991

Andrel Adoptions, Inc.
3908 Manchaca Rd.
Austin, TX 78704
512-448-4605

Bright Dreams International
4931 Cape Coral Dr.
Dallas, TX 75287
972-380-9183
www.brightdreams.org

Buckner Adoption and Maternity Services
4830 Samuell Blvd.
Dallas, TX 75228
866-236-7823
www.bucknerinternationaladoption.org

Christian Homes of Abilene
P.O. Box 270
Abilene, TX 79604
1-800-592-4725
www.christianhomes.com

Cradle of Life Adoption
245 North 4th St.
Beaumont, TX 77701-1920
409-832-3000

The Gladney Center
6300 John Ryan Dr.
Fort Worth, TX 76132
817-922-6088
www.adoptionsbygladney.com

Homes of St. Mark
3000 Richmond Ave. #570
Houston, TX 77006
713-522-2800

Hope Cottage Adoption Center
4209 McKinney Ave.
Dallas, TX 75205-4543
1-800-944-4460
www.hopecottage.org

Limiar
111 Broken Bough
San Antonio, TX 78231
210-479-0300
www.limiar.org

Los Ninos
2408 Timberlock Place, Ste. D-1
The Woodlands, TX 77380
281-363-2892
www.losninos.org

New Life Children's Services
19911 SH 249
Houston, TX 77070
281-955-1001

Smithlawn Home and Adoption
Agency
P.O. Box 6451
Lubbock, TX 79493
806-745-2574

Utah

Adopt an Angel
254 West 400 South, Ste. 320
Salt Lake City, UT 84101
801-537-1622

LDS Social Services
National Headquarters
10 East South Temple St., Ste. 1250
Salt Lake City, UT 84133
801-240-6500

Wasatch International Adoption
3725 Washington Blvd., Ste. 9
Ogden, UT 84403
801-334-8683
www.wiaa.org

Vermont

Friends in Adoption
44 South Street
Middletown Springs, VT 05757
1-800-844-3630
www.friendsinadoption.org

Wide Horizons for Children
P.O. Box 53
Monkton, VT 05469
802-453-2581

Virginia

Adoption Service Information
Agency (ASIA)
1305 North Jackson St.
Arlington, VA 22201
703-312-0263
www.asia-adopt.org

Bethany Christian Services
287 Independence Blvd. #241
Virginia Beach, VA 23462-5473
757-499-9367

Children's Home Society of VA
4200 Fitzhugh Ave.
Richmond, VA 23230-3829
804-353-0191

Commonwealth Catholic Charities
1512 Willow Lawn Dr.
Richmond, VA 23230-0565
804-285-5900

United Methodist Family Services
3900 West Broad St.
Richmond, VA 23230
804-353-4461

Washington

Adoption Advocates International
401 East Front St.
Port Angeles, WA 98362
360-452-4777
www.adoptionadvocates.org

Americans Adopting Orphans
12345 Lake City Way NE, Ste. 2001
Seattle, WA 98125
206-524-5437
www.orphans.com

Bethany Christian Services
19936 Ballinger Way NE, Ste. 2001
Seattle, WA 98125
206-367-4064

Catholic Community Services
100 23rd Ave. South
Seattle, WA 98144-2302
206-323-1950

Eurasian Adoption Services
1111 Main St. #600
Vancouver, WA 98660
Toll-free: 1-888-916-2229
www.eurasianadoption.org

Faith International Adoptions
535 East Dock St. #103
Tacoma, WA 98402
253-383-1928
http://faithadopt.org

New Hope Child & Family Agency
19304 King's Garden Drive North
Seattle, WA 98133
206-363-1800
www.newhopekids.org

WACAP
P.O. Box 88948
Seattle, WA 98138
206-575-4550
www.wacap.org

West Virginia

Adoptions from the Heart
7014 Grand Central Station
Morgantown, WV 26505
304-291-5211

Burlington United Methodist
P.O. Box 370
Scott Depot, WV 25560
304-757-9127

Global Adoption Services
50 E. Loucks, Ste. 205
Sheridan, WY 82801
307-674-6606
www.adoptglobal.org

Wisconsin

Adoption Services, Inc.
911 North Lynndale Dr., Ste. 2C
Appleton, WI 54914-3086
920-735-6750
www.adoptionservices.org

Bethany Christian Services
2312 North Grandview Blvd.
Waukesha, WI 53188
262-547-6557

Evangelical Child & Family Agency
1617 South 124th St.
New Berlin, WI 53151-1803
414-789-1881

Lutheran Social Services
647 West Virginia St., Ste. 300
Milwaukee, WI 53204
414-325-3222

Wyoming

Catholic Social Services of Wyoming
P.O. Box 1468
Cheyenne, WY 82003
307-638-1530

Focus on Children
405 Sage St.
Cokeville, WY 83114
1-888-801-7295
http://focusonchildren.com

Selected National Adoption Organizations

The following national adoption organizations provide information and support on adoption and adoption-related issues. Some specialize in a particular area, such as children with special needs, whereas other organizations provide information on children from specific countries. Some organizations are interested in the adoption of all types of children. Contact the organizations for more information. Note that this list is only a sampling of the many groups that directly or indirectly deal with adoption. Some organizations provided addresses and phone numbers, but several prefer to be contacted by e-mail or their website.

Adoption Exchange Association
8015 Corporate Drive, Suite C
Baltimore, MD 21236
1-800-200-4005
www.adoptea.org

The main contractor for The Collaboration to AdoptUSKids, a federal project promoting the adoption of foster children in the United States by recruiting adoptive parents.

American Academy of Adoption Attorneys
P.O. Box 33053
Washington, DC 20033-0053
202-832-2222
www.adoptionattorneys.org

The American Academy of Adoption Attorneys was formed in 1990 by a group of attorneys wishing to improve adoption laws and practice in the United States and abroad. Membership by invitation.

American Academy of Pediatrics Section on Adoption and Foster Care
141 Northwest Point Blvd.
Elk Grove, IL 60007
847-434-4000
www.aap.org/sections/adoption

This organization, a division of the American Academy of Pediatrics, is a professional association for pediatricians and offers a nationwide directory of pediatricians interested in adoption and foster care medicine.

Dave Thomas Foundation for Adoption
4288 West Dublin Granville Rd.
Dublin, OH 43017
1-888-ASK-DTFA
www.davethomasfoundationforadoption.com

This organization supports public awareness of adoption. It was founded by the late Dave Thomas, an adopted person. It has been instrumental in promoting the importance of adoption grants and loans to corporations.

Families for Russian and Ukrainian Adoption (FRUA)
P.O. Box 2944
Merrifield, VA 22116
703-560-6184
www.frua.org
info@frua.org

This is an active international parent support network of families who have adopted children from Eastern Europe and who seek to adopt. FRUA offers chapters nationwide and sponsors conferences and an updated website.

Families Like Ours
P.O. Box 3137
Renton, WA 98056
206-441-7602 or 425-793-7911
www.familieslikeours.org

This is a nonprofit group devoted to the needs and support of nontraditional adoptive families.

Families with Children Adopted from Bulgaria (FaCAB)
7933 NE 124th St.
Kirkland, WA 98034
425-823-8018
http://groups.yahoo.com/group/FaCAB1

This is a national support group for families with children adopted from Bulgaria.

Families with Children from China
www.fwcc.org

This valuable website provides comprehensive information on adopting from China, as well as links or addresses for the many state and city organizations of Families with Children from China.

Families with Children from Vietnam
10009 Whitestone Rd.
Raleigh, NC 27615
www.fcvn.org

This is a national support group for people who wish to adopt or have adopted children from Vietnam. It has chapters throughout the United States and offers a newsletter and many resources.

Guatemala Adoptive Families Network
P.O. Box 176
Watertown, MA 02471
www.guatefam.org
info@guatefam.org

This is a national organization for families who have adopted or seek to adopt children from Guatemala.

Korean American Adoptee Adoptive Family Network (KAAN)
P.O. Box 5585
El Dorado Hills, CA 95762
916-933-1447
www.kaanet.com

This is a national group for adoptive parents of Korean children, Korean-born adopted adults, and Korean Americans to meet and share perspectives. Offers a national conference, a weekly e-mail newsletter, and a resource website.

National Adoption Center
1500 Walnut St., Ste. 701
Philadelphia, PA 19102
1-800-TO-ADOPT
www.nac.adopt.org

This organization provides information and agency referrals to people interested in adopting children with special needs. Also works actively to promote public awareness of children who need families. Provides a photo-listing service of "waiting children."

National Adoption Information Clearinghouse
330 C St. SW
Washington, DC 20447
1-888-251-0075 or 703-352-3488
www.acf.hhs.gov

The National Adoption Information Clearinghouse offers a broad array of adoption information for adoptive parents, adoptees, and birthparents, much of which is free of charge.

National Council For Adoption
225 North Washington St.
Arlington, VA 22314
703-299-6633
www.ncfa-usa.org

This organization is a national advocacy and information group comprised of agencies, attorneys, and individuals. It provides information and assistance on many adoption-related areas, lobbies on adoption issues, and answers media queries about a broad array of adoption topics.

North American Council on Adoptable Children (NACAC)
970 Raymond Ave., Ste. 106
St. Paul, MN 55114
612-644-3036
www.nacac.org

NACAC concentrates on laws, issues, and policies related to adoptive placements of children with special needs. Provides information and assistance. Holds an annual conference in either the United States or Canada. Publishes an informational newsletter.

National Center for Adoption Law & Policy
Capital University Law School
303 East Broad Street
Columbus, OH 43215
614-236-6593
www.adoptionlawsite.org/main_cur.asp

This organization offers updated legal information on adoption laws and legal news throughout the United States.

National Resource Center for Special Needs Adoption
16250 Northland Drive, Ste. 120
Southfield, MI 48075
248-443-0306
www.nrcadoption.org

This organization provides practical and helpful information and assistance on adopted children with special needs.

RESOLVE, Inc.
1310 Broadway
Somerville, MA 02144-1731
1-888-623-0744
www.resolve.org

This is the headquarters of the national infertility information group. They also offer information on adoption. RESOLVE has chapters nationwide.

Stars of David International, Inc.
3175 Commercial Ave., Ste. 100
Northbrook, IL 60062-1915
1-800-STAR-349 or 773-274-1527
www.starsofdavid.org
starsdavid@aol.com

Stars of David is a nonprofit information and support network for Jewish prospective parents, adoptive families, adopted adults, birth families, and the Jewish community, with chapters in many states nationwide as well as abroad.

Selected Adoption Attorneys

All attorneys listed here are members of the American Academy of Adoption Attorneys and/or the National Council For Adoption. Listing in this appendix does not constitute endorsement of any particular individual; you should carefully screen any attorney with whom you are considering working.

Alabama

Beth Marietta Lyons
56 Saint Joseph St. #711
Mobile, AL 36602
251-690-9111

Bryant A. Whitmire, Jr.
215 Richard Arrington, Jr.
Blvd. N, Ste. 501
Birmingham, AL 35203
205-324-6631
www.whitmireadoptions.com

Alaska

Robert B. Flint
717 K Street
Anchorage, AK 99501
907-276-1592

Arizona

Michael J. Herrod
1221 East Osborn Rd., Ste. 105
Phoenix, AZ 85014
602-277-7000

Scott E. Myers
3180 East Grant Rd.
Tucson, AZ 85716
520-327-6041

Kathryn A. Pidgeon
3131 East Camelback Rd. #200
Phoenix, AZ 85016
602-522-8700

Arkansas

Eugene T. Kelley
303 West Walnut St.
Rogers, AR 72756
479-636-1051
www.anewworldawaits.com

Kaye H. McLeod
210 Linwood Court
Little Rock, AR 72205
501-663-6224

California

David H. Baum
16255 Ventura Blvd., #704
Encino, CA 91436-2311
1-800-795-2367 (outside California)
818-501-8355 (in California)
www.adoptlaw.com

Timothy J. Blied
19712 MacArthur Blvd.
Irvine, CA 92612
949-863-0200
www.sbsmlaw.com

D. Durand Cook
8383 Wilshire Blvd., Ste. 1030
Beverly Hills, CA 90211
323-655-2601
www.adoption-option.com

Douglas R. Donnelly
427 East Carrillo St.
Santa Barbara, CA 93101
805-962-0988
www.adoptionlawfirm.com

Randall B. Hicks
6690 Alessandro Blvd., Ste. D
Riverside, CA 92506
909-789-6800

Allen C. Hultquist
43980 Mahlon Vail Circle #403
Temecula, CA 92592
909-302-7777
www.aadoption.net

Diane Michelsen
3190 Old Tunnel Rd.
Lafayette, CA 94549
925-945-1880
www.lodm.com

David Radis
1901 Avenue of the Stars #1900
Los Angeles, CA 90067
310-552-0536

Jed Somit
1440 Broadway, #910
Oakland, CA 94612
510-839-3215

Felice Webster
4525 Wilshire Blvd. #201
Los Angeles, CA 90010
323-664-5600

Marc D. Widelock
1801 Oak St.
Bakersfield, CA 93301
1-800-MRSTORK
www.thestork.com

Colorado

W. Thomas Beltz
Adoption Choice Center
729 South Cascade Ave.
Colorado Springs, CO 80903
719-473-4444

Seth A. Grob
31425 Forestland Dr.
Evergreen, CO 80439
303-679-8266

Susan Beth Price
730 Seventeenth St. #230
Denver, CO 80202
303-893-3111

Daniel A. West
729 South Cascade Avenue
Colorado Springs, CO 80903
719-473-4444

Connecticut

Janet S. Stulting
One American Row
Hartford, CT 06103-2819
860-251-5115
www.shipmangoodwin.com

Delaware

Ellen S. Meyer
521 West St.
Wilmington, DE 19801
302-429-0344

District of Columbia

Mark T. McDermott
1050 17th St. NW, Ste. 700
Washington, DC 20036
202-331-1955
www.theadoptionadvisor.com

Peter J. Wiernicki
1050 17th St. NW, Ste. 700
Washington, DC 20036
202-331-1955

Florida

Mikal Grass
701 West Cypress Creek Rd. #302
Ft. Lauderdale, FL 33309
954-202-7889

Madonna Finney Hawken
660 East Jefferson St.
Tallahassee, FL 32301
850-577-3077

Linda West McIntyre
2929 University Dr. #204
Coral Springs, FL 33065
954-344-0990

Mary Ann Scherer
2734 East Oakland Park Blvd. #102
Ft. Lauderdale, FL 33306
954-564-6900

Susan Stockham
1800 Siesta Dr.
Sarasota, FL 34231
941-924-4949
www.StockhamLaw.com

Jeanne Trudeau Tate
418 West Platt St.
Tampa, FL 33606
813-258-3355

Georgia

Rhonda L. Fishbein
17 Executive Park Dr., Ste. 290
Atlanta, GA 30329
404-248-9205
www.rfishbeinadoption-law.com

Richard A. Horder
1100 Peachtree St., Ste. 2800
Atlanta, GA 30309-4530
404-815-6500

Irene A. Steffas
4343 Shallowford Rd., Bldg. H-1
Marietta, GA 30062
770-642-6075
www.SteffasLaw.com

Hawaii

Laurie A. Loomis
American Savings Bank Tower
1001 Bishop St., Ste. 2010
Honolulu, HI 96813
808-524-5066

Idaho

John T. Hawley, Jr.
202 North Ninth St., Ste. 205
Boise, ID 83702
208-336-6686
www.adoptionIdaho.com

Illinois

Daniel Azulay
One East Wacker Dr., #2700
Chicago, IL 60601
312-832-9200

Shelley B. Ballard
208 South LaSalle Street, Ste. 2079
Chicago, IL 60604
312-673-5312
www.infertility-law.com

Victoria Bush-Joseph
208 South LaSalle St., Ste. 2079
Chicago, IL 60604
312-673-5312
www.infertility-law.com

Deborah Crouse Cobb
515 West Main
Collinsville, IL 62234
618-344-6300

Susan Grammer
P.O. Box 111
Bethalto, IL 62010-0111
618-259-2113

Theresa Rahe Hardesty
7513 North Regent Place
Peoria, IL 61614
309-692-1087

Richard A. Lifshitz
203 North LaSalle St., Ste. 2210
Chicago, IL 60601
312-236-7080
www.mandellipton.com

Glenna J. Weith
116 North Chestnut St., Ste. 230
Champaign, IL 61820
217-398-1200

Sally Wildman
180 North LaSalle St., Ste. 2310
Chicago, IL 60601
312-726-9214

Indiana

Timothy J. Hubert
P.O. Box 916
Evansville, IN 47706-0916
812-424-7575

Joel D. Kirsh
2930 East 96th St.
Indianapolis, IN 46240
317-575-5555
www.indianaadoption.com

Steven M. Kirsh
2930 East 96th St.
Indianapolis, IN 46240
317-575-5555
www.indianaadoption.com

Iowa

Maxine M. Buckmeier
600 Fourth St. #304
P.O. Box 634
Sioux City, IA 51102
712-233-3660

Lori L. Klockau
402 South Linn St.
Iowa City, IA 52240
319-338-7968

Kansas

Martin W. Bauer
100 North Broadway, Ste. 500
Wichita, KS 67202
316-265-9311

Jill Bremyer-Archer
P.O. Box 1146
McPherson, KS 67460-1146
620-241-0554
www.bwisecounsel.com

Richard A. Macias
100 North Broadway, Ste. 500
Wichita, KS 67202
316-265-5245
www.martinpringle.com

Kentucky

Carolyn S. Arnett
401 West Main St, Ste. 1708
Louisville, KY 40202
502-585-4368
www.adoptionsofkentucky.com

Mitchell A. Charney
3000 National City Tower
Louisville, KY 40202
502-589-4440

Elisabeth Goldman
106 West Vine St., Ste. 304
Lexington, KY 40507
859-381-1145

Louisiana

Terri Hoover Debnam
500 North 7th St.
West Monroe, LA 71291
1-800-286-6046
www.centerforadoption.com

Edith H. Morris
1515 Poydras St., Ste. 1870
New Orleans, LA 70112
504-524-3781

Noel E. Vargas II
146 North Telemachus St.
New Orleans, LA 70119
504-488-0200

Maine

Judith Berry
28 State St.
Gorham, ME 04038
207-839-7004

Maryland

Jeffrey Ewen Badger
P.O. Box 259
Salisbury, MD 21803-0259
410-749-2356

John R. Greene
156 South St.
Annapolis, MD 21401
410-268-4500

Carolyn Thaler
29 West Susquehanna Ave., Ste. 205
Towson, MD 21204
410-828-6627

Massachusetts

Herbert D. Friedman
125 High St. #2601
Boston, MA 02110
617-951-9980, ext. 205
www.massadoption.com

Karen K. Greenberg
110 Cedar St.
Wellesley Hills, MA 02481
782-237-0033

Michigan

Herbert A. Brail
930 Mason St.
Dearborn, MI 48124
313-278-8779
www.keanelaw.com

Monica Farris Linkner
121 West Washington, Ste. 300
Ann Arbor, MI 48104
734-214-0200

Minnesota

Judith D. Vincent
111 Third Ave. South, Ste. 360
Minneapolis, MN 55402
612-332-7772
www.adoptionlaw-mn.com

Wright S. Walling
121 South Eighth St., Ste. 1100
Minneapolis, MN 55402
612-335-4283
www.WBDLAW.com

Mississippi

Dan J. Davis
P.O. Box 7262
Tupelo, MS 38802
662-841-1090

Lisa Milner
2000 AmSouth Plaza
Jackson, MS 39201
601-948-6100

Missouri

Allan F. Stewart
222 South Central Ave., Ste. 900
Clayton, MO 63105
314-863-8484

F. Richard Van Pelt
1524 East Primrose #A
Springfield, MO 65804
417-886-9080

Nebraska

Michael C. Washburn
10330 Regency Parkway Drive
Omaha, NE 68114
402-397-2200

Nevada

Israel "Ishi" Kunin
3551 East Bonanza Rd. #110
Las Vegas, NV 89110
702-438-8060

Eric A. Stovall
200 Ridge St., #200
Reno, NV 89501
775-329-4111

New Hampshire

Margaret Cunnane Hall
37 High St.
Milford, NH 03055
603-673-8323

Ann McLane Kuster
One Capital Plaza
P.O. Box 1500
Concord, NH 03302-1500
603-226-2600
www.rathlaw.com

Patricia B. Quigley
67 Central St.
Manchester, NH 03101
603-644-8300

New Jersey

Donald C. Cofsky
209 Haddon Ave.
Haddonfield, NJ 08033
856-429-5005

Robin A. Fleischner
374 Millburn Ave., Ste. 303 E
Millburn, NJ 07041
973-376-6623

Elizabeth A. Hopkins
766 Shrewsbury Ave.
Tinton Falls, NJ 07724
732-933-7777

Suzanne Nichols
336 Tucker Ave.
Union, NJ 07083
908-964-1097

Steven B. Sacharow
1810 Chapel Avenue
Cherry Hill, NJ 08002-4609
856-661-2272

Toby Solomon
354 Eisenhower Parkway
Livingston, NJ 07039
973-533-0078

Deborah Steincolor
295 Montgomery St.
Bloomfield, NJ 07003
973-743-7500

New Mexico

Harold O. Atencio
3809 Atrisco NW #B
P.O. Box 66468
Albuquerque, NM 87193-6468
505-839-9111

New York

Aaron Britvan
7600 Jericho Turnpike, Ste. 300
Woodbury, NY 11797
516-496-2222
www.aaronbritvan.com

Anne Reynolds Copps
126 State St., 6th Floor
Albany, NY 12207
518-436-4170

Robin A. Fleischner
11 Riverside Dr., #14 MW
New York, NY 10023
212-362-6945

Gregory A. Franklin
95 Allens Creek Rd.
Building 1
Rochester, NY 14618
585-442-0540 ext. 3007
www.AdoptionNY.com

Michael S. Goldstein
62 Bowman Ave.
Rye Brook, NY 10573
914-939-1111

Flory Herman
260 Creekside Dr. #200
Amherst, NY 14228
716-691-1706

Cynthia Perla Meckler
8081 Floss Lane
East Amherst, NY 14051
716-741-4164

Chana Mesberg
1 River Place #29-19
New York, NY 10036
646-345-6909

Suzanne Nichols
70 West Red Oak Lane
White Plains, NY 10604
914-697-4870

Brendan C. O'Shea
102 Hackett Blvd.
Albany, NY 12209
518-432-7511

Douglas H. Reiniger
630 Third Ave.
New York, NY 10017-6705
212-972-5430

Benjamin J. Rosin
630 Third Ave.
New York, NY 10017-6705
212-972-5430

Deborah Steincolor
845 Third Ave. #1400
New York, NY 10022
212-421-7807

Golda Zimmerman
711 East Genesee St., Ste. 200
Syracuse, NY 13210
315-475-3322

North Carolina

Bobby D. Mills
P.O. Box 1677
Raleigh, NC 27602
919-821-1860 X 227
www.hermcb.com

W. David Thurman
301 South McDowell St. #608
Charlotte, NC 28204
704-377-4164

North Dakota

William P. Harrie
1800 Radisson Tower
201 North 5th St.
P.O. Box 2626
Fargo, ND 58108
701-237-5544

Ohio

James S. Albers
88 North Fifth St.
Columbus, OH 43215
614-464-4414

Susan G. Eisenman
336 South High St.
Columbus, OH 43215
614-222-0540

Ellen Essig
105 East Fourth St., #400
Cincinnati, OH 45202
513-721-5151

Carolyn Mussio
3411 Michigan Ave.
Cincinnati, OH 45208
513-871-8855
www.privateadoptionservice.com

Oklahoma

Barbara K. Bado
1800 Canyon Park Circle, #301
Edmond, OK 73013
405-340-1500

John O'Connor
15 West 6th St., Ste. 2700
Tulsa, OK 74119
918-587-0101

Jack H. Petty
6666 NW 39th Expressway
Bethany, OK 73008
405-787-6911

Oregon

John Chally
825 NE Multnomah, Ste. 1125
Portland, OR 97232-2148
503-238-9720
www.adoptionnorthwest.com

Catherine M. Dexter
25260 SW Parkway Ave., Ste. C
Wilsonville, OR 97070
503-582-9010
www.oregonadopt.com

Sandra L. Hodgson
825 NE Multnomah, Ste. 1125
Portland, OR 97232-2148
503-238-9720
www.adoptionnorthwest.com

Susan C. Moffet
25260 SW Parkway Ave., Ste. C
Wilsonville, OR 97070
503-582-9010
www.oregonadopt.com

Robin Elizabeth Pope
1834 SW 58th Ave., Ste. 101
Portland, OR 97221
503-297-6150
www.robinpope.com

Laurence H. Spiegel
4040 SW Douglas Way
Lake Oswego, OR 97035
503-635-7773
www.adoption-Oregon.com

Pennsylvania

Craig Bluestein
200 Old York Rd.
Jenkintown, PA 19046
215-576-1030

Debra M. Fox
355 West Lancaster Ave.
Haverford, PA 19041
610-896-9972

Tara E. Gutterman
4701 Pine St., #J7
Philadelphia, PA 19143
215-748-1441

Samuel J. Totaro, Jr.
Four Greenwood Square #200
Bensalem, PA 19020
215-638-9330

South Carolina

Frederick M. Corley
1214 King St.
P.O. Box 2265
Beaufort, SC 29901
843-524-3232

Dale Dove
P.O. Box 907
Rock Hill, SC 29731
803-327-1910

James Fletcher Thompson
P.O. Box 1853
Spartanburg, SC 29304
864-573-5533, extension 5

South Dakota

John R. Hughes
431 North Phillips Ave., Ste. 330
Sioux Falls, SD 57104
605-339-3939

Tennessee

Lisa L. Collins
One Belle Meade Place
4400 Harding Rd., Ste. 502
Nashville, TN 37205
615-269-5540

S. Dawn Coppock
P.O. Box 388
Strawberry Plains, TN 37871
865-933-8173

Michael Jennings
130 Jordan Dr.
Chattanooga, TN 37421
423-892-2006

Robert D. Tuke
3708 Wimbledon Rd.
Nashville, TN 37215
615-256-8585
www.tntlaw.com

Texas

Vika Andrel
3908 Manchaca Rd.
Austin, TX 78704
512-448-4605

Gerald A. Bates
3200 River Front Dr. #204
Fort Worth, TX 76107
817-338-2840

Carla M. Calabrese
311 North Market St., #300
Dallas, TX 75202-1846
214-939-3000

David Cole
3631 Fairmount St., Ste. 201
Dallas, TX 75219
214-363-5117

Susan I. Paquet
320 Purcey
Ft. Worth, TX 76102
817-596-3337

Mel W. Shelander
245 North Fourth St.
Beaumont, TX 77701
409-833-2165

Ellen A. Yarell
1900 St. James Place #850
Houston, TX 77056
713-621-3332

Utah

Larry S. Jenkins
60 East South Temple, Ste. 500
Salt Lake City, UT 84111
801-366-6060

Vermont

Kurt M. Hughes
131 Main Street
P.O. Box 363
Burlington, VT 05402
802-864-9811
www.adoptvt.com

Virginia

Jennifer Brust
2000 North 14th St., #100
Arlington, VA 22201
703-525-4000

Barbara C. Jones
7016 Balmoral Forest Rd.
Clifton, VA 20124
703-222-1101

Robert H. Klima
9257 Lee Ave.
Manassas, VA 22110
703-361-5051

Rosemary O'Brien
109 South Fairfax St.
Alexandria, VA 22314
703-549-5110

Stanton Phillips
1921 Gallows Rd., Ste. 110
Tysons Corner
Vienna, VA 22182
703-891-2400

Washington

Rita L. Bender
1301 Fifth Ave., #3401
Seattle, WA 98101
206-623-6501
www.skellengerbender.com

Mark Demaray
145 Third Avenue South, Ste. 201
Edmonds, WA 98020
425-776-4100

J. Eric Gustafson
222 North Third St.
Yakima, WA 98901
1-800-238-KIDS

Michele Gentry Hinz
33035 52nd Ave. South
Auburn, WA 98001
253-735-0928

Joyce Robson
2511 South Hood St.
Tacoma, WA 98402
253-572-5104

Marie Tilden
1111 Main St., Ste. 600
P.O. Box 61566
Vancouver, WA 98666
360-699-4780

West Virginia

David Allen Barnette
500 Lee St.
Charleston, WV 25301
304-340-1327

Wisconsin

Lynn J. Bodi
434 South Yellowstone Dr.
Madison, WI 53719
608-821-8200
www.law4kids.com

Carol M. Gapen
434 South Yellowstone Dr.
Madison, WI 53719
608-821-8211
www.law4kids.com

Stephen W. Hayes
20800 Swenson Dr. #475
Waukesha, WI 53186
262-798-8220

Judith Sperling Newton
434 South Yellowstone Dr.
Madison, WI 53719
608-821-8200
www.law4kids.com

Theresa L. Roetter
2010 Eastwood Dr., Ste. 301
P.O. Box 3006
Madison, WI 53704
608-244-1354 ext. 325
www.hill-law-firm.com

Victoria J. Schroeder
2574 Sun Valley Dr. #200
Delafield, WI 53018
262-646-2054

Wyoming

Peter J. Feeney
P.O. Box 437
Casper, WY 82602
307-266-4422

Douglas H. Reiniger
54 Bartek Rd.
Bondurant, WY 82922
307-859-8811

State Public Adoption Agencies

Each state has a central adoption office based in the state social services headquarters. These offices are primarily concerned with the adoption of foster children, but in most cases, state adoption personnel are also aware of adoption laws and proposed changes to laws. State personnel probably can't recommend individual adoption agencies, but they might be able to tell you about complaints or allegations against specific agencies. If the individuals you contact cannot answer your question, ask whether they know of an organization or group who might know the answer.

Alabama

Alabama Office of Adoption
Department of Human Resources
50 North Ripley St.
Montgomery, AL 36130
334-242-1374

Alaska

Alaska Division of Family and Youth Services
P.O. 110630
Juneau, AK 99811-0630
907-465-2145

Arizona

Arizona Department of Economic Security
Children, Youth and Families Division
P.O. Box 6123
Phoenix, AZ 85005
602-542-5499

Arkansas

Arkansas Department of Human Services
Division of Children and Family Services
P.O. Box 1437, Slot 808
Little Rock, AR 72203-1437
501-682-8462

California

Adoptions Branch
California Department of Social Services
744 P St., M/S 19-69
Sacramento, CA 95814
916-323-2921

Colorado

Colorado Department of Human Services
1575 Sherman St., 2nd Floor
Denver, CO 80203
303-866-3197

Connecticut

Department of Children and Families
505 Hudson St.
Hartford, CT 06106
860-550-6350

Delaware

Delaware Division of Child Protective Services
1825 Faulkland Rd.
Wilmington, DE 19805
302-633-2655

District of Columbia

District of Columbia Child and Family Services
400 Sixth Street, SW
Washington, DC 20024
202-727-3655

Florida

Florida Department of Children & Families
1317 Winewood Blvd., Bldg. 7
Tallahassee, FL 32399
850-921-2177

Georgia

Georgia Department of Human Resources
Division of Family and Child Services
2 Peachtree St. NW, Ste. 3-323
Atlanta, GA 30303
404-657-3558

Hawaii

Hawaii Department of Human Services
810 Richards St., Ste. 400
Honolulu, HI 96813
808-586-5698

Idaho

Department of Health and Welfare
Division of Family and Community Services
P.O. Box 83720
Boise, ID 83720-0036
208-334-5700

Illinois

Department of Children & Family Services
406 East Monroe St., Station 25
Springfield, IL 62701-1498
217-524-2422

Indiana

Division of Family and Children
Bureau of Family Protection/Preservation
402 W. Washington St., Room W364
Indianapolis, IN 46204-2739
1-888-204-7466

Iowa

Iowa Department of Human Services
Adult, Children and Family Services
Hoover State Office Building, 5th Floor
Des Moines, IA 50319
515-281-5358

Kansas

Kansas Department of Social and Rehabilitative Services
915 SW Harrison, Fifth Floor
Topeka, KS 66612
785-296-0918

Kentucky

Kentucky Cabinet for Human Resources
275 East Main St., 6th Floor
Frankfort, KY 40621
502-564-2147

Louisiana

Louisiana Department of Social Services
Office of Community Services
P.O. Box 3318
Baton Rouge, LA 70821
225-216-6925

Maine

Department of Human Services
Bureau of Child and Family Services
221 State Street
11 State House Station
Augusta, ME 04333-0011
207-287-5062

Maryland

Maryland Department of Human Resources
Social Services Administration
311 West Saratoga St.
Baltimore, MD 21201
410-767-7506

Massachusetts

Massachusetts Department of Social Services
24 Farnsworth St.
Boston, MA 02210
617-748-2267

Michigan

Michigan Family Independence Agency
Child and Family Services Administration
235 South Grand Ave.
P.O. Box 30037
Lansing, MI 48909
517-373-3513

Minnesota

Adoption Unit, Minnesota Department of Human Services
444 Lafayette Road North
St. Paul, MN 55155
651-296-3740

Mississippi

Mississippi Department of Human Services
Division of Family and Child Services
750 North State St.
Jackson, MS 39202
601-359-4981

Missouri

Missouri Division of Family Services
P.O. Box 88
Jefferson City, MO 65103
573-751-0311

Montana

Montana Department of Public Health & Human Services
1400 Broadway, Cogswell Building
P.O. Box 8005
Helena, MT 59620
406-444-5919

Nebraska

Nebraska Department of Social Services
P.O. Box 95044
Lincoln, NE 68509
402-471-9331

Nevada

Department of Human Resources
Division of Child and Family Services
6171 West Charleston Blvd., Bldg. 15
Las Vegas, NV 89102
702-486-7633

New Hampshire

Department of Health and Human Services
Children, Youth and Families
129 Pleasant Street
Concord, NH 03301
603-271-4707

New Jersey

New Jersey Division of Youth and Family Services
50 East State St., CN 717
Trenton, NJ 08625
609-984-2380

New Mexico

Central Adoption Unit
P.O. Drawer 5160
PERA Building, Room 252
Santa Fe, NM 87502
505-841-7932

New York

New York State Department of Social Services
40 North Pearl St.
Albany, NY 12243
518-474-9406

North Carolina

North Carolina Department of Health and Human Resources
Children's Services Section
2408 Mail Service Center
Raleigh, NC 27699
919-733-4622

North Dakota

North Dakota Department of Human Services
State Capitol
600 East Blvd.
Bismarck, ND 58505
701-328-4805

Ohio

Department of Job and Family Services
Office for Children and Families
255 East Main Street, Third Floor
Columbus, OH 43215
614-466-9274

Oklahoma

Oklahoma Department of Human Services
P.O. Box 25352
Oklahoma City, OK 73125
405-521-2467

Oregon

Oregon Department of Human Resources
Permanency and Adoption Services
500 Summer St. NE
Salem, OR 97301
503-945-5677

Pennsylvania

Department of Public Welfare
Office of Children, Youth and Families
P.O. Box 2675
Harrisburg, PA 17105-2675
717-705-2912

Rhode Island

Rhode Island Department of Children and Their Families
530 Wood Street
Bristol, RI 02805
401-254-7010

South Carolina

Department of Social Services
P.O. Box 1520
Columbia, SC 29202-1520
803-898-7707

South Dakota

Department of Social Services
Richard F. Kneip Building
700 Governors Dr.
Pierre, SD 57501-2291
605-773-3227

Tennessee

Tennessee Department of Children's Services
436 Sixth Avenue North
Cordell Hull Building, 8th Floor
Nashville, TN 37243
615-532-5637

Texas

Texas Department of Protective and Regulatory Services
Agency Mail Code E-557
701 West 51st St.
P.O. Box 149030
Austin, TX 78717-9030
512-438-3412

Utah

Department of Human Services
Division of Child and Family Services
120 North 200 West, Ste. 225
Salt Lake City, UT 84103
801-538-4078

Vermont

Vermont Division of Social and Rehabilitation Services
103 South Main St.
Waterbury, VT 05671
802-241-2142

Virginia

Department of Social Services
Division of Family Services
730 East Broad St.
Richmond, VA 21219
804-692-1290

Washington

Department of Social and Health Services
Children's Administration
14th & Jefferson
P.O. Box 45713
Olympia, WA 98504-5713
360-902-7959

West Virginia

West Virginia Department of Health and Human Services
Office of Social Services
350 Capitol Street, Room 621
Charleston, WV 25301
304-558-4303

Wisconsin

Department of Health and Family Services
Division of Child and Family Services
1 West Wilson St.
P.O. Box 8916
Madison, WI 53708-8916
608-266-3595

Wyoming

Department of Family Services
Hathaway Building, Third Floor
2300 Capitol Avenue
Cheyenne, WY 82002
307-777-3570

Appendix E

Selected Adoptive Parent Groups

Adoptive parent groups are self-help groups for people who want to adopt or who have already adopted children. The majority of parent groups are managed by volunteers who want to help others. They don't have massive budgets or endless time. Some groups are large, but the majority are small groups that hold monthly meetings, often in sites such as a local library. Some groups wanted their addresses and phone numbers published, but others wanted only a phone number, an e-mail, or a website listed.

This list is just a sampling of the many groups available nationwide, and I hope I have not offended anyone by omission. I've done my best to verify all the information here; however, keep in mind that addresses and phone numbers are subject to change.

Arkansas

River Valley Adoption Support Group
1005 West 18th Terrace
Russellville, AR 72801
479-967-1641

California

Families Adopting in Response (FAIR)
P.O. Box 51436
Palo Alto, CA 94303
650-856-3513
www.fairfamilies.org

Pact, an Adoption Alliance
4179 Piedmont Ave., Ste. 330
Oakland, CA 94611
510-243-9460
www.pactadopt.org
info@pactadopt.org

Colorado

Adoptive Family Resources
1155 Sherman St., Ste. 201
Denver, CO 80203
303-881-7630
www.adoptivefamilyresources.org

Families for Russian & Ukrainian Adoption—Colorado Central/Mountains
6763 East Long Ave.
Centennial, CO 80112

Connecticut

Adoptions: A Gathering of Families
212 Mansion Rd.
Wallingford, CT 06492
203-679-0888
www.optionsforadoption.org

Latin American Parents Association of Connecticut, Inc.
P.O. Box 523
Unionville, CT 06085
LAPAofCT@comcast.net

Delaware

Adoptive Families with Information and Support (AFIS)
Contact: Mary Jo Wolfe
P.O. Box 7504
Wilmington, DE 19803
302-571-8784

Florida

A Bond of Love: Tallahassee Families Touched by Adoption
850-671-5793
www.abondofloveinc.com

Families with Asian Children, Brevard County, Florida Chapter
www.woodcellar.com/facbrevard

Gatherings of International Adoptive Families
839 SW 13th St.
Cape Coral, FL 33991
239-574-4590

Parents Adoption Lifeline, Inc.
13833 E-4 Wellington Trace
PMB 116
Wellington, FL 33414
561-844-8200
www.adoptionlifeline.org

Tallahassee Families with Asian Children
c/o Steve Foley
3940 Leane Drive
Tallahassee, FL 32309
850-915-7797
chinafoley@comcast.net

Georgia

Adoption Support of North Georgia (ASONG)
Contact: Linda Morehead
1432 Arbor Bluff Ct.
Lawrenceville, GA 30045

Families with Children from China—Atlanta
6300 Powers Ferry Rd. NW, Ste. 600-318
Atlanta, GA 30339
1-877-483-9778
www.fccatlanta.org
fccatlanta@bellsouth.net

Journey Home
Adoption Guidance and Support
Contact: Diane Simmering
415 Dunhill View Court
Alpharetta, GA 30005
770-845-7659
www.JourneyHomeInc.com

Hawaii

Shaloha Chapter
Stars of David
P.O. Box 61595
Honolulu, HI 96839
808-988-1989

Idaho

Idaho Families with Children from Asia (IFCA)
www.idahofca.org

Illinois

Adoptive Families Today
P.O. Box 1726
Barrington, IL 60011-1726
847-382-0858
www.adoptivefamiliestoday.org

Central Illinois Adoptive Families (CIAF)
Bloomington, IL
309-828-2692
www.ciafadopt.org
ciaf@ciafadopt.org

Chicago Area Families for Adoption
1212 South Naper Blvd., Ste. 119
Naperville, IL 60540
630-585-4680
www.caffa.org

Families with Children from China, Chicago Metropolitan Area
1341 West Fullerton Ave., PMB 338
Chicago, IL 60614
www.fcchicago.org

Indiana

Central Indiana FRUA
1209 Rowin Rd.
Indianapolis, IN 46220
317-259-7449

Indiana Foster Care and Adoption Association
Indianapolis
1-800-468-4228
www.ifcaa.org

Iowa

Iowa Foster and Adoptive Parents Association
6864 NE 14th St., Ste. 5
Ankeny, IA 50021
1-800-277-8145
www.ifapa.org

Ours thru Adoption
Contact: Jean Hess
2618 Arlington Ave.
Davenport, IA 52803
563-322-6469

Western Iowa Adoptive Families
712-676-2288

Kansas

Families with Children from China—Kansas
fcckansas@yahoo.com

Friends of Adoption
www.friendsofadoptionkc.com
foa@friendsofadoptionkc.com

Kentucky

Foster and Adoptive Families of Fayette County
Contact: Virginia Sturgeon
1843 Donco Court
Lexington, KY 40505
859-299-2749

Louisiana

Families with Children from China, Louisiana
P.O. Box 7362
Metairie, LA 70010-7362
www.fccl.org
info@fccl.org

Latin American Adoptive Families of Southeast Louisiana
Contact: Paulette Rodehorst
3516 Upperline St.
New Orleans, LA 70125
504-821-6434
www.laafonline.net

Louisiana Families with Children from Asia
Contact: Shannon Seymour
116 Nottaway Dr.
Destrehan, LA 70047
985-764-5027
www.lfca.netfirms.com

Southwest Louisiana Forever Families
Contact: Denise Reeves
1937 Adams Rd.

Ragley, LA 70657
337-855-9451
http://members.tripod.com/slforeverfamilies/index.htm

Maine

Adoptive Families of Maine
294 Center St., Unit 1
Old Town, ME 04468
207-827-2331
www.affm.net

Maine Families with Children from Asia
59 Park Road
Windham, ME 04062
www.mefca.org

Maryland

Families Adopting Children Everywhere (FACE)
P.O. Box 28058
Northwood Station
Baltimore, MD 21239
410-488-2656
www.faceadoptioninfo.org

Families with Children from China, Central Maryland
P.O. Box 2392
Columbia, MD 21045
410-730-1975
www.geocities.com/fccmd

Massachusetts

Adoptive Families Together, Inc.
418 Commonwealth Ave.
Boston, MA 02215
617-929-3800
www.adoptivefamilies.com

Families for Russian and Ukrainian Adoption (FRUA)—New England
669 Main St.
Lancaster, MA 01523
978-368-1966
info@fruanewengland.org

Families with Cambodian Children
20 Oakhurst Ave.
Ipswich, MA 01938
978-356-5186
www.famcam.org

ODS Adoption Community of New England, Inc.
1750 Washington St.
Holliston, MA 01746-2234
508-429-4260
www.odsacone.org
info@odsacone.org

Michigan

Adoptive Family Support Network
Contact: Janice Fonger
233 East Fulton, Ste. 108
Grand Rapids, MI 49503
616-458-7945
www.afsn.org

Kalamazoo-Battle Creek Families with Children from China
Contact: Judy Scott
269-665-4750

Minnesota

Peruvian Adoptive Families
(some out of state families)
PeruAdoptFAm@cohousing.org

Minnesota Adoption Support and Preservation (MN ASA)
430 Oak Grove St., Ste. 404
Minneapolis, MN 55403
612-861-7112
www.mnasap.org

Stearns County Adoptive/Resource Parent Support Group
320-656-6118

Wright-Sherburne Counties Adoptive Parent Support Group
Contact: Carol Askew at Sherburne County Social Services
1-800-433-5239 or 763-241-2656

Missouri

Families with Children from China—St. Louis
P.O. Box 220373
St. Louis, MO 63122
www.fccstl.org
fccstl@earthlink.net

International Adoptive Families of Southwest Missouri
Contact: Jessica Gerard
4349 East Kensington St.
Springfield, MO 65809
417-882-2515

International Families
(Greater St. Louis)
314-423-6788
www.interfam.org

Parkland Foster Adopt Families Support Group
408 North Allen St.
Bonne Terre, MO 63628
573-358-3512

Montana

Montana State Foster/Adoptive Parents Association
Contact: Melody Blendu
1740 Augsburg Dr.
Billings, MT 59105
406-245-7543
www.msf-apa.org

Nevada

Southern Nevada Adoption Association
1600 Campbell Dr.
Las Vegas, NV 89102
702-647-0201 or 702-649-8464

New Hampshire

Granite State Chapter of ODS Adoption Community of New England, Inc.
1-800-93ADOPT
www.odsacone.org

New Jersey

Adoptive Parents Committee—New Jersey Chapter
P.O. Box 725
Ridgewood, NJ 07451
201-689-0995

Concerned Persons For Adoption
P.O. Box 179
Whippany, NJ 07981
908-273-5694 or 973-625-8440
www.cpfanj.org

New York

Adoption Resource Network, Inc.
P.O. Box 178
Pittsford, NY 14534
585-586-9586
www.arni.org

Adoptive Parents Committee (Headquarters)
P.O. Box 3525
Church St. Station
New York, NY 10008-3525
1-800-207-0660
www.adoptiveparents.org

Adoptive Parents Committee
Hudson Region Chapter
P.O. Box 625
Hartsdale, NY 10530
914-997-7859

Latin America Parents Association
P.O. Box 339-340
Brooklyn, NY 11234
718-236-8689
www.lapa.com

North Carolina

Families with Children from China, Charlotte
3307 Mara Court
Matthews, NC 28105
www.FCC-charlotte.org

Grafted Families
Contact: Dody Lucarini
113 Drawbridge Court
Mooresville, NC 28117
704-660-3909

Rainbow Families of the Outer Banks—Multicultural
P.O. Box 2615
Kill Devil Hills, NC 27948
252-207-4565

Southern Piedmont Adoptive Families of America (SPAFA)
P.O. Box 221946
Charlotte, NC 28222-1946
704-399-1616 or 877-772-3292
www.spafa.org

Ohio

Adoption Network Cleveland
Contact: Betsie Norris
1667 East 40th St., Ste. B-1
Cleveland, OH 44103
216-881-7511
www.AdoptionNetwork.org

Families with Children from China—Greater Cincinnati
www.fcc-cincinnati.org
president@fcc-cincinnati.org

Interracial Families in Friendship
P.O. Box 82628
Columbus, OH 43202
www.simplyliving.org/ifif

New Roots Adoptive Families Support Group
P.O. Box 14953
Columbus, OH 43214
614-470-0846
www.simplyliving.org/newroots

United by Adoption
St. Anthony Church
6104 Desmont St.
Cincinnati, OH 45227
513-271-0920

Oklahoma

Adopt Older Kids Support Group
Contact: Erin Porter
11719 South 91st E. Ave.
Bixby, OK 74008
918-369-1901
adoptolderkids@aol.com

Oregon

Northwest Adoptive Families Association
P.O. Box 25355
Portland, OR 97298-0355
503-243-1356
www.nafaonline.org
information@nafaonline.org

Pennsylvania

Mission Adoption
Contacts: Russ and Kelly McCurdy
538 Dendron Drive
Coraopolis, PA 15108
412-859-3478

Pittsburgh Adoption Support Group
105 Church Lane
Pittsburgh, PA 15238
Contacts: Patty Bontempo at 412-767-4250
or Lynn Mischen at 412-373-0418

Together as Adoptive Parents, Inc. (TAP)
478 Moyer Rd.
Harleysville, PA 19438
215-256-0669
www.taplink.org

South Carolina

Adoptive Families Group
(Midlands area)
803-808-6315
www.adoptivefamiliesgroup.org

South Carolina Council on Adoptable Children
2005 Hampton St., Ste. F
Columbia, SC 29204
803-256-2622

Texas

Born From My Heart
Contact: Jennifer Edwards
P.O. Box 604
China Spring, TX 76633
254-722-6622

Council on Adoptable Children of Texas, Inc.
P.O. Box 14932
Austin, TX 78761
www.texas-coac.org

Families with Children from China Austin
9208 Trowbridge Cove
Austin, TX 78717
512-733-2268

Virginia

Adoptive Families in the Valley
245 Franklin St.
Harrisonburg, VA 22801
540-434-0452

Families of the China Moon
Richmond, VA
804-364-5734
kristenaball@comcast.net

Washington

Adoptive Friends and Family of Greater Seattle
206-903-9664
www.affgs.org

Families for Russian and Ukrainian Adoption, Including Neighboring Countries
Contact: Karen Graham
16208 NE 95th Court
Redmond, WA 98052
425-883-3262
www.frua.org/WA-state

Families with Children from China, Pacific Northwest Chapter
1001 4th Avenue, Ste. 4500
Seattle, WA 98154
jenniferfdavis@msn.com

Friends in Adoption
206-264-5136
www.friends-in-adoption.org

Kitsap Adoption Group
www.geocities.com/kitsapadoptiongroup

West Virginia

From China with Love—FCC WV
455 Vine Street
St. Albans, WV 25177

Guatemala Adoptive Family Association of West Virginia (GAFA of WV)
c/o Crystal S. Stump
Swartz & Stump
P.O. Box 673
Charleston, WV 25323
304-345-9001

Wisconsin

Adoption Adventure Support Group
(northern Wisconsin)
tjokinen@baysat.net

Adoption Resources of Wisconsin
Contact: Colleen Ellingson
6682 West Greenfield Ave., Ste. 310
Milwaukee, WI 53214
414-475-1246
www.wiadopt.org

Latin American Adoptive Families of Wisconsin (LAAF-WI)
Contact: Judy Devine Smies
W148 N7094 Terriwood Dr.
Menomonee Falls, WI 53051
262-253-0669
http://groups.yahoo.com/group/Latin_America_Adopt_WI

Milwaukee Area Families with Children from China
6115 Willow Circle
Sullivan, WI 53178
chinas3roses@aol.com
262-593-2118

Post-Adoption Resource Center
Family Services
300 Crooks St.
Green Bay, WI 54301
920-436-4360, extension 1264
www.familyservicesnew.org

Transracial Families of Milwaukee
Transracial Families
Milw@hotmail.com
Doug H.
P.O. Box 370961
Milwaukee, WI 53237-2061

Voices United
Contact: Co-president Dawn Kilts
270 Vista Dr.
Oconomowoc, WI 53066
262-569-5138
kilts@netwurx.net

Wisconsin Foster and Adoptive Parents Association
Contact: Sherry Benson
715-735-3879
tbwcrew@cybrzn.com

Selected International Adoption Medical Experts

Several international adoption medical experts (all of them pediatricians) in the United States can answer most medical questions and may be willing to review medical records and/or videotapes of children for a fee. Here is a selected list of the most prominent physicians. The information is based on what was provided by the doctors themselves. Listing a physician in this book does not guarantee the quality of that physician.

Andrew Adesman, M.D.
Adoption Evaluation Center
Schneider Children's Hospital
1983 Marcus Ave., Ste. 130
Lake Success, NY 11042
516-802-6150
FAX: 516-616-5801

Dr. Jane Aronson
International Pediatric Health Services, PLLC
151 East 62nd St., Ste. 1
New York, NY 10021
212-207-6666
FAX: 212-207-6665
www.orphandoctor.com

Karin M. Belsito, M.D., DMD
Developmental Pediatrician
University of Florida
910 North Jefferson St.
Jacksonville, FL 32209
904-360-7070, extension 265

Julia M. Bledsoe, M.D.
(Contact: Cyndi Musar or Heather Blumer, Patient Care Coordinators)
The Center for Adoption Medicine
University of Washington Pediatric Care Center
4245 Roosevelt Way NE
Seattle, WA 98105
206-598-3006
206-598-3040

Deborah Borchers, M.D.
Eastgate Pediatric Center
4357 Ferguson Drive, Ste. 150
Cincinnati, OH 45245
513-753-2820
FAX: 513-753-2824

Gail Farber, M.D.
International Adoption Health Program
Children's Hospital of Philadelphia
34th and Civic Center Blvd.
Philadelphia, PA 19104
267-426-5005
FAX: 215-590-3198

Jerri Ann Jenista, M.D.
551 Second St.
Ann Arbor, MI 48103
734-668-0419
FAX: 734-668-9492

Dana Johnson, M.D., Ph.D.
International Adoption Clinic
University of Minnesota
MMHC 211, D-136 Mayo
Minneapolis, MN 55455
612-624-1989
FAX: 612-624-8176

Edward M. Kolb, M.D.
International Adoption Medical Consultants
13110 Birch Drive
Suite 148, Box 366
Omaha, NE 68164
402-680-3269
FAX: 402-496-7126

Robin Krause Blitz, M.D.
Arizona Child Study Center
The Children's Health Center-St. Joseph's Hospital
350 West Thomas Rd.
Phoenix, AZ 85013
602-406-3543
FAX: 602-406-6135

Patrick Mason, M.D., Ph.D.
International Adoption Center
Inova Fairfax Hospital for Children
8505 Arlington Blvd., Ste. 100
Fairfax, VA 22031
703-970-2651
www.adoptionclinic.org

Laurie Miller, M.D.
Box 286
New England Medical Center
750 Washington St.
Boston, MA 02111
617-636-4285
FAX: 617-636-8388

Jennifer Nobles Chambers, M.D.
UAB International Adoption Clinic
MTC 201
1600 7th Avenue South
Birmingham, AL 35233
205-939-6964
www.adoption.chsys.org/default.asp?ID=137

Todd J. Ochs, M.D.
Ravenswood Medical Professional Group
1945 West Wilson
Chicago, IL 60613
773-769-4600
FAX: 773-769-6242

Heidi Schwarzwald, M.D., M.P.H.
Baylor College of Medicine, Department of Pediatrics
Texas Children's Health Center for International Adoptions
6621 Fannin St., CCC 1570
Houston, TX 77030
832-822-1038
FAX: 832-825-1281

Boris Skurkovich, M.D.
International Adoption Clinic
Rhode Island Hospital
593 Eddy St.
Providence, RI 02903
401-444-8360
FAX: 401-444-5650

Selected Adoption Magazines and Books

A variety of publications are available for adoptive parents. I've listed some magazines and books that I think would interest many readers nationwide.

Magazines

Adoption Today
541 East Garden Dr., Unit N
Windsor, CO 80550
888-924-6736
www.adoptinfo.net/index2.html

A bimonthly magazine for adopting and adoptive parents that covers numerous adoption-related topics. $24.00.

Adoptive Families
42 West 38th St., Ste. 901
New York, NY 10018
1-800-372-3300
www.AdoptiveFamilies.com

Bimonthly magazine with articles on a variety of issues of interest to adoptive parents, adopted adults, and birthparents. Six issues, $29.95.

Books

The Encyclopedia of Adoption by Christine Adamec and William Pierce (Facts On File, Inc., 2000)

An A to Z reference book on adoption, which covers historical, legal, medical, psychological, social, and other aspects of adoption.

Inside Transracial Adoption by Gail Steinberg and Beth Hall (Perspectives Press, 2000)

An important resource for parents who adopted their children in transracial and intercountry adoptions, offering insights and good advice.

Parenting Your Adopted Child: A Positive Approach to Building a Strong Family by Andrew Adesman, M.D. with Christine Adamec (McGraw-Hill, 2004)

Most problems adoptive parents face are the same ones all parents experience, but additional challenges exist, such as coping with teachers who think a child isn't doing well in school just because he was adopted. This book is filled with helpful hints for coping with parenting challenges that occur at all ages.

Patterns of Adoption by David Howe (Blackwell Science, 1998)

If you're curious about genetic predispositions, environmental influences, and adoption research, this book is for you. It summarizes studies of children adopted as babies separately from children adopted as older children.

Tell Me Again About the Night I Was Born by Jamie Lee Curtis (HarperCollins Juvenile Books, 1996)

A lovely children's book about adoption that may become your child's—and your—favorite.

Glossary

adoptee   The person who was adopted. Some people prefer the terms "adopted child," or "adopted adult" because adoptive status is a means of family membership, not an identity.

adoption   The complete transfer of parental rights and obligations from one family to another family. The adoptive family assumes all the legal obligations and responsibilities of the family to whom a child was born, and the birth family no longer has any rights and obligations.

adoption agencies   Organizations licensed by the state to place children with adoptive families. They are usually staffed by social workers.

adoption attorneys   Lawyers who arrange adoptive placements. Some attorneys manage adoptions from start to finish, and others assist adoption agencies.

adoption facilitators or **adoption consultants**   People who help adopters identify birthmothers. Some adoption consultants are social workers; some are unlicensed in any capacity. Adoption facilitators are not allowed to work in some states.

adoption mind-set   A goal-oriented attitude in which the adopter not only wants to adopt a child but *needs* to adopt a child. The adopter is fully prepared to act on this need.

adoption obsession A state of mind in which the adopter is constantly thinking about adopting a child. This is common behavior among people who are seeking to adopt.

adoption ritual A ceremony that acknowledges that the child has been (or will be) adopted into the family. Adoption rituals may be religious or secular.

adoption-readiness An attitude in which the adopter feels ready to explore adoption.

adoptive parent group Sometimes called an **adoptive parent support group;** a group of adoptive parents or prospective adoptive parents who meet to obtain and share information about adopting as well as to socialize and/or to discuss issues related to adoption.

adoptive parents People who have been legally approved by a court to be parents to a child. Some adoptive parents are biologically related to the child, but many are not.

agency adoption A form of adoption arranged by workers at a licensed adoption agency. This term usually refers to private adoption agencies, rather than state or county public agencies.

biracial A term used to describe a child who has biological parents of different races and is often used when one parent is black or African American and one is white.

birthfather A man who, with a woman, conceives a child who is later adopted or for whom an adoption is planned. He may also be called the **biological father.**

birthfather registry An opportunity whereby unmarried men who believe they have fathered children may register their alleged paternity. Registered birthfathers then may register their protest to a birthmother's adoption plans. Also called **putative father registries.** Many states have birthfather registries.

birthgrandparents The parents of the birthmother or birthfather. They may or may not become involved in the adoption. Although there may be an emotional involvement, birthgrandparents have no legal right to be involved in the adoption decision.

birthmother A woman who has given birth to a child whom she places for adoption. She may also be called the **biological mother.** Some people use this term to describe pregnant women who are considering adoption for their children.

black market adoption An adoption that is arranged outside the law and usually involves very large sums of money paid to an attorney, agency worker, or other individual.

confidential adoption   An adoption in which neither the adopter nor the birth-parents know identifying information about each other. Some people use the term **closed adoption.**

consent to an adoption   A voluntary agreement on the part of the birthmother and sometimes the birthfather that allows their child to be adopted. **Surrender** and **relinquishment** are terms that are sometimes used by attorneys instead of consent, but the use of these negative-sounding words is discouraged by adoption experts.

disruption   Generally refers to an adoption that fails before finalization, although many people also use the term for any failed adoption. (See **dissolution.**)

dissolution   Refers to adoptions that fail after finalization.

dossier   The collection of legal documents that must be compiled to adopt a child from another country.

entitlement   Describes the attitude of adopted parents who feel worthy and ready to take on all the responsibilities and obligations of parenthood.

finalization   The procedure in which the adopter goes to court to receive legal permission and recognition for the adoption.

foster child   A child in the primary custody of a state, county, or private adoption agency. Foster children often live with foster families for varying periods. A foster child cannot be adopted unless a judge terminates the parental rights of the biological parents or they willingly sign consent to the adoption.

genetic predisposition   A probability that a child may inherit some genetic feature that occurred in the biological family. A genetic predisposition does not mean a child will develop traits, only that the likelihood is increased.

gray market adoption   Connotes an adoption that is not quite "on the level," usually involves questionable payments, and is often used in association with nonagency adoptions. In reality, however, an adoption is either legal, or it is not legal. There is no middle ground.

Hague Convention on Intercountry Adoption   A multilateral treaty that was signed by 66 nations in 1993 and by the United States in 1994. It covers adoptions between countries. The United States Congress passed a bill for implementation of the Convention in 2000 with the Intercountry Adoption Act of 2000.

home study   The approval process for prospective adopters that includes interviewing prospective parents, talking to them in their homes, checking their references, and reviewing medical, financial, and other relevant information. Some agencies use the term **family study** instead.

independent adoption   A nonagency adoption. Sometimes it is also called **private adoption.**

independent contractors   Social workers who are hired by adoption agencies to handle the home study process.

institutionalized child   A child in another country who lives in an orphanage.

international adoption   The process of adopting a child from another country. Also called "intercountry adoption." The term "foreign adoption" is considered negative and obsolete.

The Interstate Compact on the Placement of Children   An agreement between all states in the United States that governs the adoptive placement of children across state lines. Interstate adoptions cannot legally occur without the approval of interstate compact officials, who are employed by the state social services department of each state.

irrevocable consent   A type of agreement that means that, once signed, consent to an adoption may not be taken back by a birthparent. There may be some exceptions, such as if fraud or duress is proven.

legal guardian   A person who can make legal and often parental decisions for a minor child. The legal guardian can't adopt the child unless the biological parents (or whomever has custody) agrees.

multiracial   A child with a heritage of more than two races in his or her background.

namesake   Naming a child after someone in the family.

nonrelative adoption   An adoption in which the adoptive parent is a "biological stranger" to the child.

nonsectarian adoption agencies   Adoption agencies that are not sponsored by a religious organization.

open adoption   An adoption in which there is an exchange of identities, typically first and last names, between the adopting parents and the birthparents. Both parties also often meet in person, but they may or may not decide to have a continuing relationship as the child grows up.

open record   A system wherein an adopted adult can request the original sealed birth certificate and it will be provided so that he or she may obtain the identities of the birthparents. No court order is required in such a system. Most states do not have open records.

orphan A child who doesn't have any living parents. It is also a term used in international adoption and usually refers to a child in another country who either has no parents or who has only one parent who cannot care for him or her.

orphan petition A request submitted to the U.S. Citizenship and Immigration Services by the prospective adoptive parents on the behalf of a specific child from another country, so that the adopted child may be admitted to the United States and reside with adopting parents.

positive adoption language Words or phrases that depict adoption in a favorable, or at least neutral, manner. For example, the word "birthmother" or "biological mother" is preferred over "natural mother" or "real mother."

positive adoption mind-set (PAM) An attitude that an adopter will succeed with the adoption and become a parent.

postplacement home study A background investigation and interview of the adopting parents after the child has already been placed with the family.

prebirth consent Consent by the biological father to an adoption before the baby is born. Many states allow prebirth consent to an adoption.

private agencies Nongovernmental agencies licensed by the state to arrange adoptions. They usually are run by someone with an advanced degree in social work or psychology.

public agencies State social services agencies that are run by state or county governments. These agencies usually deal with foster children.

putative father The alleged birthfather.

rapture of the adoption An emotional state in which adopters suspend all normal judgment and common sense, often because they have little information or time to make a decision—a kind of sensory overload.

readoption A process in which international adopters adopt their children a second time, in front of a U.S. judge. (The first time was in the country of the child's birth.)

relative adoption An adoption in which the adopter is biologically related to the adopted child.

reunion A face-to-face meeting of an adopted adult with a birth relative, such as a birthmother or birthfather.

revoke To take back consent to an adoption. Some states allow birthparents to revoke consent for varying time periods, while others do not.

sealing of the birth certificate   A process by which the original birth certificate with the birthparents' names on it is made unavailable for viewing except through a court order. A new birth certificate is issued, listing the adoptive parents' names as the parents to the child.

search   The process of an adopted person seeking a biological relative, usually a birthmother, birthfather, or a birth sibling. Sometimes birthparents seek adopted adults.

search group   An organization that assists adopted adults and/or birthparents with the search process.

second-parent adoption   A relatively recent phenomenon in which the gay or lesbian partner of a biological parent adopts his or her partner's child. Thus, if the couple breaks up, they both still retain parental rights. If one person dies, the other person has legal rights and will not lose custody of the child. This is not legal in every state.

sectarian agencies   Adoption agencies that are sponsored by a religious organization. They sometimes only serve families with particular religious interests.

semi-open adoption   An adoption in which the adopters and birthparents may meet once or twice and on a first-name-only basis. It's always important to ask the agency for their definition of this term because agencies vary greatly on how they define the phrase.

social worker or **caseworker**   A person who performs the home study. A social worker also interviews the birthparents who are considering adoption and gathers social and medical information.

special needs   Used to describe children whom agencies consider hard to place. Children with illnesses or impediments often are referred to as children with special needs. Older children, sibling groups, and minority children are considered to have special needs. Each agency has its own definition of what constitutes "special needs."

stepparent adoption   The process by which a person adopts the child of his or her spouse, usually with the permission of the other biological parent.

termination of parental rights   The legal process by which the birthparents' parental rights are terminated (usually voluntarily, but sometimes involuntarily). An adoption cannot occur until the parental rights of the birthparents have been terminated.

transracial adoption   A situation in which a family adopts a child who is of another race.

waiting children   A term sometimes used to describe children in foster care and for whom adoption is sought.

wrongful adoption   An adoption that theoretically would not have taken place had the adopters been given information that was known to the adoption arranger. The information was (or is alleged to have been) purposely withheld or misrepresented.

Bibliography

Adamec, Christine. *The Adoption Option Complete Handbook 2000-2001*. Rocklin, CA: Prima Publishing, 1999.

——. "The Fear Factor," *Adoptive Families*. January/February 1995, pp. 29–31.

——. *Is Adoption for You? The Information You Need to Make the Right Choice*. New York: John Wiley & Sons, 1998.

——. *There ARE Babies to Adopt: A Resource Guide for Prospective Parents*. New York: Kensington, 2002.

——. "What's In a Name?" *National Adoption Reports*. Vol. XVIII, Issue No. 4, April 1997, p. 7.

Adamec, Christine, and William L. Pierce, Ph.D. *The Encyclopedia of Adoption*. Second Edition. New York: Facts on File, Inc., 2000.

Adesman, Andrew, M.D., with Christine Adamec. *Parenting Your Adopted Child: A Positive Approach to Building a Strong Family*. New York: McGraw-Hill, 2004.

Altstein, Howard, et al. "Clinical Observations of Adult Intercountry Adoptees and Their Adoptive Parents," *Child Welfare.* May–June 1994, Vol. 73, No. 3, pp. 261–269.

Benson, Peter L., Ph.D., Anu R. Sharma, Ph.D., L.P., and Eugene C. Roehlkepartain. *Growing Up Adopted: A Portrait of Adolescents and Their Families.* Minneapolis, MN: The Search Institute, 1994.

Bothun, Linda. *Dialogues About Adoption: Conversations Between Parents and Their Children.* Chevy Chase, MD: Swan Publications, 1994.

Brodzinsky, David M., and Marshall D. Schechter. *The Psychology of Adoption.* New York: Oxford University Press, 1990.

Chesey, Gordon. "Adoption for the Disabled," *Accent on Living.* Fall 1995, Vol. 40, No. 2, pp. 86–91.

Child Welfare League of America, *Issues in Gay and Lesbian Adoption: Proceedings of the Fourth Annual Peirce-Warwick Adoption Symposium.* Washington, DC: 1995.

De Simone, Michael, Ph. D., BCD. "Birth Mother Loss: Contributing Factors to Unresolved Grief," *Clinical Social Work Journal.* Vol. 24, No. 1, Spring 1996.

Donovan, Denis M., and Deborah McIntyre. *Healing the Hurt Child.* New York: W. W. Norton Co., 1990.

Duggan, Paul. "A Baby Arrives Amid Joy, Departs Amid Heartache," *Washington Post.* April 2, 1997, p. A1.

Fioto, Lou. "Domestic Adoption Is Their Choice," *Accent on Living.* Winter 1996, Vol. 41, No. 3, p. 62(5).

Forman, Deborah L. "Unwed Fathers and Adoption: A Theoretical Analysis in Context," *Texas Law Review.* April 1994, Vol. 72, No. 5, pp. 967–1045.

Freivalds, Susan. "Nature & Nurture: A New Look at How Families Work," *Adoptive Families.* Vol. 35, No. 2, March/April 2002, pp. 28–30.

Gaber, Ivor, and Jane Aldridge, Eds. *In the Best Interests of the Child: Culture, Identity and Transracial Adoption.* London: Free Association Books, 1994.

Garn, Stanley M., et al. "Similarities Between Parents and Their Adopted Children," *American Journal of Physical Anthropology.* Nov. 1976, Vol. 45, No. 3, Part 2, pp. 539–543.

Grotevant, Harold D., Ph.D. "Adoptive Families: Longitudinal Outcomes for Adolescents. Final Report to the William Grant Foundation," April 30, 2001.

Groze, Victor. *Successful Adoptive Families: A Longitudinal Study of Special Needs Adoption.* Westport, CN: Praeger, 1996.

Howard, Jeanne A., and Susan Livingston Smith. *After Adoption: The Needs of Adopted Youth.* Washington, DC: CWLA Press, 2003.

Howe, David. *Patterns of Adoption: Nature, Nurture and Psychosocial Development.* London: Blackwell Science, 1998.

Jenista, Jerri Ann, M.D. "Medical Primer for the Adoptive Parents," in *Handbook for Single Adoptive Parents.* Chevy Chase, MD: National Council of Single Adoptive Parents, 1996.

Johnson, Jill, et al. "Sociobiology and the Naming of Adopted and Natural Children, *Ethnology and Sociobiology.* Vol. 12, 1991, pp. 365–375.

Johnston, Patricia Irwin. *Launching a Baby's Adoption: Practical Strategies for Parents and Professionals.* Indianapolis, IN: Perspectives Press, 1997.

Keck, Gregory, C., Ph.D., and Regina M. Kupecky, L.S.S. *Parenting the Hurt Child: Helping Adoptive Families Heal and Grow.* Colorado Springs, CO: Pinon Press, 2002.

Koepke, Jean E., et al. "Becoming Parents: Feelings of Adoptive Mothers," *Pediatric Nursing.* Vol. 17, No. 4, July–August 1991, pp. 333–336.

Kowal, Katherine, A., Ph.D., and Karen Maitland Schilling, Ph.D. "Adoption Through the Eyes of Adoptees," *American Journal of Orthopsychiatry.* July 1985, Vol. 55, No. 3,pp. 354-362.

Lazare, Aaron, M.D. "A Family's Adoption of Eight Children of Three Races," unpublished paper, University of Massachusetts Medical School, 1996.

Levine, Elaine S., Ph.D., and Alvin L. Sallee, M.S.W. "Critical Phases Among Adoptees and Their Families: Implications for Therapy," *Child and Adolescent Social Work*. June 1990, Vol. 7, No. 3, pp. 217–232.

Lichtenstein, Tovah. "To Tell or Not to Tell: Factors Affecting Adoptees' Telling Their Adoptive Parents About Their Search," *Child Welfare*, January–February 1996, pp. 61–72.

Mason, Mary Martin. *Designing Rituals of Adoption for the Religious and Secular Community*. Minneapolis: Resources for Adoptive Parents, 1995.

McDermott, Mark T. "It's the Law: Health Insurance for Adopted Children," *Adoptive Families*, March/April 2002, www.adoptivefamilies.com/pdf/health_ins.pdf.

McGue, Matt, et al. "Parent and Sibling Influences on Adolescent Alcohol Use and Misuse: Evidence from a U.S. Adoption Cohort," *Journal of Studies on Alcohol*. January 1996, Vol. 57, No. 1, pp. 8–19.

Melina, Lois Ruskai, and Sharon Kaplan Roszia. *The Open Adoption Experience*. New York: HarperPerennial, 1993.

Mishra, Debjani. "The Road to Concord: Resolving the Conflict of Law Over Adoption by Gays and Lesbians," *Columbia Journal of Law and Social Problems*. Fall 1996, Vol. 30, No. 1, pp. 91–136.

Moran, Ruth. "Stages of Emotion: An Adult Adoptee's Postreunion Perspective," *Child Welfare*. May 1994, Vol. 73, No. 3, pp. 249–260.

National Council For Adoption. *The Adoption Factbook*, Washington, DC, 1999.

Nickman, Steven L., M.D., and Robert G. Ewis, M.Ed., M.S.W. "Adoptive Families and Professionals: When the Experts Make Things Worse," *Journal of the American Academy of Child and Adolescent Psychiatry*. June 1994, Vol. 33, No. 5, pp. 753–755.

Oppenheim, Elizabeth. "Adoption Assistance," *Public Welfare*. Winter 1996, Vol. 54, No. 1, pp. 8–9.

Patterson, Charlotte J., and Richard E. Redding. "Lesbian and Gay Families with Children: Implications of Social Science Research for Policy," *Journal of Social Issues*. Vol. 52, No. 3, 1996, pp. 29–50.

Raynor, Lois. *The Adopted Child Comes of Age*. London: George Allen & Unwin, 1980.

Reitz, Miriam, Ph.D, L.C.S.W., and Kenneth W. Watson, M.S.W., L.C.S.W., *Adoption and the Family System: Strategies for Treatment*. New York: The Guildford Press, 1992.

Rutter, Michael, and the English and Romanian Adoptees (ERA) Study Team. "Developmental Catch-up, and Deficit, Following Adoption After Severe Global Early Privation," *Journal of Child Psychology and Psychiatry and Allied Disciplines*. 1998, Vol. 39, No. 4, pp. 465–476.

Sanford, Donna. "Since You Asked …" *EXPO*. May 1997, Vol. 9, No. 5, p. 6.

Scarr, Sandra, Elizabeth Scarf, and Richard A. Weinberg. "Perceived and Actual Similarities in Biological and Adoptive Families: Does Perceived Similarity Bias Genetic Inferences?" *Behavior Genetics*. 1980, G. 10, No. 5, pp. 445–458.

Sharma, Anu R., Matthew K. McGue, and Peter L. Benson. "The Emotional and Behavioral Adjustment of United States Adopted Adolescents: Part II. Age at Adoption," *Children and Youth Services Review*. 1996, Vol. 18, No. 1/2, pp. 101–114.

Silber, Kathleen, and Phylis Speedlin. *Dear Birthmother: Thank You for Our Baby*. San Antonio, TX: Corona, 1982.

Silverman, Phyllis R., et al. "Reunions Between Adoptees and Birth Parents: The Adoptive Parents' View," *Social Work*. Sept. 1994, Vol. 39, No. 5, pp. 542–549.

Simon, Rita J., and Howard Altstein. *Adoption Across Borders: Serving the Children in Transracial and Intercountry Adoptions*. Lanham, MD: Rowman & Littlefield Publishers, Inc., 2000.

Simon, Rita J., Howard Altstein, and Marygold S. Melli. *The Case for Transracial Adoption*. Washington, DC: The American University Press, 1994.

Steinberg, Gail, and Beth Hall. *Inside Transracial Adoption*. Indianapolis, IN: Perspectives Press, 2000.

Townsel, Lisa Jones. "Neither Black Nor White,'" *Ebony*. November 1996, Vol. 52, No. 1, pp. 44–48.

U.S. Census Bureau. "Adopted Children and Stepchildren: 2000," U.S. Department of Commerce, Economics, and Statistics Administration, U.S. Census Bureau, August 2003.

Varon, Lee. *Adopting on Your Own: The Complete Guide to Adopting as a Single Parent.* New York: Farrar, Straus and Giroux, 2000.

Ward, Margaret, M.A., and John H. Lewko, Ph.D. "Support Sources of Adolescents in Families Adopting Older Children," *American Journal of Orthopsychiatry*. Oct. 1987, Vol. 57, No. 4, pp. 610–612.

Watkins, Mary, and Susan Fisher. *Talking with Young Children About Adoption*. New Haven, CN: Yale University Press, 1993.

Index

B

government funding, 107
  federal laws on health
    insurance, 109-110
  income tax credit, 108
  state deductions, 109
  sliding-scale systems, 104
  standard payment terms,
    105-106
fetal alcohol syndrome.
  See FAS
finalization day, 236
finalizing adoption, rights
  of adoptive parents, 128
financial considerations,
  26-28, 103-110
  average fees, 104
  benefits to society, 27
  financial plans, 106-107
  flat fees, 104
  government funding, 107
    federal laws on health
      insurance, 109-110
    income tax credit, 108
    state deductions, 109
  health-care costs, 26-27
  sliding-scale systems, 104
  standard payment terms,
    105-106
financial materials, home
  studies, 169
finding a child, international
  adoptions, 150-151
flat fees, 104
FMLA (Family Medical
  and Leave Act), 107
food issues, 271
foreign travel, international
  adoptions, 144
foster care, 9
  fost/adopt programs, 41-42
  how kids enter foster care,
    40-41

legal risk adoptions, 41-42
parental reunification laws,
  36
waiting children, 37-39
foster children
  explaining adoption to
    children, 262-263
  medical history, 201
friends and family
  networking, 92-94
  revealing plans to adopt,
    190-192
  waiting time, 224

G

gathering information about
child, 198-199
  genetic predispositions,
    202-203
  health and environment,
    198-199
  medical background infor-
    mation, 199
    foster children, 201
    international adoptions,
      202
    U.S.-born children, 200
  prenatal information,
    203-204
gay and lesbian adopters, 180
  objections, 180-182
  tips, 182-183
genetic predispositions,
  202-203
Gerbner, Dr. George, media
  bias evidence, 12
Gibbs v. Ernst, 129
Gladney Center, Adoption
  Information Sheet, 160
gorging on food, 271

government funding, 107
  federal laws on health
    insurance, 109-110
  income tax credit, 108
  state deductions, 109
grandparents, impact of birthparents' parents, 220-221
gray market adoptions, 82
guardianship, 9
"Guatemala Travel and
  Etiquette: A Guide for
  Adoptive Parents," 150
guilt trips (scams), 114-115

H

Hague Convention on
  Intercountry Adoption, 140
Hall, Beth, *Inside Transracial
  Adoption*, 46
*The Handbook for Single
  Adoptive Parents*, 177
Healing the Hurt Child, 253
health and environment,
  gathering information about
  potential child, 198-199
health care, preparing for
  child, 235-236
health insurance
  federal laws, 109-110
  preparing for child, 234
Health Insurance Portability
  and Accountability Act. *See*
  HIPPA
health-care costs, 26-27
HIPPA (Health Insurance
  Portability and
  Accountability Act), 109,
  164
hoarding and hiding food,
  271

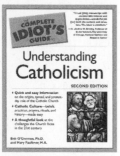

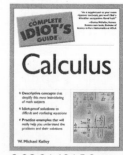